IFUGAO LAW

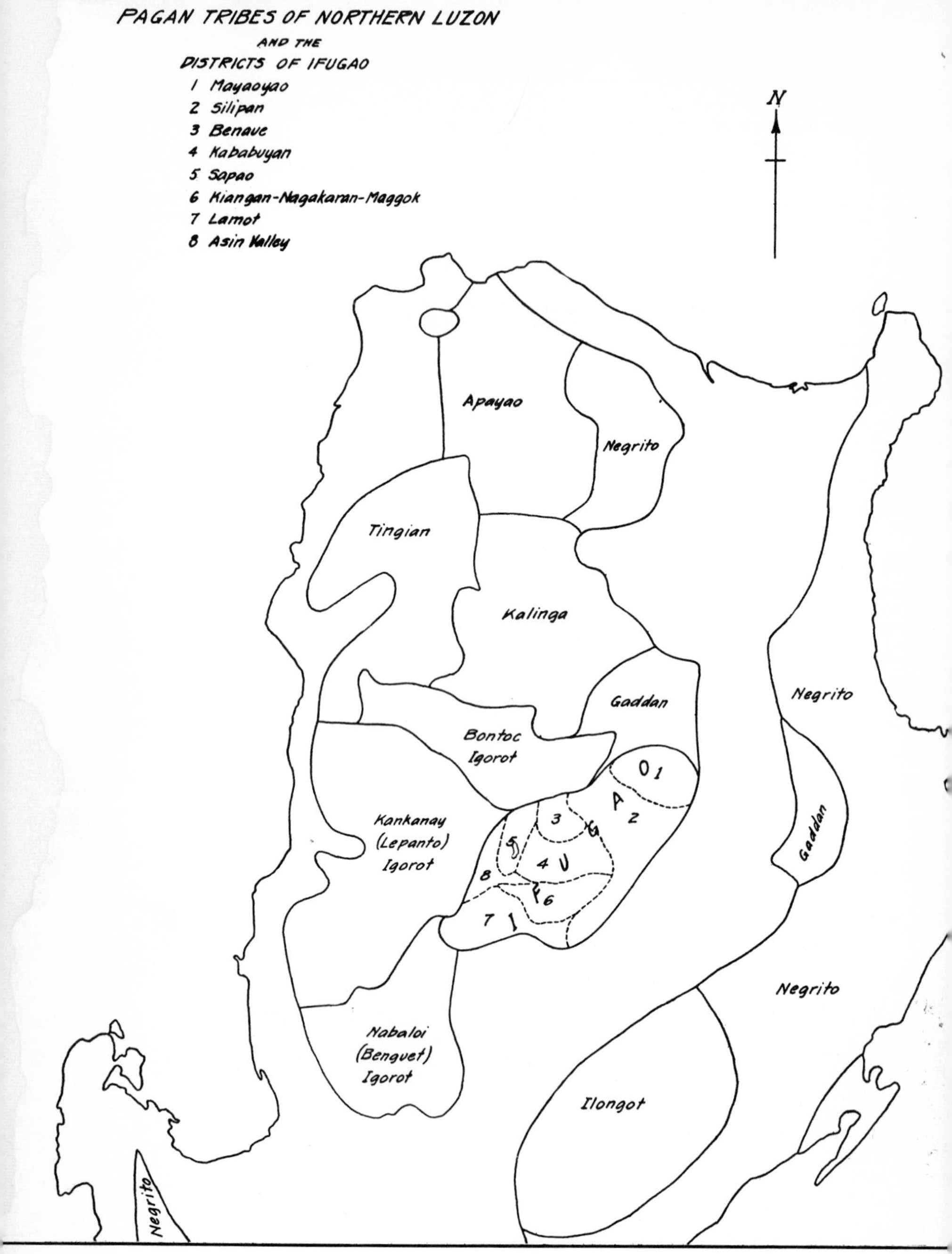

PAGAN TRIBES OF NORTHERN LUZON
AND THE
DISTRICTS OF IFUGAO
1 Mayaoyao
2 Silipan
3 Benave
4 Kababuyan
5 Sapao
6 Kiangan-Nagakaran-Maggok
7 Lamot
8 Asin Valley

N

Apayao

Negrito

Tingian

Kalinga

Gaddan

Negrito

Bontoc
Igorot

Gaddan

Kankanay
(Lepanto)
Igorot

0 1
A 2
3
5
4
8
6
7

Nabaloi
(Benguet)
Igorot

Negrito

Ilongot

Negrito

Map 1

IFUGAO LAW

R. F. Barton

by Franklin

With a New Foreword by

Fred Eggan

UNIVERSITY OF CALIFORNIA PRESS

Berkeley and Los Angeles · 1969

First printing: University of California Publications
in
American Archaeology and Ethnology
Vol. 15, No. 1   1919

University of California Press
Berkeley and Los Angeles, California

University of California Press, Ltd.
London, England

Library of Congress Catalog Card Number: 78-76334
Printed in the United States of America

"We are likely to think of the savage as a freakish creature, all moods—at one moment a friend, at the next moment a fiend. So he might be were it not for the social drill imposed by his customs. So he is, if you destroy his customs, and expect him nevertheless to behave as an educated and reasonable being. Given, then, a primitive society in a healthy and uncontaminated condition, its members will invariably be found to be on the average more law-abiding, as judged from the standpoint of their own law, than is the case in any civilized state.

"Of course, if we have to do with a primitive society on the down-grade—and very few that have been 'civilizaded,' as John Stuart Mill terms it, at the hands of the white man are not on the down-grade—its disorganized and debased custom no longer serves a vital function. But a healthy society is bound, in a wholesale way, to have a healthy custom."

R. R. MARRETT, in *Anthropology.*

FOREWORD

With this reprinting of Barton's *Ifugao Law,* a classic in Philippine ethnology and the law of primitive peoples is again available, and anthropologists and other readers will find it as fresh and interesting today as it was when the University of California Press first brought it out a half century ago.[1] Roy Franklin Barton had just spent some eight years among the Ifugao as a supervising teacher, where his interest and curiosity had led him to learn their language and begin recording their ways of life. *Ifugao Law* was his first major publication, but it was much more than a dry systematization of the rules and regulations that control social life and conduct, for it provided in addition a compact outline of Ifugao society and culture and reflected their basic values and motivations. As such it is an indispensable introduction to Barton's later and more detailed studies of Ifugao and Kalinga culture. Taken together these studies provide a corpus on the Ifugao that matches in comprehensiveness and interest anything in the whole range of ethnological literature.

The specifically legal contributions of *Ifugao Law* to the study of primitive law are well known through the work of E. A. Hoebel, who was a friend of Barton's and one of our foremost students of primitive legal institutions. In his "Introduction" to Barton's study of Kalinga law he characterizes that contribution as follows:

> The great theoretical interest that resides in the Ifugao way of life is that it presents us with an anarchistic political organization, i.e., a system controlling intergroup relations within the tribe and between the tribe and the alien world that operates with little or no institutionalization of government, yet this condition prevails in a technologically sophisticated society whose rice terraces on the ragged mountainsides of Luzon evoke expressions of awe from outside visitors. Further they have developed through the ages a most elaborate system of substantive property law and personal law—a system that operates almost entirely without benefit of government. The Ifugaos are the star example of how far a system of private law can go. They demonstrate that anarchy is not necessarily synonymous with disorder. Their system also shows up nicely the limitations in a legal order that depends primarily upon the kinship group for its operation.[2]

And in his later volume, *The Law of Primitive Man, A Study in Comparative Legal Dynamics* (1954), Hoebel devotes a chapter to the Ifugao in which he abstracts the basic legal postulates and their corollaries

---

[1] University of California Publications in American Archaeology and Ethnology, XV, No. 1 (1919), 1–186.

[2] E. A. Hoebel, "Introduction," in *The Kalingas, Their Institutions and Custom Law,* by R. F. Barton (Chicago: University of Chicago Press, 1949), pp. 2–3.

from Barton's account and illustrates them from the case studies and in modern legal terminology.

While Barton never claimed adherence to any school of anthropology or jurisprudence, his work made him an anthropological behaviorist and a jurisprudential realist. Barton not only analyzed the structure of Ifugao law but made it a living reality through the use of case studies, so that we come to understand Ifugao behavior much better than we could otherwise do. And the use of case materials makes it possible for other scholars to utilize the data in terms of their own analytical frames of reference. As Hoebel notes, *Ifugao Law* stands as "one of the few shining examples of what can be harvested in the way of legal enlightenment through purposeful and intelligently conceived study of law-ways among primitive peoples."[3]

This praise does not mean that the technical aspects of *Ifugao Law* are acceptable to legal specialists in the form or terminology in which Barton presented them. Thus Kroeber notes that Max Radin protested Barton's use of the term "crime" for Ifugao injuries. And more recently Max Gluckman has written that "while Barton, in his classic books on the Kalinga and Ifugao of the Philippines, makes very good analyses of the body of rules of the tribe and illustrates these with records of cases, I do not think he deals adequately with processes of and pressures towards, settlement."[4] Here, I think Gluckman is unjustified in his criticism, but I will leave it to the readers to judge for themselves.

How Barton came to be an anthropologist is not at all clear and what little we know about his early life is contained in A. L. Kroeber's obituary[5] and in occasional revelatory passages scattered here and there in his later writings. As Kroeber notes, Barton "produced some of the most gifted ethnography ever written in English," and "possessed an unusual insight into the salient physiognomy of institutions, an intense interest in their functioning, and consuming curiosity as to human motives within this functioning." He was wholly self-taught, which was both a limitation and an advantage.

Barton was born near the Spoon River country in west central Illinois, the son of a physician and well-to-do farmer. He graduated from

---

[3] *Ibid.*, p. 1.
[4] Max Gluckman, *Politics, Law and Ritual in Tribal Society* (Chicago: Aldine Press, 1965), pp. 175–176.
[5] A. L. Kroeber, "Roy Franklin Barton, 1883–1947," *American Anthropologist*, LI (1949), 91–95. I have drawn freely on Kroeber's account in the following paragraphs.

the Illinois State Normal University in preparation for a teaching
career and was a student in the University of Chicago when as he
says, "the notion seized me of going to the Philippines as a teacher."
The U.S. government was recruiting a large contingent of teachers in
an earlier version of the Peace Corps to staff the new educational system which was being established in the Philippines, and in 1906, at
the age of twenty-three, Barton arrived in Manila.

He was first sent to Pangasinan in central Luzon as a supervising
teacher, but one day he met some mountaineers who had come down
to trade and immediately applied for a transfer to the Mountain Province. He went to Cervantes, where there was an Industrial School for
Igorots, but soon volunteered for a post in Ifugao sub-province, which
his predecessor, who had been speared there, was anxious to leave. Here
he lived for eight years, and as Kroeber puts it, "quickly clicked into
his life work." In *The Half-Way Sun* Barton provides a fascinating
account of his life during this period, as well as of the problems involved in the administration of the Mountain Province.

The Mountain Province had just emerged from the disorders of the
revolt against Spain and was being administered by a picked group
of Americans under the direction of Dean C. Worcester, as Secretary
of the Interior for the Philippines. Ifugao Sub-Province was in the
charge of Jeff D. Gallman, an ex-army officer who was restoring peace
and order and building trails with a firmness and tact which Barton
came greatly to admire. David P. Barrows, an anthropologist who had
come earlier to the Philippines as Chief of the Bureau of Non-Christian
Tribes and was now Director of Education, also encouraged his early
studies. With H. Otley Beyer, a fellow teacher who was stationed at
Banaue, Barton set out to learn Ifugao and to master native life and
culture in the Kiangan region. As he grew more proficient it was natural
that disputes would be brought to his attention as he made the rounds
of the district schools and their adjudication brought him to the heart
of Ifugao society and culture.

As a youth Barton had exhibited a gift for observing people and
entering sympathetically into their lives. As a lonely young man in
Ifugao, he opened his home to the community, and particularly to the
children. "Throughout my eight and a half years in Ifugaoland my
house was a boys' agamang [sleeping place]. The youngsters came in
at dusk without any by-your-leave, would help my houseboys with their
chores if asked to, would scuffle with each other, romp and banter for
awhile, would quiet down a bit when tired, lie on the floor, scuffle again

and play pranks with each other's bodies, tell stories and obscene jokes, and finally fall asleep, several under a blanket."[6]

Ifugao religion first caught his attention; among the Ifugao almost every man is a priest and the pantheon of deities rivals that of India. By 1912 he had published two articles on Ifugao rituals and had completed a preliminary manuscript, "The Religion of the Kiangan Ifugaos." During the summer of 1912 he went as a cinematographer on an expedition to Korea and Japan with Frederick Starr, which broadened his perspective. Together with H. Otley Beyer, he had begun the assemblage of the data available on the history and ethnography of the Ifugao people, and he now began a systematic study of various aspects of Ifugao society and culture which was to continue to the end of his life. The Ifugao, who are surely one of the most interesting and original of primitive groups, could have found no better or more sympathetic interpreter.

In 1916, at the end of his first period among the Ifugao, Barton spent four months as supervising teacher among the Kalinga, a related headhunting group in the northern part of the Mountain Province. Here he found similar institutions, but often in different or more developed form, which enabled him to see Ifugao life in clearer perspective. He began to record Kalinga disputes and he later returned to the Kalinga in 1941 for a more systematic recording of legal cases for his well-known study of Kalinga customary law.[7]

Barton left the Philippines in 1916 and returned to the United States. The rapid Filipinization of the civil service and the onset of World War I led to a general exodus of Americans and Barton came to the University of California, where he decided on dentistry as a more adequate way to make a living. Both Kroeber and Barrows were at Berkeley and together they encouraged Barton to complete his "Ifugao Law" and "Ifugao Economics" which were published, along with papers by C. R. Moss on the Nabaloi and Kankanay, in Volume 15 of the University of California Publications in American Archaeology and Ethnology, 1919–1922.

During the 1920's Barton practiced dentistry in a variety of places, including Manila, and managed to spend another period with the Ifugao, in the meantime writing *The Half-Way Sun*, which Barrows later characterized as the most valuable book published on any of the mountain peoples. He returned to America in 1930 but did not feel

---

[6] Barton, *Philippine Pagans*, p. 10.
[7] Barton, *The Kalingas, Their Institutions and Custom Law*.

at home. His marriage broke up and in his resentment over what he considered an unjust divorce judgment he went to Europe, and then to the Soviet Union where he spent a decade, first in dentistry and then at the Institute of Ethnography of the Academy of Sciences, where he took an advanced degree and became a member of the staff, with responsibility for the Indonesian area. He remarried in Russia but maintained his U.S. citizenship, and, in 1937, returned to the Philippines for field research supported by both the Institute of Ethnography and American research organizations. Here he collected the Ifugao autobiographies which were published in *Philippine Pagans* (London, 1938) and which gave a new dimension to his studies.

In 1940, with the onset of World War II, Barton left Russia and went directly to the Philippines. He taught briefly at Sagada in the Mountain Province before being awarded a Guggenheim Fellowship which enabled him to continue his field researches and begin the recording of the *hudhud*, an extensive series of epics sung on various occasions. It was during this period that I first began corresponding with him about planning a systematic survey of the social and political institutions of the various mountain peoples, a project which was interrupted by the Japanese invasion in December 1941. Barton was interned in Baguio, and later at Los Baños, but was able to retain his notes and a number of his manuscripts. During internment he completed *The Religion of the Ifugaos* (published in 1946 as a Memoir of the American Anthropological Association) and largely completed *The Mythology of the Ifugaos* (which was published as a Memoir of The American Folklore Society in 1955). The manuscript on the Kalinga had been completed in preliminary form just before the war and was brought to this country by E. D. Hester, then economic advisor to the High Commisioner, who came out by submarine from Corregidor in 1942.

After the war Barton returned to his brothers, sisters, and mother in the San Joaquin valley for recuperation from starvation and beriberi, and then taught briefly at the University of California before coming to the University of Chicago as a Lichtstern Fellow in Anthropology. With a renewal of his Guggenheim fellowship he set out to prepare himself for further field work, and to do the final editing on his manuscripts. But an operation for gall bladder difficulties led to an embolism and he unexpectedly died in April, 1947. As Kroeber says, "he was indeed always memorable: courageous, candid, forthright, self-reliant, alert but kindly, hewing his own way. Above all, he forgot himself over the objectives that rose in his view: his soul never rusted."

Important as are Barton's contributions to the study of primitive
law, it is his contributions to the understanding of Ifugao—and Mountain Province—institutions that have aroused the greatest interest
among social scientists. He recognized that the cultures of all the mountain peoples of northern Luzon are basically similar, and that there
were numerous parallels with the lowland Filipinos in both language
and custom. But in common with his contemporaries he overemphasized
the role of multiple migrations in the settlement of the mountains and
the probable length of time required for the development of Ifugao
culture. And while aware of regional variations in Ifugao through the
researches of Father Francis Lambrecht on Mayawyaw and H. Otley
Beyer on Banaue he was not particularly concerned with their explanation.

In the two decades since Barton's death much progress has been
made in our knowledge of Mountain Province life and culture. Teams
of linguists from the Summer Institute of Linguistics have been engaged in the study of selected languages and dialects for over a decade
and their researches will extend and correct Barton's and Beyer's preliminary efforts. Father Lambrecht's continuing studies of ritual chants
and religious beliefs are modifying certain of Barton's conclusions regarding Ifugao origins and development.[8] And Harold C. Conklin's
comprehensive studies of Ifugao agriculture and ecology promise to
extend greatly the preliminary studies of both Barton and Beyer, when
they are completed.[9]

Here I would like to pay particular tribute to Barton's contributions
to our understanding of bilateral social systems. Since World War II
there has been a revival of interest in the "long neglected" field of bilateral descent—but part of the neglect is of Barton's writings, in
which he describes with clarity and economy the structure of bilateral
social systems and their operation. The Philippines, along with large
portions of Indonesia, provide one of the most important regions of the
world for the study of bilateral systems and considerable research has
already been accomplished or is underway. But many of the findings,

---

[8] Francis Lambrecht, "The Hudhud of Dinulawan and Bugan at Gonhadan," *Saint
Louis Quarterly,* V (1967); especially Part II, "Historical, Social and Cultural
Aspects."

[9] See particularly, H. C. Conklin, "Ifugao Ethnobotany 1905–1965" in *Studies in
Philippine Anthropology,* M. D. Zamora (ed.), Quezon City: 1967, pp. 204–262; and
"Some Aspects of Ethnographic Research in Ifugao," *Transactions* of the New York
Academy of Sciences (Series II), XXX, No. 1 (1967), 99–121. Conklin has also
recently compiled a comprehensive bibliography of over 650 titles on the Ifugao.
(Harold C. Conklin, *Ifugao Bibliography,* Bibliography Series, No. 11, Southeast
Asia Studies, Yale University, 1968.)

both conceptual and substantive, are present or implicit in *Ifugao Law,* and in Barton's companion study of the Kalinga.

Barton's major finding was that kinship is the primary basis for social relations and that each individual or sibling group is the center of a kinship or family group whose "unity must at all hazards be preserved."[10] This "kinship circle" or personal kindred includes all the descendants of the eight pairs of great-great-grandparents, extending laterally to include the third cousins, and is both the exogamous group and the feuding group. The local or neighborhood tie in contrast is relatively weak, and local groups unite only against distant regions where there are no close kinsmen. Marriage is an alliance between two such kinship groups, but the alliance is weak or tentative until children are born. Inheritance of rice lands and heirlooms is in terms of primogeniture, the oldest child receiving the bulk of the inherited property, and being responsible for the support of his parents and siblings.

Hoebel, in his analysis of the basic postulates of legal significance for the Ifugao, at the same time summarizes their social and cultural system.[11]

Postulate I. The bilateral kinship group is the primary social and legal unit, consisting of the dead, the living, and the yet unborn.

Postulate II. Men and women are of equal social and economic worth.

Postulate III. Supernatural forces control most activities, and the actions of human beings are either compatible or incompatible with the predilections of the supernaturals.

Postulate IV. Capital goods may be lent at interest.

Postulate V. Rice is the one *good* food.

Postulate VI. Propinquity of residence ameliorates the absoluteness of the primacy of kinship ties and, conversely, outside the kinship group responsibility to others diminishes with distance.

Professor Hoebel expands each of these postulates with a series of corollaries, and it might be useful to look at those he provides for Postulate I, concerned with the bilateral kinship group.

Corollary 1. An individual's responsibility to his kinship group takes precedence over any self-interest.

Corollary 2. The kinship group is responsible for the acts of its individual members.

Corollary 3. The kinship group shall provide protection for its members and punish outside aggression against them.

Corollary 4. The kinship group shall control all basic capital goods.

Corollary 4.1. Individual possession of rice lands and ritual heirlooms is limited to trust administration on behalf of the kin group.

---

[10] Barton, *Ifugao Law,* p. 8.

[11] E. A. Hoebel, *The Law of Primitive Man* (Cambridge: Harvard University press, 1954), pp. 104–105.

Corollary 5. Marriage imposes strict and limiting reciprocal obligations on husband and wife, but the obligations of each to his own kinship group take priority.

Corollary 5.1. Sex rights in marriage are exclusive between husband and wife.

Corollary 6. Because children provide the continuity essential to the perpetuation of the kinship group, the small family exists primarily for its child members.

It is clear that these "kinship groups" have both continuity and a corporate character, so far as inherited property and responsibility are concerned. It is also clear that they differ for each sibling group and that in neighboring localities they overlap in varying degrees, thus influencing the outcome of controversies and feuds in predictable ways.

Barton was aware of the extensive genealogical knowledge of the Ifugaos: "Many Ifugaos know their ancestors back to the tenth or even the fourteenth generation, and in addition, the brothers and sisters of these ancestors."[12] But he never recorded these genealogies and so missed another important group—the regional bilateral descent group or cognatic stock. Father Lambrecht has recorded these for both Mayawyaw and Kiangan[13]—they include all the descendants in both lines from early deified culture heroes and include much of the population in particular regions. These genealogical networks were utilized by priests and "go-betweens" in keeping track of economic and other transactions and in maintaining proper relationships with the ancestors in the Skyworld. They are thus of great importance in the settlement of disputes over land and other inherited property. We do not yet know how these cognatic stocks were integrated with the personal kindreds, but it seems clear that they are interrelated in a systematic way and serve to unite different regions into the larger society.

Ifugao society operates without any formal political organization and the families are sovereign in most situations. Rice lands are the source of wealth and prestige and social classes are important in terms of leadership and ceremonies. Feuds were common and were mediated by temporary "go-betweens" in related regions or by headhunting and vengeance with regard to more distant districts. Barton initially underestimated the tie of propinquity but in his Introduction to *Philippine Pagans* he notes that the local or geographic unit is "extremely important despite the fact that it is obscure, undefined, and rarely has a place in the Ifugao's consciousness."[14] More recently discrete "agricultural districts"[15] with rice chiefs and rituals have been

---

[12] Barton, *Ifugao Law*, p. 3.
[13] F. Lambrecht, "Genealogical Trees of Mayawyaw," *Journal of East Asiatic Studies*, Manila: Vol. II, 1953; "Genealogical Trees of Kiangan," *Ibid.*, Vol. III, 1954.
[14] Barton, *Philippine Pagans*, p.8.
[15] Cf. Conklin, "Ifugao Ethnobotany," p. 215.

identified and promise to further our understanding of local ties, even though it is clear that "kinship solidarity transcends geography."

Barton's autobiographies, collected some twenty years after *Ifugao Law*, offer both a remarkable confirmation of his earlier generalizations and an insight into the workings of another society and culture which is both illuminating and rare. Here the reader can feel what it is like to live in an anarchic society surrounded by endless feuds and responsible to and for a kinship group. We see the kinship system in action and the training in genealogical knowledge and kinship behavior that made for survival. Of particular significance are the accounts of courtship in the girls' *agamang*, where trial mating is carried out at a level of intensity which surprised even Barton. But once marriage is entered into—a process that requires many sacrifices and ceremonies involving both family groups—adultery becomes one of the most serious of offenses requiring very heavy indemnities. Barton suggests that the best definition of Ifugao marriage would be: "an agreement between kinship groups for the procreation of children by a man from one of the groups and a woman from the other."

The Kalinga, who are geographically separated from the Ifugao, but with a similar social base, have solved certain of the problems which plague the Ifugao by developing endogamous regions which have some of the characteristics of small states. Barton studied the Southern Kalinga who have wet rice agriculture and a rather dense population. Here a class of political leaders (*pangats*) had arisen who settled disputes within the region, and a system of peace pacts had been developed between regions to reduce the headhunting and feuding tendencies. Coming from the Ifugao, Barton saw the Kalinga as politically organized.[16]

Edward Dozier's recent study of the Northern Kalinga has both clarified and corrected Barton's earlier views. The Northern Kalinga are dry rice cultivators who reside in small hamlets that are grouped into endogamous regions. Within the region there are overlapping kinship circles or personal kindreds similar to those of the Ifugao, but outsiders treat the region as a kinship unit and may kill any member to satisfy vengeance. Here authority was in the hands of leading warriors, but the development of peace pacts has led to the rise of influential headmen who adjust disputes within the region and act as pact holders. But Dozier found that in the last analysis the pact holder represents his kinship group rather than the territorial unit, and that kinship is

---

[16] This and the following paragraphs are summarized from F. Eggan, "Some Aspects of Bilateral Social Systems in the Northern Philippines," in *Studies in Philippine Anthropology* (1967), pp. 186–203.

still the basic bond. By comparing Barton's data with his own investigations of the Northern and Southern Kalinga, Dozier was able to define the effects of wet rice cultivation on population density and community size in the south and to clarify the changes which were going on in the socio-political system.[17]

For the Bontok and Northern Kankanay regions, which lie between Ifugao and Kalinga, the social organization becomes more complex. Kinship is still important but a ward organization has developed in the relatively large towns which are characteristic of these regions. Barton had made a brief study of Sagada, a Northern Kankanay community west of Bontoc, the capital of the Mountain Province, and after his death I continued his researches. Here I found a series of cognatic or bilateral descent groups which had certain corporate features such as ownership of hill farmlands and pine forests. Certain ritual positions are likewise controlled by these descent groups, and today these "main families" are active in municipal politics, as well. In addition, Sagada is divided into twelve contiguous wards, each with a name and corporate property such as a ward center for the performance of rituals, a sleeping hut for old men and boys, and a council of old men for the settlement of disputes and the organization of rituals. Each ward has its own household membership, without reference to kinship ties, but individuals can shift from one ward to another. Here we can see that the territorial aspects of the village have developed at the expense of kinship ties, and the wards offer discrete groups which simplify the problems of organization and the settling of disputes. There is still no central political structure, except that provided by the modern Philippine state, but unity is further achieved by a communal ceremonial calendar administered by the councils of old men.

These are only three of the variant combinations of social institutions found in the Mountain Province. The lowland Christian groups show further variations as a result of Spanish and American acculturation, but the personal kindred and bilateral descent and inheritance are still important, along with *compradrazgo* and other added features. In the lowlands the social system has become more flexible and kinship relationships have to be implemented with regard to more distant kin, but the family group is still of central importance and marriage is utilized to extend the kinship network. Even the Moslem Filipinos in the south have built their political structure on a bilateral social system.

---

[17] E. P. Dozier, *Mountain Arbiters*, Tucson: The University of Arizona Press, 1966.

By careful study and comparison of these and other groups within the Indonesian-Pacific region we will ultimately be able to understand better the nature of bilateral social systems. The early societies of northern Europe had similar social systems, and what we learn will throw light on the structural features and development of our own modern European and American societies, as well as on the evolution of social structure generally.

There is much else that is of interest in Barton's *Ifugao Law* and his later studies, but I have tried to suggest some of the scientific results which have resulted from his pioneer researches and from his inspiration. As with Malinowski's writings on the Trobriands, the reader is here brought into the Ifugao world, and once he has sampled its contents he will never view his own culture in quite the same ethnocentric way. In the Preface to *Philippine Pagans* Barton takes his credo from Geoffrey Gorer: "Anthropologists of today [1938] want to see 'not only the generalized objective culture as conceived by a foreign investigator, but also the individual *in* that culture, the individual as a product of that culture, and that culture through the individual's eyes.'"

Barton had great faith in the Ifugao but he worried as to whether the processes of acculturation would be for the better: "It might have been more propitious to have merely helped them out of the trap of headhunting and to have left them the rest of their culture. . . ."[18] I think he would be reassured if he could revisit Ifugaoland today. The population has recovered from the effects of the Japanese occupation and its aftermath, in which they lost a considerable number of people and set a standard of loyalty which was unsurpassed. The Ifugao have also largely maintained their unique culture and have developed political skills which have enabled them to establish their region as a full-fledged province, despite the lack of a traditional political system. And the famous rice terraces which Barton so greatly admired still have a sweep and grandeur unequalled anywhere in the world.

Barton addressed his writing to a wider audience than anthropologists or social scientists. He hated all intolerance—the prejudice that rears barriers between human beings—and he hoped that his Ifugao studies would contribute to that broader understanding of the human condition which is essential if we are to survive. *Ifugao Law* is the keystone to these studies and it is particularly appropriate that the University of California, which played such an important role in Bar-

---

[18] Barton, *The Half-Way Sun,* p. 296.

ton's scientific development, should again make it available to a new audience through its Press.

I have added a bibliography of Barton's writings on the Philippines to facilitate a further acquaintance with his work.

FRED EGGAN

June 1, 1968
Director, Philippines Studies Program
University of Chicago

PUBLICATIONS OF
ROY FRANKLIN BARTON

"The Harvest Feast of the Kiangan Ifugao," *Philippine Journal of Science*, VI-D, No. 2 (April 1911), 81–105.

"An Ifugao Burial Ceremony" (with H. Otley Beyer), *Philippine Journal of Science*, VI-D, No. 5 (November 1911), 227–252.

"The Funeral of Aliguyen," in *The Headhunters of Northern Luzon*, (pp. 126–138), by Cornelis DeWitt Willcox. Kansas City: Franklin Hudson Co., 1912.

"Ifugao Law," *University of California Publications in American Archaeology and Ethnology*, XV, No. 1 (1919), 1–186.

"Ifugao Economics," *University of California Publications in American Archaeology and Ethnology*, XV, No. 5 (1922), 385–446.

"Lawsuit and Good Custom a la Ifugao," *Asia*, XXIX, No. 8 (August 1929), 598–607.

"My Ifugao Brother's Gods," *Asia*, XXIX, No. 10 (October 1929), 806–814, 822–824.

"Hunting Soul-Stuff," *Asia*, XXX, No. 3 (March 1930), 188–195, 225–226.

"White Man's Law among Filipino Tribesmen," *Asia*, XXX, No. 6 (June 1930), 410–416, 445–448.

The Half-Way Sun. New York: Brewer and Warren, Inc., 1930.

"Paths of Vengeance in Luzon," *Travel*, LV, No. 1 (October 1930), 24–29, 53.

"Ifugao, Malaiskoe plemia nagornoi chasti Filippin" [Ifugao, a Malayan tribe in the mountainous section of the Philippines], *Sovetskaia Etnografiia* I–II (1931), 116–149. Moscow: Akademia Nauk.

"Ispol'zovanie mifov kak magii u gornykh plenem Filippin" [The use of myths as magic among the mountain tribes of the Philippines], *Sovetskaia Etnografiia*, III (1935), 77–95. Moscow: Akademia Nauk. (English translation from the Russian, by Joshua Kunitz, for the Human Relations Area Files, New Haven, Conn., 1956.)

Philippine Pagans: The Autobiographies of Three Ifugaos. London: George Routledge & Sons, 1938. (Also New Hyde Park, N.Y.: University Books, 1963.)

"How Marriage Prohibitions Arose," *Philippine Magazine*, XXXV, No. 8 (August 1938), 380–381, 394.

"Myths and Their Magic Use in Ifugao," *Philippine Magazine*, XXXVII, No. 9 (September 1940), 348, 351.

"Numputol—the Self-Beheaded," *Philippine Magazine*, XXXVII, No. 10 (October 1940), 384–386, 394–396.

"Ifugao Somatology," (with J. J. Roginsky). *Philippine Journal of Science*, LXXIV, No. 4 (April 1941), 349–365.

"Primitive Kalinga Peace-Treaty System," *Philippine Magazine,* XXXVIII: No. 5 (May 1941), 190–191; No. 6 (June 1941), 235–237.

"Igorots Today," *Asia,* XXXXI, No. 6 (June 1941), 307–310.

"Reflections in Two Kinship Terms of the Transition to Endogamy," *American Anthropologist,* XXXIII, No. 4 (October/December 1941), 540–549.

The Religion of the Ifugaos. (Memoir 65, American Anthropological Association.) Menasha, Wisconsin: American Anthropological Association, 1946.

"The Philippines," (with F. Eggan), *American Anthropologist,* XXXXIX, No. 3 (July–September 1947), 532–533.

The Kalingas, Their Institutions and Custom Law. Chicago: University of Chicago Press, 1949.

The Mythology of the Ifugaos. (Memoirs of the American Folklore Society, Volume 46.) Philadelphia: American Folklore Society, 1955.

PREFACE

There is no law so strong as custom. How much more universal, willing, and spontaneous is obedience to the customary law that a necktie shall be worn with a stiff collar than is obedience to the ordained law against expectoration on sidewalks; notwithstanding that the latter has more basis in consideration of the public weal and even in aesthetics.

This little paper shows how a people having no vestige of constituted authority or government, and therefore living in literal anarchy, dwell in comparative peace and security of life and property. This is owing to the fact of their homogeneity and to the fact that their law is based entirely on custom and taboo.

The Ifugaos are a tribe of barbarian head-hunters. Nevertheless, after living among them for a period of eight years, I am fully satisfied that never, even before our government was established over them, was the loss of life from violence of all descriptions nearly so great among them as it is among ourselves. I do not, however, wish to be understood as advocating their state of society as ideal, or as in any way affording more than a few suggestions possibly to our own law-makers. Given dentists and physicians, however, I doubt gravely if any society in existence could afford so much advantage in the way of happiness and true freedom as does that of the Ifugaos.

But we must realize that probably neither security of the individual life nor even happiness are the chief ends of existence. The progress and evolution of our people are much more important in all probability, and this seems to demand the sacrifice of ease and freedom and of much happiness on the part of the individuals composing our society.

Acknowledgments are due first to my teacher and friend, Professor Frederick Starr, for his encouragement and assistance, and, above all, for his inculcation of respect for and tolerance toward customs other than our own.

Captain Jeff D. Gallman, whose work among the Ifugaos stands to the credit of our government of the Philippines second to that of no other man in the archipelago, assisted me in many ways. He is a man learned in the ''lore of men,''

> ''Who ha' dealt with men
> In the new and naked lands.''

Dr. David P. Barrows, now Major Barrows, also rendered me

indispensable aid and encouragement. Dr. A. L. Kroeber of the chair of anthropology, University of California, and his associates, Dr. T. T. Waterman and Mr. E. W. Gifford, have read the manuscript and proofs and have made valuable suggestions which are incorporated in the paper as finally published. These gentlemen have been unstintedly generous in welcoming a newcomer in the field in which they are so preëminent.

Dr. George W. Simonton has kindly assisted in preparing the manuscript for the printer.

The photographs, with one exception, were taken by myself.

SAN FRANCISCO, CALIFORNIA, January 14, 1918.

CONTENTS

APPENDIXES

PLATES

INTRODUCTION

Philippine ethnologists generally agree to the hypothesis that the Negritos, a race of little blacks, remnants of which now inhabit mountain regions of many of the larger islands, were the original inhabitants of the Philippine Archipelago. They advance the hypothesis that these little blacks were driven by Malay immigrants from their former homes in the fertile plains to the mountains; and that these first Malay invaders were driven from the lowlands into the mountain regions by succeeding immigrations of Malays superior to them in organization and weapons.[1] By and by, no one cares to hazard how long afterward, the Spaniards came. They christianized the lowlanders, except the Mohammedan populations of Mindanao and Sulu. But at the time of the American occupation the mountaineer descendants of the first immigration, for the most part, had not received the spiritual ministrations of Her Most Catholic Majesty's missionaries, on account of the inaccessible character of their habitat. True, garrisons and missions had been established in a few localities among them; but owing to the scattered character of the population, the independent spirit of the people, their natural conservatism, and the lack of tact and consideration on the part of the Spanish officials and missionaries, practically no progress had been made in christianizing or civilizing them.

The great majority of the non-Mohammedan, non-Christian Malays inhabit the island of Luzon. The Luzon non-Christian tribes and their estimated numbers are: Apayaos, 16,000; Benguet Igorots, 25,000; Bontoc Igorots, 50,000; Wild Gaddanes, 4000; Ifugaos, 120,000; Ilongots, 6000; Kalingas, 60,000; Tingianes, 30,000; Lepanto Igorots, 35,000; total, nearly a quarter million. All these tribes inhabit the mountain ranges of the northern third of the island.

The habitat of the Ifugaos is situated in about the center of the area inhabited by the non-Christian tribes. In point of travel-time,

---

[1] The present population of the Philippine Islands is about 10,000,000. Notwithstanding, there are vast stretches of unoccupied lowlands. At the coming of the Spaniards the population of the tribes that now are Christian has been estimated at 500,000. These second Malay immigrants undoubtedly gained the principal part of their livelihood from agriculture, for which they needed little land. Why, then, is it hypothesized that any immigration *drove* another to the mountains? My own belief is that the first immigrants went to the mountains of their own volition for the reason that they had been a mountain people and a terrace-building people in their former home.

as we say in the Philippines, for one equipped with the usual amount of baggage, Ifugao-land is about as far from Manila as New York from Constantinople. To the northeast are the Wild Gaddan, to the north the Bontoc Igorot, to the northwest, west, and southwest the Lepanto and Benguet Igorots; to the east, across the wide uninhabited river basin of the Cagayan, are the Ilongots. This geographic isolation has tended to keep the Ifugao culture relatively pure and uninfluenced by contact with the outside world. Two or three military posts were fitfully maintained in Ifugao by the Spaniards during the last half century of their sovereignity; but the lives of the natives were little affected thereby.

Ifugao men wear clouts and Ifugao women loin cloths, or short skirts, reaching from the waist to the knees. Wherever they go the men carry spears. Both sexes ornament their persons with gold ornaments, beads, agates, mother of pearl, brass ornaments, and so forth. Ifugao houses, while small, are substantially built, of excellent materials, and endure through many generations.

It may safely be said that the Ifugaos have constructed the most extensive and the most admirable terraces for rice culture to be found anywhere in the world. The Japanese terraces, which excite the admiration of tens of thousands of tourists every year, are not to be compared with them. On these steep mountains that rise from sea-level to heights of six to eight thousand feet—mountains as steep probably as any in the world—there have been carved out, with wooden spades and wooden crowbars, terraces that run like the crude but picturesque "stairsteps" of a race of giants, from the bases almost to the summits. Some of these terrace walls are fifty feet high. More than half are walled with stone. Water to flood these terraces is retained by a little rim of earth at the outer margin. The soil is turned in preparation for planting with a wooden spade. No mountain is too steep to be terraced, if it affords an unfailing supply of water for irrigation. The Ifugao, too, makes clearings on his mountains in which he plants sweet potatoes, and numerous less important vegetables. Without his knowing it, he bases his agriculture on scientific principles (to an extent that astounds the white man) and he tends his crops so skillfully and artistically that he probably has no peer as a mountain husbandman.

Of political organization the Ifugao has nothing—not even a suggestion. Notwithstanding, he has a well-developed system of laws. This absolute lack of political government has brought it about that the Ifugao is a consummate diplomat. After an eight years' residence among them, I am convinced that the Ifugaos got along very well in the days before a foreign government was established among them. Through countless generations the Ifugao who has survived and prospered has been the one who has carried his point, indeed, but has carried it without involving himself in serious trouble with his fellows.

The Ifugao's religion is a mixture of an exceedingly complex polytheism, ancestor worship, and a mythology that is used as an instrument of magic. His religion seems to be far more highly developed than that of the other non-Christian tribes.

Attempts made by Spain to colonize the Ifugao in the lowlands invariably met with failure. The Ifugao is a hillman, and loves his hills. He is of an independent nature and cannot stand confinement. A great many prisoners jailed by American officials have courted death rather than endure incarceration.

While there are well defined tribal divisions that mark off the various mountain-Malay populations of northern Luzon, the cultures of all of the tribes are basically similar. Numerous parallelisms, too, are found with the lowland Filipinos, even now, in features of daily life, religion, taboo, law, and marital relation. The dialects of all the tribes inhabiting the islands are branches of the great family of Malay languages—languages spoken over more than half the circumference of the globe. The linguistic differences that exist between the mountain and the lowland tribes seem to be not much greater than the linguistic differences between the various mountain tribes themselves.

Many things lead us to believe that the culture of the Ifugaos is very old. We have to do with a people who possess both as individuals and collectively a most remarkable memory. Ifugao rich men lend to considerable numbers of clients and others every year during the "hungry time"—to these, varying numbers of bundles of rice, to this one a skein of yarn, to that one a pig, and to another again a chicken. All these bargains and their amounts and their varying terms, our wealthy Ifugao remembers, unaided by any system of writing or other artificial means. Many Ifugaos know their ancestors back to the tenth or even the fourteenth generation, and, in addition, the brothers and sisters of these ancestors. If we consider the racial or tribal memory of these people, we find a mythology fully as voluminous as that of the Greeks. But the Ifugaos have no recollections of having ever migrated. Unless they have lived for many centuries in their present habitat, it seems certain that they would have retained at least in mythical form the memory of their migration.

Another consideration that is significant lies in a comparison of the rate of rice-field building in these peaceful times, when such work is not hindered but instead vigorously stimulated by the government, with the amount of such work accomplished by past generations. One who stands on some jutting spur of the mountain-side in Asin, Sapao, or Benaue can scarcely help being impressed with the feeling that he is looking upon a work of tens of centuries. Any calculation must be based on vague and hazardous figures of course, but, without having any theories to prove, and making due allowance for increased rate of building during peaceful times and for the pressure of the needs of increased population, from a comparison of the estimated area of voluntary rice-field building with the areas already constructed, I come to the conclusion that the Ifugaos must have lived in their present habitat for at least two thousand years, and I believe that these figures are too small.

SOURCES OF IFUGAO LAW AND ITS PRESENT STATUS OF DEVELOPMENT

The Ifugaos have no form of writing: there is, consequently, no written law. They have no form of political government: there is, therefore, no constitutional or statutory law. Inasmuch as they have no courts or judges, there is no law based on judicial decisions.

Ifugao law has two sources of origin: taboo (which is essentially religious) and custom. The customary law is the more important from the greater frequency of its application.

1. *Relation of taboo to law.*—The Ifugao word for taboo is *paniyu.* The root, which appears under the varying forms *iyu, iho, iyao,* and *ihao,* means in general "evil" or "bad." The prefix *pan* denotes instrumentality or manner. The word *paniyu* means both by derivation and in use, "bad way of doing," or "evil way." By far the greater number of taboos have their origin in magic. A very large number of them concern the individual, or those closely related to him by blood ties, and for this reason have no place in a discussion of law. Thus a pregnant woman may not wear a string of beads, since the beads form a closed circle and so have a magic tendency to close her body and cause difficult childbirth. This, however, is not a matter that concerns anybody else, and so could be of no interest

at law. It is taboo for brothers to defecate near each other, but only they are harmed thereby, and the matter is consequently not of legal interest.

The breaking of a taboo that concerns the person or possessions of an individual of another family is a crime. The following instances will illustrate:

In nearly all districts[2] of Ifugao it is taboo for persons of other districts[2] to pass through a rice field when it is being harvested. It is also taboo for foreigners to enter a village when that village is observing its ceremonial idleness, *tungul,* at the close of harvest time. One who broke this taboo would be subject to fine. In case it were believed that the fine could not be collected, he would be in danger of the lance.

It is taboo to blackguard, to use certain language, and to do certain things in the presence of one's own kin of the opposite sex that are of the degrees of kinship within which marriage is forbidden or in the presence of another and such kindred of his, or to make any except the most delicately concealed references to matters connected with sex, sexual intercourse, and reproduction. Even these delicately concealed references are permissible only in cases of real necessity. The breaking of this taboo is a serious offense. One who broke the taboo in the presence of his own female kin would not be punished except in so far as the contempt of his fellows is a punishment. In Kiangan, before the establishment of foreign government, breaking the taboo in the presence of another and his female kin of the forbidden degrees is said to have been sometimes punished by the lance (see sec. 123).

It is taboo for one who knows of a man's death to ask a relative of the dead man if the man is dead. The breaking of this taboo is punishable by fine.

If asked, Ifugaos say that it is taboo to steal; to burn or destroy the property of another; to insult, or ruin the good name of another; to cause the death or injury of another by sorcery or witchcraft; in short, to commit any of those acts which among most peoples constitute a crime.

The word *taboo* as understood among ourselves, and as most often used among the Ifugaos, denotes a thing rather *arbitrarily* forbidden. It seems likely that moral laws—from which most criminal laws are an outgrowth—originate thus: the social conscience, learning that some act is antisocial, prohibits it (often in conjunction with religion) or some feature of it, or some *semblance* of it, arbitrarily, harshly, and sometimes unreasonably. Thus the first taboo set forth above has the semblance of being aimed against interruption in the business or serious occupation of another, or against his worship. The mere passing near a rice field when it is being harvested or the mere entrance into a village during the period of ceremonial idleness are

---

[2] I use the word "district" to denote the inhabitants of one of the many smaller culture sections into which the habitat of the Ifugaos is divided.

arbitrarily seized upon as acts constituting such interruptions. The second taboo arose from the purpose of the social consciousness to prevent marriage or sexual intercourse between near kin.[3] It is most sweeping and unreasonable in its prohibitions. A third person may make no remark in the presence of kin of the opposite sex as to the fit of the girl's clothing; as to her beauty; nor may he refer to her lover, nor play the lover's harp. Many ordinary things must be called by other than their ordinary names. Even the aged priests who officiate at a birth feast must refer in their prayers to the foetus about to be born as "the friend" and to the placenta as "his blanket." A great number of things are forbidden in the presence of kindred of opposite sex that would not shock even the most prudish of our own people. The third taboo seems to be aimed against the bandying or the taking in vain of the name of the dead.

It would seem that a primitive society, once it has decided a thing to be wrong, swings like a pendulum to the very opposite extreme, adds taboo upon taboo, and hedges with taboo most illogically. With the ardor of the neophyte, it goes to the other limit, becoming squeamish in the extreme of all that can in the remotest conception be connected with the forbidden thing.[4]

Ultimately reason and logic tend to triumph and eliminate the illogical, impertinent and immaterial taboos, remove the prohibitions contained in the useful taboos from their pedestal of magic, and set them upon a firmer base of intelligence, or at least practical empiricism.

A small part of Ifugao law consists even yet of taboos that are arbitrary and, except in essence, unreasonable. But the greater part has advanced far beyond this stage and is on a firm and reasonable basis of justice. Much of it originated from taboo—even yet the taboos are remembered and frequently applied to acts that constitute crimes among ourselves—but the immaterial and arbitrary taboos have been eliminated. Although the Ifugaos say that adultery and theft and arson are tabooed, nevertheless their attitude of mind is not the same as that toward things that are *merely* tabooed. It is the attitude of

---

[3] The possibility that these sex taboos are survivals of a former clan system in which exogamy was the rule does not in the least invalidate this statement.

[4] Taboo is for the most part undoubtedly derived from magic. Indeed, there are not wanting those who hold that all taboo has its origin in magic. While doubting if so sweeping an assertion as this can be true, especially when we consider that even in its most primitive phases human life is exceedingly complex and intricate, I invite attention to the fact that magic is such an all-embracing thing in primitive society, and is so closely connected with matters of morality and public policy, that there is nothing in this paragraph that can offend even those who hold that the field of taboo is one wholly of magic prohibitions.

the human mind toward things that are prohibited by law and by conscience.

2. *Scope of customary law.*—The customary law embraces that which pertains to property, inheritance, water rights, and to a great extent, family law and procedure. There is a certain amount of variation in customs and taboos throughout Ifugao land. This accounts to a certain extent, perhaps, for the reserved behavior of visitors to a district distant from their own. Visitors are afraid of unwittingly breaking some taboo. In general, however, it may be said that laws are very nearly uniform throughout the Ifugao country.

3. *Connection of law and religion.*—Religion and law appear conjointly in (*a*) transferals of family property; (*b*) ordeals; (*c*) certain taboos; (*d*) payments of the larger fines; (*e*) peace-making. The Ifugaos state that a large part of their customary law and procedure was given them by Lidum, their great teacher, a deity of the Skyworld, and an uncle of their hero-ancestor, Balitok.

4. *General principles of the Ifugao legal system.*—*Its personal character.* Society does not punish injuries to itself except as the censure of public opinion is a punishment. This follows naturally from the fact that there is no organized society. It is only when an injury committed by a person or family falls on another person or family that the injury is punished formally.

Collective responsibility. Not only the individual who commits an act but his kin, in proportion to the nearness of their kinship, are responsible for the act. Their responsibility is slightly less than his. This applies not only to crimes but to debts and civil injuries.

Collective procedure. Legal procedure is by and between families; therefore a family should be "strong to demand and strong to resist demands." *A member of an Ifugao family assists in the punishment of offenders against any other member of his family, and resists the punishment of members of his family by other families.* A number of circumstances affect the ardor with which he enters into procedures in which a relative is concerned and the extent to which he will go into them. Among these are: (*a*) the nearness or remoteness of his relationship to the relative concerned in the action; (*b*) relationship to the other principal in the action; (*c*) the loyalty to the family group of the relative principally concerned in the procedure and the extent to which this relative discharges his duty to it; (*d*) evidence in the case bearing on the correctness of the relative's position in the controversy.

A corollary of the above principle. Since legal procedure is between families, and never between individuals, nor between a family and an individual, crimes of brother or sister against brother or sister go unpunished. The family of the two individuals is identical. *A family cannot proceed against itself.* But in the case of incest between a father and a daughter the father might be punished by the girl's mother's family on the ground that he had committed a crime against a member of that family. It is true that just as great an injury would have been committed against the family of the father, since the relationship of the daughter to that family is the same as to her mother's family. But the father, the perpetrator of the crime, being a nearer relative of his own family than his daughter, his family certainly would not take active steps against him. Were the crime a less disgraceful one, the father's kin would probably contest his penalty.

The family unity must at all hazards be preserved. Clemency is shown the remoter kin in order to secure their loyalty to the family group. A large unified family group is in the ideal position of being "strong to demand and strong to resist demands." The family is the only thing of the nature of an organization that the Ifugao has, and he cherishes it accordingly.

Collective recipiency of punishment. Just as the family group is collectively responsible for the delinquencies of its members, but in less degree than the delinquent himself, so may punishment be meted out to individuals of the group other than the actual culprit, although naturally it is preferred to punish the actual culprit; and so may debts or indemnities be collected from them. But only those individuals that are of the nearest degree of kinship may be held responsible; cousins may not *legally* be punished if there be brothers or sisters.

Ifugao law is very personal in its character. For the different classes of society there are in the Mampolia-Kababuyan area five grades of fines in punishment of a given crime, four in the Hapao-Hunduan area, and three in the Kiangan area.

Might is right to a very great extent in the administration of justice. For a given crime, one family, on account of superior war footing, or superior diplomacy, or on account of being better bluffers, will be able to exact much more severe penalties than another. Especially is Ifugao administration of justice likely to be unfair when persons of different classes are parties to a controversy. I doubt very much, however, whether this characteristic of Ifugao administration of justice be more pronounced than it is in our own.

5. *Stage of development of Ifugao law.*—Reasons have already been given for believing the Ifugao's culture to be very old. His legal system must also be old. Yet it is in the first stage of the development of law. It is, however, an example of a very well developed first-stage legal system. It ranks fairly with Hebrew law, or even with the Mohammedan law of a century ago. R. R. Cherry in his lectures on the *Growth of Criminal Law in Ancient Communities* demonstrates these stages of legal development: First, a stage of simple retaliation—"an eye for an eye, a tooth for a tooth, a life for a life." Second, a stage in which vengeance may be bought off "either by the individual who has inflicted the injury or by his tribe." Third, a stage in which the tribe or its chiefs or elders intervene to fix penalty-payments and to pronounce sentence of outlawry on those who refuse to pay proper fines. Fourth, a stage in which offenses come to be clearly recognized as crimes against the peace and welfare of the king or the state.

No Ifugao would dream of taking a payment for the deliberate or intentional murder of a kinsman. He would be universally condemned if he did so. However, he would usually accept a payment for an accidental taking of life. There is still, however, an element of doubt as to whether even in such a case payment would be accepted. For nearly all other offenses payments are accepted in extenuation. Ifugao law, then, may be said to be in the latter part of the first stage of legal development.

THE FÁMILY LÁW

6. *Polygamy.*—The extent to which personality affects what an Ifugao may or may not do without being considered an offender is illustrated in the matter of polygamy. Any Ifugao, except one of the most powerful, who might try to take a plural wife would only bring upon himself heavy punishment—punishment that would be administered by the kin of the first wife. But men who are very wealthy and who are also gifted with a considerable amount of force of character sometimes take a second or even a third wife, and compel the kin of the first wife to recognize her and her children. In other words, they *make* polygamy legal for themselves. The first wife is of higher class than succeeding wives. Her children have inheritance rights to all the property their father had at the time of the taking of the plural wife. The following is a typical instance of the taking of a plural wife:

> Guade of Maggok, an extremely wealthy man, after marrying and having a number of children by his first wife, began habitually to have illicit intercourse with another woman. The kin of the first wife demanded a heavy indemnity. Such was their *bungot* (ferocity) that they succeeded in making Guade think that he was in imminent peril of losing his life, and in collecting double the amount usual in such cases. But having paid the fine, Guade rallied to his support all his kin and kept up the relations with the woman, taking her as a second wife. Nor did the kin of the first wife attempt to prohibit this, well knowing that they had gone far enough. The second wife is recognized, and her children are recognized, as legitimate. Guade informed me recently that he was thinking seriously of taking a third. Guade is admired and envied by every one in the community apparently; whereas a man of less force would be condemned by public opinion.

When a plural wife is taken a heavy payment must be made the first wife and her kin. This may amount to about 500 pesos.

7. *Nature of marriage.*—Marriage among the Ifugaos is a civil contract of *undefined* duration. It may last a month, a year, a decade, or until the death of one of the parties to it. *It has no essential connection with the tribal religion.* True, at almost every step in its consummation the family ancestral spirits and the other deities are besought to bless the union in a material way in the matter of children and wealth and by giving the two parties long life. But this is a matter of self interest, and not of hallowing or consecrating the union. Should the omens be bad, the two people do not marry because they

are afraid that in the shape of sickness or death or childlessness, ill
fortune may overtake them if they do so. And even after the marriage has been fully consummated should it happen that at any one
of three certain feasts performed by the parents of the couple during
the year in connection with their rice crop, the omen of the bile sac[4a]
should promise ill, the marriage is dissolved. No promises are made
by the contracting parties to each other or to anybody else. Nor do
the contracting parties take any part in any religious ceremonials
or in any marriage ceremonials of any kind. Marriage may be terminated at any time by mutual agreement. But that marriage is considered a contract is shown by the fact that if either party terminates
the marriage against the will of the other the injured party has the
right to assess and collect damages.

The theory that marriage should be permanent in order to provide
the better for the training and rearing of children has no legal em-
bodiment.[5] It is, however, established by custom that in case of
divorce a property settlement according to the wealth of the family
must be made on the children.

8. *Eligibility to marriage.*—Any person of any age may marry.
The consent of the parents is not necessary. But there is a taboo
on the marriage of cousins within the third degree. This taboo may
be rendered inoperative, except in the case of full cousins, by an
exchange of animals ranging from two pigs in the case of the nearer
relationships to one small pig or a chicken in the case of the remoter.
The girl's kin in all cases receive the more valuable animals in this
exchange. But the marriage of first cousins is absolutely tabooed and
never occurs. It is said that children are sometimes coerced into
marriage against their will; but I have heard of only one case in
which physical force was used, and even in this case the attempt ended
in failure.

9. *The two ways in which marriage may be brought about.*—
Those children that will inherit a great deal of property are married

---

[4a] When the Ifugao sacrifices a chicken or pig, he always consults the omen
of the bile sac. A full distended bile sac normally placed is a good omen. An
empty one, or one abnormally placed is a bad omen. Needless to say, most
omens are good.

[5] There is a feeling on the part of the social consciousness that marriages
ought to be permanent—that it is better when such is the case. Inasmuch,
however, as all the uncles and aunts consider themselves, and, in the scheme of
the reckoning of Ifugao relationships are considered, *in loco parentis* with respect
to their nephews and nieces, and almost equally bound with the parents themselves to impart instruction and give training, the removal of one parent is of
little detriment to the mental and moral phase of the rearing of children.

usually, but by no means always, by a *contract*[6] marriage; those who
will inherit no property, or but a small amount, and those who, married by the preceding method, have lost their spouses, or who on
reaching a maturer age, do not find themselves compatible with their
spouses, and consequently remarry, are married by a *trial* marriage.
However, it should be said that even a *contract* marriage is a trial
marriage to a great degree. In fact, one inclined to be prudent in
his speech would never pronounce an Ifugao marriage a permanent
one until the death of one of the parties to it.

The trial marriage is merely a primitive sexual mating in the
dormitories of the unmarried. It might be called a courtship, it being
understood that, except in its very incipiency, Ifugao courtship postulates an accompaniment of sexual intercourse. It is very reprehen-
sible, but not punishable, for a girl to enter into two such unions
contemporaneously. The moral code is hardly so strict with respect
to the male.

In case the two individuals are satisfied with each other, that is,
in case they find themselves compatible, and nearly always in case
the girl becomes pregnant and the youth has no reason for misgivings
as to the parentage of the child, the youth, after consultation with
his parents, sends a distant relative or friend, *who is not related to
the girl,* with betels for a ceremonial conference in which the hand of
the girl is asked in marriage. Generally it requires two or more trial
marriages to select for a person his *more permanent* mate.

10. *Contract marriage.*—The contract marriage is usually arranged
for, and its first ceremonies at least performed while the children are
quite small. Its purpose is to guard against the commission of such
a folly on the part of the child who will be wealthy as marriage to a
less wealthy spouse. The danger is that such a child, sleeping in the
common dormitory, will give way to the ardor of youth and tempor-
arily mate with one below him in station, and that the union so begun
prove permanent.

As a rule the couple married by a contract marriage while yet
children are elevated by the *uyauwe* feast to the category of the
kadangyang (upper class). The *uyauwe* feast is not an essential part
of the marriage ceremonials, but is an addition to them.

The following is the history of a typical marriage of this kind:

---

[6] I prefer using the term contract marriage to using antenuptial agreement.
The latter is an occidental institution of which the reader has a definite notion.
The contract marriage is different in motive and nature.

Dulinayan of Ambabag, when his son was about two years old, sent a go-between to Likyayu, also of Ambabag, whose daughter was somewhat younger than Dulinayan's son, with betels for a ceremonial conference looking toward a marriage between the two children. He stated that he would contract to give his son his fields at Takadang, and wished to know what fields Likyayu would give his daughter. The go-between returned, stating that Likyayu's people did not consider Dulinayan's fields at Takadang seriously, and asked that he assign the boy his fields at Banggo and Dayukong in order that they might consider the union of their daughter with his son. The go-between stated that Likyayu was considering bestowing on his daughter his field at Takadang.

Dulinayan returned the go-between to state that he did not take as being very serious Likyayu's statement that he intended to give his daughter only the field at Takadang. He made the proposal that Likyayu add to the field at Takadang the one at Danok, and stated that if Likyayu would do so he would give his son the fields at Banggo and Dayukong, as Likyayu suggested. Likyayu accepted this proposal.

After two or three more conferences, it was agreed that Dulinayan was to assign his son the following movable family property: 1 rice-wine jar, 1 *gansa*, 1 gold ornament. Likyayu was to assign his daughter 1 rice-wine jar, 1 gold ornament, and 1 *pango* (string of ancient beads). Besides the above, Likyayu would give, at the proper time, a house for the young couple. Each of the two men would present his child a granary.

The above agreement made, Dulinayan sent a pig called *tokop di mommon* and a pig called *imbango*. These pigs were sacrificed by Likyayu and his kin. The omens of the bile sacs promised well. Likyayu returned 1 *natauwinan* (4 spears), as the *mangdad* of the *imbango*.

About three years elapsed before anything further was done toward the completion of the marriage. During this period Dulinayan on behalf of his son furnished Likyayu's household with what firewood was needed and kept his granaries in repair. Whenever his son's betrothed fell ill, or whenever her parents or grandparents fell ill, Dulinayan furnished a pig for sacrifice. And whenever Dulinayan's son or his son's parents or grandparents fell ill Likyayu furnished a pig. Likewise when one of the direct ascendants of either of the young couple died the other family furnished a pig for the funeral and a death blanket as one of the burial robes.

In the year 1912—that is, three years after the contract was made—Dulinayan sent a man to propose an *uyauwe*. Each family performed a granary feast to determine whether the time was propitious. The omens being good, each family notified the other of the fact. Dulinayan then sent a large pig as the *hingot*. Likyayu's people returned a small pig as *hulul di hingot*. Then Dulinayan furnished a large pig for the *bubun*, and the two families met for the first time during the period of the negotiations and sacrificed and prayed together.

A short time afterward the children were made *kadangyang* by the giving of an *uyauwe* feast. At this feast Dulinayan gave *hakba* (marriage presents) to Likyayu and his kin.

In a contract marriage there is always an assignment to the children of the property that they will inherit. The amount of property settled upon either of them is equal or very nearly equal to that settled on the other. Nor may the parent of one of the children sell any of this property except for the purpose of providing animals for sacrifice in case of the illness or death of the child or one of his direct ascendants, or in case of the illness or death of the child's betrothed, or one of his direct ascendants (see sec. 13).

11. *Marriage ceremonials.*—The following are the steps taken to consummate a typical marriage in the Kiangan-Maggok area:

(*a*) The boy's kin send the girl's kin a pig. This pig is sacrificed by the girl's kin. The omen of the bile sac is consulted. The pig is eaten. This feast is called *mommon.*

(*b*) The boy's kin send another pig to the girl's kin. The girl's kin sacrifice this pig. The omen of the bile sac is consulted. This feast is called *imbango.*

A non-essential part of the ceremonials, but an important matter in some contingencies, is the return by the girl's kin of a gift to the boy's kin in exchange of the pig sent for this feast. This return gift is called *mangdad.* Its effect is to nullify any right on the part of the boy's kin to demand a repayment of the pig sent for this ceremony in case the marriage should for any reason whatever fail to be effected. Even though the failure to complete or effect the marriage be the girl's fault, if the *mangdad* has been sent, the boy's kin have no right to ask a return of the *imbango.* The return gift is of much less value than that made by the boy's parents.

(*c*) The boy's kin send the girl's kin a pig, which pig is sacrificed by the girl's kin. The omen of the bile sac is consulted. This feast is called *hingot.*

A non-essential part of the ceremonials, but one important in the same way as in the preceding ceremony, is the return by the girl's kin of a small pig, called the *hulul di hingot* (exchange of the *hingot*).

(*d*) The kin of both the contracting principals meet at the girl's house and sacrifice a large pig furnished by the boy's kin. This feast is called *bubun,* and has for its especial purpose to obtain from the gods of animal fertility long life, health, and many children for the young couple. It is attended by a giving of gifts by the kin of the boy to the kin of the girl, except that in the case of a contract marriage between *kadangyang* (the upper class) the giving of these gifts is often deferred till the *uyauwe* ceremony, which, while not part of the marriage ceremonials, often follows immediately after them.

The programme of marriage ceremonials among the northern Ifugao is somewhat different.

(*a*) Same as (*a*) above. This ceremonial is omitted except in marriages between the wealthy.

(*b*) The boy's kin sacrifice a pig at his home, sending half of it, if the omen of the bile sac promises well, to the kin of the girl in a back basket, called *bango,* whence originates the term *imbango,* meaning "carried in a *bango.*"

(*c*) The boy's kin take a pig to the girl's home. The girl's kin furnish another and smaller pig. Both families participate in a religious feast. This feast is called *tanig,* and seems to include both the *bubun* and the *hingot* of the Kiangan people.

(*d*) Ceremonial idleness for the boy and the girl is required during a period of five days. On the third day the couple go to one of their fields, it being taboo for either of them to stumble on the way. The trip is in one respect somewhat like the time-honored cutting of the cakes in one of our own marriage feasts to secure a prognostication as to which of the two spouses will die first. Stumbling on the part of one of the couple, however, would indicate that that one would die not only first but soon, and would probably lead to a refusal on his or her part to go ahead with the marriage.[7] Arrived at the field, the girl weeds a part of it, and the boy gathers some wood from a near-by forest. Then they go home, the boy carrying the bundle of wood.

In case a bad omen of the bile sac is encountered in any of these ceremonies, the marriage is not proceeded with, since the belief is that misfortune would surely attend it.

In the case of the poor, some of the above ceremonies may be omitted; or chickens or smaller pigs may be substituted for any or all the pigs. The above programme is simply that which is to be followed out if the groom be financially able to do the "right thing."

In case the spouses are related, two pigs—a male and a female—are sacrificed, and the ceremony called *ponga* is performed. The larger pig is furnished by the boy. The nearer the kinship the larger the pigs necessary for this ceremony.

At no time are any vows or promises made by the principals. At no time, except in the fourth ceremony among the Northern Ifugao, do the principals have any active part in the ceremonies. Indeed, they may not eat the meat of the pigs or chickens killed at their own wedding, for it is taboo to them.

12. *Gifts to the kin of the bride: hakba.*—In the Kiangan area, but in no other, expensive gifts are made to the kin of the bride.

---

[7] Stumbling is not merely a prognostication; it is also a cause. It would *tend to bring about* that he who stumbled would die or be unfortunate if he went ahead with the marriage.

These gifts are called *hakba*. Only in the case of the very poorest
are gifts foregone. The gifts are distributed to the girl's kin, the
nearer kin receiving the more valuable and the remote kin the less
valuable articles. But the elder of a line of cousins by a single uncle,
for example, receives a more valuable present, the next in age a less
valuable one, the next in age a still less valuable one, and so on, the
youngest getting nothing if he have many brothers and sisters. No
distinction is made between male and female kin. The gifts may
range from two death blankets, worth 16 pesos, to a spearhead worth
0.20 peso.

Except in the case of the poverty-stricken, there is nothing for it
but to pay these presents. If they be not forthcoming, the kin of
the woman seize the pig provided for the *bubun* ceremony, carry it
home and guard it well till such time as the groom comes forward
with the *hakba* gifts, when they return it for the ceremonial.

The following is a list of the *hakba* given by Dulinayan of Ambabag
to Likyayu's family of the same village on the occasion of the marriage
of the son of the former to the daughter of the latter.

12	clouts at ₱1	₱12
10	woman's skirts at ₱2	20
42	death blankets at ₱8	336
10	woman's girdles at ₱2	20
10	war knives at ₱1	10
3	iron pots at ₱5	15
1	*bayaó* (blanket) at ₱5	5
1	rice-wine jar at ₱8	8
2	*gansas* at ₱8	16
620	"irons" (spears, knives, axes, etc., at an average value of ₱.50 each)	310
	Total	₱752

Dulinayan stated at the time these notes were taken that there
were a number of things omitted from the above list that he had
forgotten; that he counted up the amount of all the *hakba* immediately
after the feast, and that it totaled over 800 pesos.

A groom whose property placed him in the upper rank of the
middle class would spend about 128 pesos as follows on *hakba:*

8	death blankets at ₱8	₱64
128	"irons" at ₱.50	64
	Total	₱128

A member of the lower middle class would spend about 92 pesos, and a member of the poorer class would spend about 36 pesos.

13. *Obligations incurred by those who enter into a marriage contract.*—First. The initial ceremony, the *mommon*, puts upon the principals in a marriage contract the obligation to abstain from sexual relations with any other persons. Sexual intercourse with any other person constitutes the crime of adultery. The degree of guilt for lapses in this respect depends on the progress that has been made toward the completion of the marriage, the culpability growing progressively with the performance of each succeeding marriage ceremonial.

Second. The obligation rests on the boy and his kin to furnish the immediate family of the girl with firewood from the time at which the first ceremony is performed until the young couple separate to live in a house by themselves.

Third. For the same period of time as that embraced in the preceding paragraph, the obligation rests on thé boy and his kin to keep the granaries of the family of the girl in repair, and to reroof them whenever needful.

Fourth. Each family helps the other in all that pertains to rice culture throughout the first year following the *bubun* ceremony. Each family furnishes the other with the pig necessary for the sacrifice at each of the three important rice-culture feasts: the *kulpe* (growth feast), the *kolating* (harvest feast), and the *tuldag* (granary feast).

Fifth. From the time at which the first ceremony is performed until the dissolution of the marriage, it is the duty of either spouse to furnish a pig to the other in the event of the sickness of the other or of any of his or her lineal ascendants.

Sixth. For the same period as that embraced in the preceding paragraph it is the duty of either spouse to furnish the other in the event of the death of any of the lineal ascendants of the other, a pig and a death blanket.

If the spouses be too young to attend to any of their respective obligations to each other or to the families concerned, it is the duty of their parents to attend to the discharge of the obligations.

The non-fulfilment or the non-discharge of any of the above obligations is sufficient cause for a demand for a divorce on the part of the injured spouse. The Ifugao does not consider it to be the duty of any person to leave his father and mother and cling to his wife

or husband. Rather does he consider the opposite to be the duty.
A good many marriages are undone between children because of the
non-fulfilment of one of these obligations on the part of one of the
families involved. It matters not that the spouse be so young as to
be of necessity innocent.

The husband has a right to have sexual intercourse with his wife.
If she does not accede to his desires, he has the right to force her
if he can, but he must not strike or injure her in his attempt. If he
cannot force her, he may demand a divorce. Ordinarily no man can
have sexual intercourse with an Ifugao woman possessed of her reason
and of normal strength, against that woman's will.

> Bugan of Baay, a very pretty girl, was married by her parents against her
> will to Pingkihan of Baay, a very rich but, unfortunately, a darkish and
> very ugly man. The marriage proceeded as far as the *hingot,* when it was
> thought wise by Pingkihan and the part of justice by the kin of the girl that
> the girl give her body before the proceeding went further. Pingkihan made
> many futile attempts to attain this purpose, but all in vain. Finally he de-
> spaired. The girl's father, however, told him to come to his house one night.
> Pingkihan did so. An uncle of the girl caught her, and held her. Pingkihan
> tried in vain to have sexual intercourse with her. The girl's resistance made
> the thing impossible. The marriage ceremonies were carried no further.

It cannot be too strongly emphasized that husband and wife *are
never united into one family. They are merely allies.* The ties that
bind each to his own family are much stronger than the ties that bind
them together. An Ifugao explained this to me by putting his hands
parallel, the forefingers together. The forefingers represent the two
spouses; the hands the two families. Should the two families separate,
should they withdraw from amity and agreement, the two spouses,
the forefingers, of necessity withdraw, because they are attached to
different hands.

Each succeeding feast in the consummation of the marriage carries
with it an added degree of obligation and of alliance; and an added
degree of culpability in cases of failure to comply with the marital
obligations and in cases of crimes against the marriage.

14. *The binawit relation.*—Oftentimes when the spouses are children and live in different villages, as soon as they are of sufficient
age to have some feeling for each other—at ten or more years, for
instance—one of them goes to the house of the other. Usually the
two espoused children live for a time at the house of the parents of
the one, and then for a time at the house of the parents of the other.

A child living thus at the house of his parents-in-law is called *binawit*. This matter is purely optional with the children, and is a matter of convenience to them.

The father of the girl has, however, a mean advantage, which he sometimes, though rarely, uses. If, for example, his son-in-law be a good worker, he counsels his daughter not to go to the house of her father-in-law, in order that she may hold her husband in his house to the end that the family profit by his labor. And even though the couple may have arrived at the age of separating from their elders and living in a house to themselves, the father of the girl refuses to give her her rice fields, putting the boy off from season to season with "Wait till next harvest" or "Wait till next spading time." It is true that the boy has in such conduct on the part of his father-in-law sufficient cause to justify him in divorcing the girl; but if he divorces her, he loses all that he has spent for sacrifices and *hakba* gifts!

15. *Property rights acquired by marriage.*—Neither spouse acquires any interest in the property that the other possesses at the time of the marriage. Each has, however, the right to veto the sale or transfer of the family property[8] of the other except where legal and sufficient reasons exist for such transfer. These legal and sufficient reasons are the necessity of selling the field: (*a*) to provide the necessary things for a funeral feast for ascendants or kinfolk; (*b*) to pay rightful debts; (*c*) to pay fines or indemnities; (*d*) to provide things necessary for feasts and sacrifices which are considered essential—a very liberal interpretation being placed upon the word "essential."

Should a man sell a field for a light or trivial cause without the permission of his wife, the validity of the transfer would not be effected by the fact of the non-consent of the wife. But the wife would have recourse for damages from her husband, and might demand: (*a*) twice the price received for the field as a settlement on their children; (*b*) a divorce; (*c*) or both. The right of each spouse to veto the sale of the other's property is equal and the same. This right is based principally or perhaps wholly on the ground that each spouse is the guardian of the interest of the children of the union, born or unborn.

The spouses have a joint right in all property acquired after marriage as the result of their joint labors; that is to say, any property whatever obtained except (*a*) by the sale of the fields of the one and the repurchase of other fields with the proceeds; (*b*) as the result of

---

[8] Family property: for definition see sec. 33.

a fine or indemnity assessed by the family of one against some person for injury done a member of that family; (*c*) ceremonial gifts such as the *hakba* and *habalag;* (*d*) inheritance.

REMARRIAGE OF THE WIDOWED

16. *The gibu payment to terminate marriage.*—Even death itself does not terminate an Ifugao marriage. It terminates neither the obligation of the widowed to the soul of the dead spouse nor the compact of alliance between the two families involved. This obligation and this compact may be terminated only by the payment known as the *gibu.*

The word *gibu* means literally "finish". In its narrowest and probably original sense it may have meant a payment to terminate all the relations and obligations growing out of a marriage. There is another explanation. From the day of the death of a spouse till the third day after the interment (when the *binokbok* ceremony is performed), the kin of the deceased and the kin of the surviving spouse are on terms of theoretical enmity. They observe with reference to each other all the taboos that are observed toward enemies. This practice may have arisen from a former belief—a belief that is current among many primitive peoples today—that every death is due to sorcery or witchcraft. Whom so naturally blamed as the surviving spouse or his kin? If this be the explanation, then the *gibu* originated as an indemnity paid for the life of the deceased.

In the present day, the *gibu* in a broader sense applies to all fines and indemnities paid in connection with the abuse or termination of a marriage.

A remarriage may not properly be effected by the widowed until he has paid the kin of the dead spouse the *gibu 'n di nate* (*gibu* of the *dead*), or the *datok,* as it is specifically called. Failure on the part of the widowed to make this payment would lead to a seizure of his property or a lance throwing. In the Kiangan area this payment is not nearly so high as in other parts of Ifugao land, and for the reason that in the former area large payments are made to the kin of the woman in the *hakba* gifts at the beginning of the marriage. In Benaue and other areas of Ifugao the payments are about five times the amounts shown in the subjoined table.

The following is the *datok* payment of the Kiangan area:

DATOK[9]

For the Wealthy

Pu-u, 1 death blanket	₱8.00
Haynub, 1 pot	5.00
Haynub, 1 pot	2.00
Natauwinan	1.00
Natauwinan	1.00
Natauwinan	1.00
Natauwinan	1.00
Natuku	.50
Natuku	.50
Na-oha	.25
Amo:	
6 irons	1.50
Paduldul (offering to the soul of the dead), 1 pig	10.00
Total	₱31.75

For the Middle Class

Pu-u, 1 death blanket	₱4.00
Haynub, 1 pot	2.00
Haynub, 1 pot	2.00
Natauwinan	1.00
Natauwinan	1.00
Natuku	.50
Natuku	.50
Nunbadi	.40
Na-oha	.25
Amo:	
4 irons	1.00
Paduldul, 1 pig	8.00
Total	₱20.65

For the Very Poor

Pu-u, 1 pot	₱4.00
Haynub	1.00
Natauwinan	1.00
Natuku	.50
Nunbadi	.40
Na-oha	.25
Amo:	
4 irons	1.00
Paduldul, 1 pig	5.00
Total	₱13.15

---

[9] For an explanation of the Ifugao's method of making payments and of reckoning fines and indemnities, see sec. 75.

It is considered an insult to the deceased and his kin for a widowed person to remarry within a year from the death of his spouse. In such an event, a larger *gibu* is demanded by the kin of the dead spouse. Should the spouses have had no children, double the amount usual is demanded as the *datok*.

If the widowed remarries without having first formally notified the kin of his dead spouse of his intention, or if he scandalously has sexual intercourse, he commits adultery according to Ifugao law, and must pay the *gibu luktap* (see sec. 75, 94). As a matter of fact, I do not believe that this law is often enforced. The Ifugaos say that it was nearly always enforced before the establishment of foreign government.

If the widowed be a woman, both she and the man with whom she contracts a second marriage are responsible for the *gibu* payment. The payment as a matter of practice is always made by the man who marries her; but it is said that, should her second husband for any reason fail to pay, the widow would be held for the payment.

In the event of the birth of a bastard child to a surviving spouse, the *gibu* must be paid.

The following is an instance of the non-payment of this indemnity, and the *sequelae:*

Piniliu of Longa married the wife of Butlong, a deceased kinsman of Timbuluy, also of Longa. Piniliu did not come forward with the usual *datok* payment, notwithstanding the fact that it was repeatedly demanded of him.

Finally Piniliu went to Nueva Viscaya, and there bought a carabao. Timbuluy gathered his kin and met Piniliu when he was bringing back the carabao. About two miles before they reached their home village Timbuluy and his kin seized the animal, hamstringing and slaughtering it before Piniliu's eyes.

The act of Timbuluy may very safely be said to have been justified by Ifugao custom, and so to have been legal.

The *gibu* is smaller if the second spouse taken be a kinsman or kinswoman of the first.

If the living spouse should not have furnished the animal required of him (see sec. 13) and a death blanket for the funeral of the dead spouse, the value of these things is added to the amount of the *gibu*.[10]

---

[10] The fact that an Ifugao spouse remains always a member of the family of his blood kindred, and that the ties binding him to his conjugal partner are light indeed is shown by the fact that, at his death, funeral expenses fall mainly on his father and mother and brothers and sisters.

DIVORCE

The following tables show some of the causes for divorce together with the payments, if any, due and to whom they are due.

17. *Divorce because of necessity.*—This is always achieved by mutual agreement.

Cause	Fine	Paid to
1. A bad omen of the bile sac of the animal sacrificed at the *mommon, imbango, hingot,* or *bubun* feasts (see sec. 17)	None	
2. A bad omen of the bile sac at any of the three principal rice feasts of either family during the year following the performance of the *bubun* ceremony (see sec. 7)	None	

It is considered that only ill fortune could come of a marriage which gave even a single ill omen in any of these cases. It is not permitted to provide another pig and consult the omen again in any of these feasts. But in all subsequent feasts this may be done, and does not lead to divorce. Divorce is unavoidable if the above occurs, and neither party would dream of opposing it.

18. *Divorce for mutual benefit.*—Childlessness is the cause. Divorce under these circumstances is considered a mutual benefit. It may be achieved by mutual consent or may be demanded by either party without liability for indemnity.

Cause	Fine	Paid to
1. Continuous dying of offspring	None	
2. Childlessness for a period of two or three years after marriage	None	

It is considered that the gods of animal fertility look with permanent disapproval on the union. This is not without some show of reason, since spouses who have lived together for a goodly number of years on separation and remarriage with other persons have each had children. Ifugao experience in this matter would indicate that there is such a matter as *biologic incompatibility.*

19. *Divorce which may be demanded by either party.*—Cruelty and incompatibility are the causes. The divorce may be by mutual consent or may be demanded by the injured.

Cause	Fine	Paid to
1. Neglect of one spouse by the other in time of sickness; the failure to "cherish"	*Hudhud* (see below)	The injured
2. Ill treatment of one of the spouses by the near kin of the other; insulting language by a father- or mother-in-law	In some cases *hudhud*	Divorcer

Cause	Fine	Paid to
3. Unwillingness of either party to have sexual intercourse with the other, and continued resistance to it, when there is the ability to perform the sexual act	*Hudhud*	Divorcer
4. The lessening of the fields of one of the spouses which it was agreed in the contract of marriage would be his, without the consent of the kin of the other spouse	*Hudhud*	Divorcer
5. Permanent inability to perform the sexual act	None	
6. Insanity	None	
7. Failure on the part of one spouse or his family in any of the obligations heretofore mentioned (see sec. 13)	*Hudhud* (not always paid)	Divorcer
8. Commission of crime by one spouse against a member of the other spouse's family	*Hudhud*	Divorcer
9. Refusal of one family to furnish the pigs necessary to complete the ceremonials; in case the spouses are related, the refusal or continued neglect of one family to produce a pig for the *ponga* (see sec. 11)	None	
10. The selling of a rice field for insufficient reasons by one spouse without the consent of the other (see sec. 14)	*Hudhud* (also see sec. 21)	Divorcer
11. Continued refusal of the father of either of the spouses to deliver the fields called for in the contract when the couple has reached a reasonable age (see sec. 10)	*Hudhud*	Divorcer
12. Continued laziness or shiftless conduct on the part of one of the spouses	Usually none	
13. The incurring of many debts or other obligations; the squandering of family resources	*Hudhud*	Divorcer
14. Unreasonable or insane jealousy	None	

20. *Cases where divorce may be demanded by one party or the other.*

Cause	Fine	Paid to
1. Desertion of lawful spouse and cohabitation with another; divorce already a *fait accompli*	*Gibu* of *hokwit* (see sec. 94)	Injured party
2. Incompatibility; continuous quarreling	*Hudhud*	The divorced
3. A change of affection or a desire not to proceed with or complete the marriage; if there be children, all the property or nearly all must be settled on them	*Hudhud*	The divorced
4. Adultery	*Gibu* of *luktap* (see sec. 94)	The injured

21. *The hudhud, or payment for mental anguish.*—This is the fine or indemnity assessed in cases of divorce at the instance of one of the parties, when uncomplicated by improper sexual relations, on the ground of mental anguish, *hakit di nemnem,* literally, "hurt of the mind." In general it may be said to be assessed against that spouse who has made necessary the dissolution of the marriage, whether or not he be the one who takes the initiative in effecting the divorce. Should the divorce be effected on account of sexual crime of one of the spouses, the *greater the injury the more severely the crime* is punished. The *hudhud* is a small fine, but its payment is said effectually to banish the mental anguish. The dignity and self-importance of the Malay are of unusual proportions in comparison with his other feelings and emotions. In Kiangan district there are three grades of the *hudhud:* one for the *kadangyang* or wealthy; one for the *tumuk* or middle class; and one for *nawatat* or poor. The following are the usual amounts of the indemnity:

THE HUDHUD INDEMNITY

For the Wealthy

1 death blanket	₱8.00
Total	₱8.00

For the Middle Class

1 iron pot	₱2.00
Natauwinan	1.00
Natuku	.60
Nunbadi	.40
Na-oha	.25
Total	₱4.85

For the Very Poor

Natauwinan	₱1.00
Total	₱1.00

In case of a change of mind leading to an unwillingness to proceed with the marriage, the following additional data are pertinent: Should the girl refuse to proceed with the marriage after the performance of the *mommon* ceremonial and before the performance of the *imbango* ceremonial, she pays simply the *hudhud;* should she refuse after the *imbango,* she pays the *hudhud,* and, unless her kin have given the boy's kin the *mangdad di imbango,* she pays back the pig given her family by the boy's family for the *imbango* ceremonial. The same is true, *mutatis mutandis,* should she refuse to proceed after the *hingot* ceremony. The boy may refuse to proceed with the marriage after the *mommon* and before the *imbango* without liability to damages; should he refuse after the *imbango,* he must pay the *hudhud.*

22. *Divorce ceremonies.*—It is only when divorce is by mutual agreement that divorce is attended by any ceremonies. The ceremonies consist of a *honga,* or general welfare feast, not greatly different in spirit from the ceremonials by which the couple were married. In other cases, the couple have separated prior to the formal divorce or have such ill feeling toward each other that concerted action is impossible.

23. *Property settlements in case of divorce.*—(1) When there are no children: Each spouse takes the property that he brought to the marriage, together with any property received since by inheritance, or solely by virtue of his relationship to his own family.

The remaining property, that is, family property such as rice fields, gold ornaments, *gansas,* etc., and personal property such as food stores, house furnishings, implements, domestic animals, and also liabilities that rightfully bear equally on both spouses are apportioned by two umpires, *monhangdad,* one chosen by each spouse. These persons make an equitable division, taking as their fee any odd articles of personal property. Thus if there be three *bolos,* they take one; if there be a chicken "left over," they take it. They may not carry this appropriation to themselves too far, however.

(2) When there are children of the union: The woman has the *right* to the children, and nearly always exercises it. In some cases, when the mother has no rice fields and the father does have rice fields, and when the children are large enough not to need a mother's care, by special agreement the father takes one or more of the children.

Whoever takes the children takes possession of the property that belongs to them. Usually the woman takes all the children and manages the husband's family property that has been allotted them.

All the property of both the spouses must be assigned to their children at the time of the divorce (except the personal property). The one who takes a child takes also the property of that child and tills it. He may not dispose of it except for the purpose of meeting legitimate obligations against it. Should the child die, its brothers and sisters inherit the property.

DEPENDENTS IN RELATION TO FAMILY LAW

24. *Adopted children.*—An adopted child is termed *inagamid,* that is, "taken to one's self"; or it may be termed *na-imbalbalayen,* "made one's child." The word *inagamid* is also used to denote a slave taken into a household.

Adoptions are rather rare; for the reason, I suspect, that it is only the propertied class who make them, and that persons of this class, being well nurtured, usually have children of their own. Usually the child adopted is the son or daughter of a brother or sister, and so is really, according to the Ifugao mode of reckoning kinship, the son or daughter of the adopter. Which family the child shall be adopted from[11] is a question that is hard for a man and his wife to agree upon, the wife naturally wishing to adopt from her family and the husband from his. Sometimes two children are adopted, one from each family. More often the adopted child is married to one of the family of the unrelated parent. The two parents by adoption then give or will give their children by adoption a large part or nearly all of their properties. They may not give the adopted children *all.* They must give something to those who would have been their heirs had they not made the adoption.

25. *Servants.*—The general term for servants is *baal.* As a rule no pay is given a servant other than his board and clothing. It is the obligation of the master, however, to furnish animals for sacrifice when the servant falls sick. It is, further, considered good form for the master to furnish animals for sacrifice in case of sickness of the servant's father or mother; but I do not believe it to be an obligation. A servant that has been a long time with his master is called *nikkop.* It is an obligation resting on the master to furnish the animals and other necessities for a marriage feast for such a servant. As a rule there is no definite time set for the termination of a contract between master and servant, and such contracts are terminable at any time at the will of either party.

Sometimes an unmarried adult goes to the house of a rich man and asks to be taken as a member of the family on such a basis; but as a rule servants are children when first taken. Oftentimes a high degree of affection is felt for a faithful member of the family of this

---

[11] The Ifugao reckons kinship by generations. Those of a contemporaneous generation are *tulang,* brothers and sisters, children of the preceding generation of blood relatives, grandchildren of the generation of ascendants twice removed, fathers of the succeeding generation, and so on (see appendix 1).

class, and if a child he is treated as a son or daughter. Sometimes a rice field is assigned to him, and he inherits as though he were the youngest son or daughter.

26. *Slaves.*—Before the American occupation, except in those few parts of the habitat that were prosperous and in which the obtaining of the daily ration was not a serious problem, the selling by parents who found themselves poverty stricken of one of their children was not at all uncommon. The price that a child brought his parents varied from five pigs to five carabaos. There was no difference in value between a male and a female child. A slave was most valuable at the age of eighteen or twenty. Some men were slave dealers, and carried great numbers of children to Nueva Vizcaya and Isabela. In those parts a slave was worth from five to twenty carabaos.

Among the Ifugao a slave was absolutely the property of his owner. The latter had power of life and death over him. Even if the master killed the slave it was not considered that the slave's family would be justified in avenging the death. But a slave's children, even though they be the children by another slave parent, were free. Frequently one of them was assigned to take the place of the father and another of the mother, and these two then became free. In the lowlands, however, the children of slaves were slaves, which accounts partly for the higher prices paid for slaves in those parts. It would be interesting to know whether the lowland (Christian) Filipino held children of slaves as slaves before his civilization and christianization by the Spaniard, or whether his practice then was that of his Ifugao brethren.

The purchase of a slave was celebrated by a very pretentious series of religious ceremonials. Oftentimes, with the Ifugao, a slave was set free, at or before the death of his master, and was given a rice field. Unless set free he was inherited by the master's heirs as any other property. Sometimes a slave child was adopted by a childless couple as their own son or daughter.

The following "Pocahontas" story is told of a slave who lived at his master's house in Anao. The master treated him ill, and the slave, a young man, ran away. He went to the enemy village of Alimit. The men of that town were going to kill him, hearing his Anao accent, and believing him to be one of their hereditary enemies. But a handsome girl, the daughter of a rich man, protected him with her own body and begged for his life. She afterward married him and bought his freedom. There was no actual necessity for her buying his freedom, since the last thing in the world the Anao master could have accomplished would have been the recovery of his property. She bought his freedom, however, in order that the children of herself and her husband might never be called the "offspring of a slave."

Mention should be made, also, of those who voluntarily entered into slavery as a means of paying a debt. The word "voluntarily" in this connection needs explanation, however. A man was usually frightened into entering into servitude by the probability that if he did not he would be killed.

In parts of Ifugao, the killing of women or children in feuds was a disgraceful thing, and rarely, if ever, practiced. Instead they were made prisoners and sold for debt. Sometimes, too, women or children were carried off and held for debt. This form of collection of debts was legal, or at least semi-legal. In case the debt was paid, the captive was returned; otherwise, he was sold as a slave.

ILLEGITIMATE CHILDREN

27. *Definition of illegitimacy; its frequency.*—A bastard is one whose father refuses to take the mother as his legal wife for any period of time, however short. The marriage of the parents after the birth of the bastard, consequently, legitimizes the child.

Bastardy is not very frequent. It is extremely frequent, however, for a girl to become pregnant before her marriage. But in such cases her lover usually marries her. It is usually in cases of doubtful parentage and in cases in which one of the parents is of vastly different status as to wealth that a marriage does not follow pregnancy. But there are also a few cases of bastardy surrounded by other circumstances.

28. *Obligations of father to bastard child.*—The father of a bastard must give his child a rice field if he has a field unassigned. He must also give the mother an *oban*, or blanket, with which to carry the child after the Ifugao fashion on her back. The value of this gift is principally in its constituting a formal recognition of the child.

The mother's rights are enforced by her kin. To a certain extent the same is true of the bastard's rights. A man is never forced to marry a woman against his will—an Ifugao woman would be ashamed to ask such a thing. Such a marriage, too, would not be congenial. The mere making of a bastard a legitimate child is not of sufficient importance to justify such a marriage. Besides, the Ifugaos have a saying, *kumadangyang di inlaglaga:* "The bastard becomes a rich man."

Except in the matter of division of estates, the bastard has the same rights as legitimate children. His father's kin back him in legal procedures and avenge his wrongs as if he were legitimate. The father and his kin assist him in his marriage feast and in other feasts that may be necessary.

29. *Determination of parentage.*—The ordeal is employed when two or more men are accused of being the father of a bastard. The woman's word is not sufficient to settle the parentage. The one she accuses may lay the matter at the door of another. The ordeals used are the duel with *runo* stalks, or eggs, and the hot water test. The woman, holding the babe in her arms, sits half way between the two controversants.

The Ifugao has the remnant of a peculiar belief that a child may be begotten by two fathers. They say, for example, that if A and B, two men, are having sexual intercourse with a woman, Z, and that if it is settled by fate that A and B each shall beget a child of the male sex, Z will conceive and the child may be the son of both of them. But if A is fated to beget a female child, and B to beget a male child, the semen of the one undoes that of the other, and the woman does not conceive. This belief is not taken seriously as a rule; but I have heard it advanced in a case of illegitimate birth.[12]

Accordingly, should each of the two men be struck by the eggs thrown in the duel to decide the parentage of the child, or should both be scalded by hot water, the Ifugao, formerly at least, held that the child belonged to each of them.

RECIPROCAL OBLIGATIONS OF PARENTS AND THEIR CHILDREN

30. *Duties of parents to children.*—The Ifugao family exists principally for the child members of it. The parents are supposed to love, and do love their children more than the children love them. The parents are under the obligation to provide food and clothing for their children, and to impart to them the tribal knowledge that is necessary to a respectable and well regulated Ifugao life. The child may be forced to assist, according to his ability, in the matter of household tasks, work in the fields, and the like.

Corporal punishment may be, but *very rarely* is, administered. It is the mothers, strange to say, rather than the fathers, who use this

---

[12] It is a Malay's pride never to be caught without an explanation or excuse. However flimsy or absurd this may be, or perhaps in proportion to its absurdity, he advances it boldly and brazenly.

form of punishment. I never saw or heard of a father whipping his child. Such a thing as a right of life and death over a child is as unthought of, as it would be abhorrent, to the Ifugao if mentioned.

The Ifugao child, even at the age of ten or twelve, begins to look upon his parents' property as his own, or at least that portion of it that will fall to his share. A little later, he becomes independent—he does not obey his parents unless he wants to do so. He is fully as likely to command them as to obey them. And the parent is under the obligation early to allow the children to displace him from his possession. He must turn over all his property to them as soon as they are able to marry or care for themselves. Should there be but a single field, he assigns it to his eldest. From the time that the fields are turned over, the father's offices are those of priest and counselor; the mother's offices are those of priestess (sometimes) and of household drudge (always).

31. *Obligations of children to parents.*—The obligations of children to their parents are:

(*a*) To provide animals and other things requisite to religious feasts that are thought necessary to keep them in good health and to restore them when sick. This obligation is by far the most burdensome one, usually.

(*b*) To provide food and clothing for them, and to care for them when sick or helpless.

(*c*) To provide requisites for a funeral feast in accord with the station of the deceased.

In case the child has not yet obtained possession of his allotment, these obligations do not rest upon the child, but are a charge upon the property alloted him. If the child has obtained possession of his share in the family estate, the obligation rests upon the child himself.

The law of primogeniture holds with respect to these obligations. Civil obligations rest more heavily upon the older children and as nearly as possible in proportion to the amounts of property received from the parents. Children who receive no family property contribute very little.

One might ask how compliance with these obligations is enforced. Compliance with them is really not enforced. They are the most sacred of all duties. Not to meet them would bring upon one's self such universal reproach as to render life unbearable.

THE PROPERTY LAW

32. *The Ifugao's classification of properties.*—The Ifugao clearly distinguishes between two classes of property. His language, and indeed his thought, is very poor in abstractions, however, and he bases his classification upon the difference in the method of transferring property by sale. The one class he calls *ma-ibuy,* "that for whose transfer by sale an *ibuy* ceremony is necessary"; and the other, *adi ma-ibuy,* "that for whose transfer by sale an *ibuy* ceremony is not necessary." Classifying them upon their essential differences in status in Ifugao law and culture, I term the former family property and the latter personal property.

FAMILY PROPERTY

33. *The Ifugao attitude toward family property.*—Family properties consist of rice lands, forest lands, and heirlooms. The Ifugao attitude is that lands and articles of value that have been handed down from generation to generation cannot be the property of any individual. Present holders possess only a transient and fleeting possession, or better, occupation, insignificant in duration in comparison with the decades and perhaps centuries that have usually elapsed since the field or heirloom came into the possession of the family. Their possession is more of the nature of a trust than an absolute ownership—a holding in trust for future generations.

It is a misfortune when family property that has long been in the possession of a family must be sold out of it. But if it be sold to a member of another branch of the same family, the misfortune is accounted less in proportion to the nearness of the kinship. However, the rights of the living and of the ancestors departed, are greater than the rights of the unborn. Consequently, a field may properly be sold and so depart from the family, if it be in order to provide animals to accompany the spirit of a deceased ancestor to the spirit world, or in order to provide animals for sacrifices to secure the recovery from dangerous sickness of some member of the family. Inherited property, however, is not to be disposed of without exhausting every effort to keep it within the family. Nor must it ever be disposed of for light or trivial reasons. Except when sold to satisfy the needs of the departed or living (in these cases, a forced sale) family properties when sold bring exorbitant prices. Fields or other properties which have been recently acquired or constructed, sell at considerably lower prices, even though their intrinsic value be the same.

Nothing that I know of in the Ifugao make-up, is so characteristically oriental as is this subordination of individual to family rights.

34. *Rice lands.*—A "field" consists of all the contiguous paddies in one place that are the property of one man. In sales and in transfers arising out of family relationship, and in *balal* (pawning), a field is never divided. If there be two heirs and only one field to be inherited, the elder of the heirs takes the entire field. The reason for this and for the rights of primogeniture (see sec. 53) in inheritance and assignment of property, is to be found in the fact that the Ifugao social consciousness considers it better—and it is better—that a family have at least one powerful member round whom the kin may rally and to whom they may look for aid, than that the family property be split into insignificant parcels that would affect but little the property of all. Aside from this consideration there is also the practical difficulty of dividing a field. In the process of dividing, the family unity— which is the dearest and most necessary thing in Ifugao society—would probably be destroyed by quarrels and squabbles. Even if an equitable division could be arranged, a great deal of the field would be taken up in dikes and division lines. It is a rare thing to find an Ifugao rice field as large as one acre in extent.

There is no formal recognition of the eldest as the head of the family. But together with the lion's share of the property, the first-born inherits certain well defined and rather stringent obligations. In this we seem to have the savor of a system of patriarchy.

35. *Forest lands.*—Such lands, valuable principally because of the woods upon them, are often the common property of a group of kinsmen and their families. They are sometimes partitioned. They are nearly sure to be partitioned if wood be scarce, or if part of the land be suitable for rice fields.

36. *Heirlooms.*—Heirlooms consist of such articles as gold neck-ornaments (intrinsic value of the gold being about 10 pesos to 20 pesos; current price among the Ifugaos, 60 pesos to 120 pesos); gongs (value 8 pesos to 250 pesos); rice-wine jars (value 60 pesos to 400 pesos); *pango*, or strings of amber colored glass beads (value 80 pesos to 160 pesos); and *bungol*, long strings of agates and bloodstones which are very rarely sold (value about 250 pesos). These articles

are used fully as much by the owner's kin as by the owner himself; for they wear the beads and ornaments, play the gongs in feasts, and brew rice wines in the jars.

37. *Sale of family property.*—The selling of rice fields, forest lands, gold neck-ornaments, rice-wine jars, and the like is a matter of practical concern to the entire family. Selling them, except in cases of necessity and after consultation with the kin, would lead to ill feeling toward the seller on the part of his kin, and a refusal to assist and back him. Since there is no form of political government in Ifugao culture, and since every man must, with the help of his kin, ''get his own justice,'' this would be no small punishment. How serious a punishment it would be, the reader will, perhaps, realize when he reads the chapter on procedure.

The sale of family property is registered by ceremonies in which the near kin of both buyer and seller take part. In comparison with the solemnity of these transfers, our real estate transfers are commonplace. In comparison with their complexity, our transfers are simplicity itself.

PERSONAL PROPERTY

38. *Definition.*—Such articles as knives, spears, dishes, baskets, pots, houses, *camote* fields, fruit-bearing trees, blankets, animals and articles of minor value, are on the same legal basis as personal property among ourselves. Three items in this list demand special attention: houses, valuable trees, and sweet potato fields.

39. *Houses.*—Dwellings are movable property in Ifugao. A man, with the aid of his kinsmen can, and frequently does, take a house to pieces, move it to a different site and set it up again before sunset. The plot on which a house stands has no value. The value of a house is usually about ten pesos, the range of prices being from six to sixty pesos.

40. *Valuable trees.*—Cocoanut trees, coffee trees, and areca palms are sold without any sale or transfer of the land on which they stand. The value of a cocoanut tree in full bearing is five pesos; of a coffee tree, one to two pesos; of an areca palm one-half peso. As a rule, the land on which these trees stand has no value. A practice presenting parallel features that leads one to believe that the same manner of selling trees must have prevailed among the Pangasinanes, one of the Christian tribes, is that, in the sale of the cocoanut groves in

central Pangasinan, the trees are sold at so much apiece; but in order to get possession of the trees, it is necessary to buy the land at so much a hectare, since the land has a value.

Camote or sweet potato fields are discussed in section 45.

No ceremonials are involved in the transfer of personal property; nor are witnesses necessary, as a general thing.

PERPETUAL TENURE

Tenure is either perpetual or transient.

41. *Rice and forest lands.*—Rice-land and forest-land tenures are perpetual.

In case an owner abandons a rice field for any period of time, however long, and another man takes up the field without interference or contrary order of the true owner, clears it of underbrush, builds up the broken dikes, levels once more the terraces, tills and plants it, the latter has the right to use the field for the same number of years that it was abandoned. At the end of this time, the field reverts to the true owner. Should the owner desire possession of his field before the expiration of the time, for which, in accordance with this rule, the field should remain in the possession of him who redeemed it from the wild mountain side, he must repurchase possession.

It is not incumbent on a man to secure permission of the owner of an abandoned field before working it; it is incumbent on the owner to prevent others from working his field against his will.

In the event a rice field is made on privately owned forest lands from which the timber has long been cut, the owner of the land, when he has proved title, demands payment for the land. But he may not take advantage of the labor that the other has spent on the land in making rice fields, to demand an exorbitant payment. To take such a course would invite danger to himself.

Forest lands that have been divested of their wood may be planted in *camotes* (sweet potatoes) by any person without asking the consent of the owner. If the owner does not want his land so planted or intends to use it himself, it is his business to inform any who may have started to work the land. But if he is tardy in making this prohibition, he must pay for the labor expended, or must allow the continuance of the work, and the harvesting of one crop of camotes from the land. I am not certain that this is the case in all parts of Ifugao.

42. *"Homesteading."*—That land which is not rice fields or forest land and which is not owned by some individual by reason of its having been one or the other formerly, becomes the property of whomsoever makes it into rice fields. The tenure so acquired is perpetual.

43. *Paghok, or landmarks.*—Whenever a rice-field terrace is walled, the terrace wall is an unfailing and unimpeachable landmark. But in many districts, the terraces are not walled. In such cases, the division lines between fields are marked by large chunks of wood or by large stones, buried three or four feet deep along the division line. A boulder is of course a most excellent landmark.

Weather and the elements are continually wearing back an unwalled terrace. The amount each year is very small. But when in the course of years the displacement is sufficient to justify it, the owner may take that part of the field in the terrace below that belongs to him.

The moving of a landmark is said never to occur, since it would take two or three men to lift the heavy stones, and would require a long time. Moreover it could not be done without leaving plain and indisputable evidence of the crime.

44. *Right of way through property owned by others.*—In order to get rid of insect pests, clay is sometimes conveyed to a field to form a layer over it about two inches thick. The clay is shovelled into a stream of water above, and carried as silt to the field and there allowed to settle. Sometimes leaf mold and other fertilizers are conveyed to a field in this manner.

It makes no difference how many fields there may be above that on which it is desired to deposit the sediment, the owner of the last has a right to cut a ditch through the upper fields as a conduit for the stream of water. He must, however, repair all the upper terraces so as to leave them as they were before.

TRANSIENT TENURE

45. *Tenure of sweet potato fields.*—Sweet potato, or *camote*, fields are clearings on the mountain sides about the village. They are nearly always steep slopes, and quickly lose their fertility. For that reason, they are abandoned after a period that varies in different districts of Ifugao according as *camotes* are a more or less important factor in the subsistence of the people. Thus in Banaue, where *camotes* form a very large part of the subsistence of the people, the fields are cul-

tivated for five or even six years, if located near the village; if more
distant, they are abandoned after about two years. In Kiangan, where
camotes do not play such an important part in subsistence, the fields
are in any case abandoned after one or two years. The reason for
abandoning the fields is that the soil wears out soon, so that the
camotes grow small, and the yield does not repay the labor spent in
cultivation. But in case a large area about the village be cultivated,
rather than face the necessity of going far from the village to make
clearings, the old fields are tended to a point at which the yield becomes
almost *nil*. After abandoning a field, the owner still has a claim on
it, but only until such time as the field grows up in weeds, in which
case the labor spent by him in making the clearing may be fairly
presumed to have been undone. After abandonment, the field regains
its fertility slowly. The first person who begins clearing the field
again becomes its possessor for a new term of years. It is exceedingly
rare that quarrels arise over *camote* fields. *Camote* fields are sometimes sold, but it is not the land that is sold, but the crop with temporary possession of the land.

TRANSFERS OF PROPERTY FOR A CONSIDERATION

There are two kinds of transfer of family property for "consideration": the *balal* (pawn), and outright sale.

46. *The balal.*—In case a man finds himself under the necessity
of raising a considerable sum of money—usually in order to provide
funds for a funeral feast or a sacrifice—he frequently borrows the
sum, giving a rice field into the hands of his creditor as a security
and as a means of paying the interest on debt. The creditor holds,
plants, and harvests the field until the debt be repaid. The field is
to all purposes his, except that he cannot sell it. He can, however,
transfer it as a *balal* into the hands of another. But he must transfer
it for the same or a less amount of money; that is, if he has loaned
fifty pesos on the field, he must not borrow more than that sum, unless,
of course, he be able to secure the owner's consent. This is a very wise
provision of Ifugao law that insures the prompt return of the field
to the owner as soon as he be able to get together the amount needed
to redeem the field. An example will make this clear. A borrows
fifty pesos of B, giving his field as a *balal* into B's charge; B gives it as
a *balal* to C for the same or a less amount, who gives it as a *balal* to D
and so on. When A is able to repay the debt, he goes to B and

delivers him the sum plus the fee of the agent through whom the deal was effected. With this amount, including the fee, B goes to C, C goes to D, and so on. Were B to have borrowed without A's consent more than fifty pesos, say seventy pesos, and were he not financially able to obtain the difference (twenty pesos) between his debt to C and the debt that A had just paid him, there would be an excellent beginning for a quarrel that might end in lance throwing.

Real estate of this kind continues in the hands of the creditor until the debt be paid. Transfers of the same piece of land may go on indefinitely. The transfers are witnessed each time by the agent who obtains the loan for the person in whose charge the field is. This agent receives as his fee about five to twelve per cent of the value of the loan obtained. He is the only witness necessary. His fee is paid him in the first place by the creditor. But the fee is added to the amount loaned, and must be returned by the debtor when the debt is paid. As soon as the agent has received his fee, it is his duty to inform his oldest son, in case he be of sufficient age, otherwise his wife or a brother, of the terms of the transaction. This is a precautionary measure against his death and the consequent leaving of the transaction without a witness.

Each creditor is liable to his debtor for the return of the field upon the payment of the sum due, the case being precisely parallel to the liability of the indorsers of a check or a note, one to another.

Suppose, however, that the field be planted in rice. In such an event, the owner must leave the creditor in possession of the field until the crop shall have been harvested. In case the field be newly planted, it is sometimes returned to the owner on the agreement that he care for the growing crop, harvest it, and give the creditor half. If the field be spaded, but not planted, the owner may pay his creditor for the cost of the labor expended in spading the field, together with a bonus as interest.

The amount loaned on a field never equals the value of the field. Usually it is about half the value. It makes no difference how long a field remain in the status known as *balal,* the field, subject to the conditions of the preceding paragraph, *must be returned to the owner or his heirs whenever the amount loaned be returned.* Sometimes a field remains a *balal* for two or three generations.

47. *Sales of family property.*—The Ifugao has a very peculiar system of buying and selling in connection with family property, by which, paradoxical as it may sound, a man has to pay for an article

almost twice its price. In order to complete the purchase of a rice field, there are "extras" almost without number, to be paid, each extra bearing as its metaphorical name, the name of some act of rice-field cultivation or of a feature of the trade itself. So far as has yet been ascertained, there is no myth or story to explain how this peculiar idiosyncracy originated.

The price is divided into ten parts, each part being represented by a *runo* stick or a notch cut in a stick, or by knots in a string. In the Banaue district, these sticks are kept for generations as records of the sale. The first two sticks are called *budut,* and represent the payment down. They are the heaviest payments, not necessarily made on the day of the transfer, but at a set time. The eight others represent some standard in the Ifugao's system of barter, and are called *gatang,* or price. They are paid at some indefinite time in the future. Possession of the field is given after the first payment. In order to make the sticks conform to the standards of barter, it is sometimes necessary to represent one payment by two sticks.

Fee of witnesses and agent. This fee is called *lukbu,* or *lagbu* (in Benaue dialect). The principal witnesses are preferably the distant kin of the seller, and the agent or agents who effected the sale. The names of the different sticks, knots, or notches are translated literally in the tables diagraming the transactions in purchasing fields.

These fees are paid and the presents made to the kin of the seller at a feast called *ibuy.* This feast is performed whenever the purchase price of the field has been paid. The kin of buyer and seller meet in the purchaser's house.

A. TRANSACTIONS IN THE PURCHASE OF A FIELD IN THE KIANGAN AREA

I. Payments on the property

Paid down at time purchase is consummated, or soon after:

Name of transaction and meaning	Article transferred	Value
Budut, or *tandong*	1 pig	₱20.00
Budut, or *tandong*	1 pig	15.00

Additional instalments (*gatang*) paid irregularly:

Gatang	1 death blanket	8.00
Nunokóp (two at a time)	1 death blanket	8.00
Nunokóp (two at a time)	1 pig	20.00
Gatang	1 pig	8.00
Gatang	1 pig	8.00

Total .... ₱87.00

II. Fees (lukbu) of the principal witnesses

Name of transaction and meaning	Article transferred	Value
Bobod (the tying)	1 pig	₱10.00
Page (rice)	1 small pig	6.00
Lanad (commission of the go-between)		5.00
Pugug (finished)		4.00
Gogod (cut)		3.00
Kinta (left over)		1.00
Total		₱ 29.00

III. Advance interest paid to the seller

Baloblad　　　　　　　　　　　　　　　　　　　　　　₱ 6.50

(If the seller is a kinsman, he may not take this amount. If taken, the seller and the purchaser may not eat together for five days, since they are on a basis of "theoretical enmity." This "theoretical enmity" exists in several other instances in Ifugao life. See section 15 and appendix 2.)

IV. Gifts to the seller's kin

Piduan di gogod (repetition of the cut)	Natauwin	₱1.00
Piduan di kinta (repetition of the surplus)*	Natauwin	1.00
Hablal (flooding of field)	Na-oha	.25
Hagaphap (chopping of grass from terrace wall)	Na-oha	.25
Ohok (sticks for beans to climb up)	Na-oha	.25
Umuhun (burning off grass)	Na-oha	.25
Aiyag (dinner call)	Na-oha	.25
Banting (flint and steel)	Na-oha	.25
Pakimáan (chewing betels together)	Na-oha	.25
Alauwin (woman's rice-field jug)	Na-oha	.25
Kalakal (edible water beetle living in rice-field)	Na-oha	.25
Tobong (spit on which kalakal are strung)	Na-oha	.25
Inipit di otak (holding bolo between toes to cut meat with)	Na-oha	.25
Banga (cooking pot)	Na-oha	.25
Hukup (lid for the same)	Na-oha	.25
Duyu (dish)	Na-oha	.25
Tayap di gatang (wings of the sale)	Natauwin	1.00
Tayap di mongatang (wings of the seller)	Natauwin	1.00
Kindut (carried under the arm)	Natauwin	1.00
Inhida (eaten chicken)	Natauwin	1.00
Total		₱9.50
Grand total		₱132.00

*This payment is based on ideas of magic. It tends to cause the field to produce in like manner: that is, to produce enough and a surplus besides.

B. Transactions in the Purchase of a Field in Benaue

I. Payments on the property

Budut nabungol (the jeweled *budnut*)	₱60.00
Budut nadulpig (additional *budut*)	10.00
Budut nadulpig (additional *budut*)	10.00
Budut nadulpig (additional *budut*)	10.00
Budut nadulpig (additional *budut*)	10.00
Budut nadulpig (additional *budut*)	10.00
Budut nadulpig (additional *budut*)	10.00
Budut nadulpig (additional *budut*)	10.00
Budut nadulpig (additional *budut*)	10.00
Budut nadulpig (additional *budut*)	10.00

Total (value of field, 15 pigs) .... ₱150.00

II. Additional payments made to the seller, his kindred, and the witnesses after payments of purchase price but before the ibuy feast

Tayap di gatang (wings of the sale)	₱30.00
Bobod (tie)	20.00
Binangwa de bobod (half of the tie)	10.00
Pinohat (carried under the arm)	8.00
Dotag (meat)	5.00
Gogod (cut)	2.00

Total .... ₱75.00

III. Payments at ibuy ceremony

To the witnesses:

1 death blanket	₱8.00
1 death blanket	8.00
Inagagong (kind of blanket)	5.00

For distribution to seller's kin:

10 chickens, *Nunpatngan* (?)	8.00
Alaag (cooking pot of Chinese origin)	2.00
Gogod, 1 *bolo* (the cutting off)	1.00
Puguy (finish)	2.50
Linuta (cooked)	2.50

Total .... ₱37.00

Grand total .... ₱262.00

One of the fine points in buying consists of an insidious hospitality on the part of the purchaser, which gets the seller and his kin drunk so that they forget some of their perquisites. At the psychological moment, that is, when a few, but not all, of the presents or *lukbu* have been made the seller and his kin, and when the latter are at the proper stage of drunkenness, one of the purchaser's kinsmen says: "Let us proceed with the praying." If he is successful in getting the religious part of the ceremonies started, and can keep the minds of the seller and his kin from the unpaid gifts or fees until they eat, then the fees never have to be paid. For when they have started eating, everything is over. They may demand the unpaid fees only if they want to make themselves laughing stocks in the eyes of their fellows. For according to Ifugao law, when the seller and the purchaser eat together at the *ibuy* feast, the transfer of ownership is complete, and irrevocable.

Although possession of the property is given before the purchase price is paid, ownership of it is not, however, complete until after the performance of the *ibuy*. *If one were to buy a field without performing the* ibuy *ceremony, the presumption would be held that the field had passed into his hands as a* balal. It has been noted already that but one or two of the unit payments are made at the time possession is given, and that no particular time is set for making the rest of the various partial payments. At any time before the *ibuy* ceremonial which forever transfers the field, the seller may demand a payment or *all* the payments, except the fees to the witnesses and his kin. He may do this as a matter of malice, or he may do it as a matter of necessity. He sends a *monkalun,* or go-between, to demand payment. The go-between and the buyer arrange a reasonable time—usually not less than ten days—within which the payment is to be raised. If it be not then forthcoming, the field may revert to the former owner, should the latter so desire, and be sold by him. He must, however, return *immediately* the entire amount of the partial payments made to date by the first purchaser.

In case of such a transfer of a field as that described in the preceding paragraph, the same rules apply to the ownership of standing crops as apply in transfers of possession arising from the *balal*.

But should the seller of a field, after having sold it to a second person, and after having received a part of the purchase price of the field from him, without consultation or notification, and without giving this second person a chance to make the final payments on the field, sell it to another, he must repay to the first purchaser double the amount of the partial payments made by the first purchaser to the date of the sale.

Personal property is transferred without formality.

48. *Responsibility of seller after property has left his hands.*—In both Ifugao and Kalinga, if a rice field after passing into the hands of a purchaser, is subject to an unusual number of slides in the terrace wall, or is wholly, or in part washed away by a freshet, the

purchaser may, at any time within the year following the purchase, relinquish the field and demand the return of his purchase price. This is on the ground that the seller may have put a curse on the field when it left his hands, or that, at least, he did not relinquish his hold on its welfare and fertility.

In Kalinga, if a water buffalo, horse, or ox, die within the year following its sale, the purchaser may demand the return of the purchase price.

TRANSFERS OF PROPERTY ARISING FROM FAMILY RELATIONSHIPS

49. *Methods of transfer.*—Property is transferred within a family by two methods: by assignment and transferal during the life of the owner; and by inheritance.

50. *Assignment and transfer of property during the lifetime of the owner.*—At some undefined time all the family property that one possesses is assigned to his children. By *"assigned,"* I mean "provisionally allotted," subject to any legitimate charge or obligation against it. A family property is always subject to sale or pawn for the purpose of providing funeral feasts, sacrifices in time of sickness or other grave necessity, payments of fines, and indemnities, made on behalf of lineal ascendants and descendants and near collateral kin. The property is usually assigned when the children are quite small.

Property is transferred (that is to say, possession is given) to the children when they marry and separate from the household of the parents. By the time the youngest child has so separated, or even before, the parents have become a charge on their children. It is only sometimes, in the case of the very rich, that a portion of the property is reserved. Childless widowed aunts or uncles usually transfer their property to those who would otherwise inherit it, and so become a charge upon those persons.

51. *Inheritance.*—It is only in case of the death of the parents when the children are very small, or of the death of a more distant relative from whom it is inherited, that the Ifugao receives property by inheritance.

52. *The passing of property between relatives because of relationship.*—The same laws govern both the assignment and transfer of property while the possessor is yet living, and the inheritance of property. Of all Ifugao laws, they are the most definite and the most invariably followed.

53. *The law of primogeniture.*—By this law, the elder children inherit a greater portion of the property than the younger ones, the proportion being governed by the ordinal rank of the children as to birth. If there be but one rice field, the eldest takes it. Because of his greater wealth, the eldest is frequently the family leader, counselor, and advocate. He has no actual authority over his brothers and sisters, however—indeed no person in Ifugao society has authority over another.

54. *The passing of property to legitimate sons and daughters by assignment or inheritance.*

(*a*) No distinction is made because of sex.

(*b*) The greatest proportion of an estate goes to the eldest child.

(*c*) If the number of children be greater than the number of rice fields, the elder children take the fields. If there be but one field, the eldest takes it.

(*d*) If all the children inherit rice fields, the heirlooms and personal property are divided in accordance with the laws of primogeniture that apply to real estate.

(*e*) If there be children that inherit no rice fields, a slight compensation is made them by giving them a larger share of the heirlooms and personal property than would fall to their lot otherwise. This compensation by no means equals the value of the real estate they would inherit under our laws.

(*f*) In the event of the death of either spouse before the property of the spouses has been allotted to the children, the living spouse allots the property to the children at the proper time. In this allotment, the brothers of the dead spouse are usually called in consultation. The living spouse may not deviate from custom in allotting the property of the deceased. All the property of both the spouses must be allotted at this time. None may be held back.

55. *The passing of property to other relatives.*—In the apportionment or inheritance of property in which blood relatives other than sons and daughters benefit, two general principles hold:

(*a*) Property received from the father goes to the father's family; property received from the mother goes to the mother's family. The families of the two parents coalesce in, and are identical in, their children and their childrens' descendants.

(*b*) So near as may be, those persons inherit who would have inherited the property had the deceased never lived. It is only in the case of the childless that others than sons and daughters have rights in the property left.

If the deceased were unmarried, his property goes to his relatives in the following order:

(1) To his brothers and sisters, if living. To the brothers and sisters descended from one parent, passes that portion of the property received from that parent; to the brothers and sisters descended from the other parent, that portion of the property received from that parent.

(2) To the nephews and nieces, the offspring of the brothers and sisters, or to their descendants.

(3) To the cousins in order, first of degree, and second of primogeniture.

If the deceased were married, in the the inheritance of his property there are the following rules:

(1) The living spouse inherits the sole right in, and possession of, half the property jointly acquired by the spouses subsequent to their marriage. It is not, properly speaking, the *property* that is inherited: it is the *sole right* in what was a joint possession before.

(2) That half of the property jointly acquired by the spouses which is the share of the deceased, goes to his heirs, being divided (if his heirs be not his brothers and sisters or their descendants) equally between the heirs on the father's side, and those on the mother's side.

(3) The property that the deceased brought to the marriage and that which he acquired subsequently owing to and by virtue of his relationship to his family, goes to the deceased's family.

Personal property acquired by the deceased and his spouse is not, however, taken from the surviving spouse. The above applies only to family property.

56. *Property rights of bastards.*—Bastards usually inherit approximately half the property of a father who dies without legitimate children, the other half going to those who would be the sole heirs had the father died childless. But if there be only one field, the bastard takes it.

Should a parent have only one legitimate child, the bastard inherits usually as if he were a *younger* legitimate child.

A bastard is entitled to a rice field from his father if the father has a rice field that is unassigned to a legitimate child. He is not entitled to any special value of fields, and as a rule, receives less than his legitimate brothers and sisters if there be such.

The above paragraphs apply equally to the bastard's right in the property of his mother. He has, however, no kin to enforce his rights against his mother. Since he is of illegitimate birth, the kin of the father are not in a position to enforce his rights against her; while his mother's kin would not take issue in any matter for him against their nearer kin, his mother. If the mother marries after the birth of the bastard, she usually makes a settlement on her bastard child before marrying. Not infrequently he who marries a woman having a bastard child recognizes that child as his own, and even assigns him a portion of his property. The following are examples:

Dulnuan and Ngahiu of Tupplak carried on a courtship, after the Ifugao fashion, in the *agamang* (dormitory). Ngahiu became pregnant; but Dulnuan refused to marry her. However, and notwithstanding the fact that he knew her to be pregnant, a third party, Baliu, married Ngahiu. From what motive he did this does not appear: it was probable that he gained financially, since Ngahiu was wealthier than he; and being pregnant as she was, she was in no position to stipulate too closely as to the property of the one who might become her husband. The bastard child, notwithstanding the fact that there were legitimate half brothers and sisters, was given fields by (*a*) his mother; (*b*) his natural father, Dulnuan; (*c*) Baliu, who recognized him as his son.

R, a Christianized Ifugao woman, and a wife who had borne five legitimate children to B, her husband, was indiscreet in her relations with a Spaniard. She bore a *mestizo* child. B, her husband, did not proceed against his wife and her paramour according to Ifugao law and recognized the child as his own. The legitimate children except one having died, the bastard child inherited from his mother and his mother's husband as if he had been of legitimate birth.

There is a Malay proverb which is used to describe the attitude of the husband in such cases as the above: "Although I did not plant the tree, yet it grew in my garden."

The amount of property that parents settle on a bastard is to a great extent a matter of caprice. His rights to any property whatever, except a single field from his father, are decidedly weaker than those of children of legitimate birth, added to which he has not the right in any case to so great a portion of property.

57. *Transfers of property to adopted children.*—Customs relating to these transfers are as follows:

(*a*) An adopted child related to only one of the spouses may inherit from that spouse only.

(*b*) If the adopted child be a niece or nephew, he inherits or has assigned him all the property of the related parent; provided that there be no brothers or sisters of the related parent except the adopted child's own blood parents. If there be other brothers and sisters, and if these brothers and sisters agree to help stand the funeral expenses of the adopting brother or sister, a small part of the property is given them. But the adopted child inherits the greater part of the property.

(c) If the adopted child be the son or daughter of a cousin, there is assigned him, or he inherits all the property that his parents would inherit in case of the death of the related parent, and a portion in addition. Should the parents not be in the position of being likely to become heirs to the related adopting parent, the adopted child inherits, or has assigned him, only a minor portion of the estate. If there be no brothers and sisters of the parent by adoption, he may have assigned him the greater portion of the estate, however.

(d) If the adopted child be not related by blood to either of the parents by adoption, he inherits, or has assigned him, a small portion of the estate of both adopting parents. The kin of these parents take the lion's share of the estate.

(e) If the adopted child marry a kinsman of the unrelated adopting parent, the unrelated parent usually settles on the spouse of the adopted child, an amount of property about equal to that settled on the adopted child by his kinsman, his other adopting parent, subject, however, to the four rules above.

(f) It is optional with the blood parents of an adopted child to settle no property on him, in case the parents by adoption provide for him in this respect.

The above settlements are customary. They can hardly be said to be rights, however. Often when a child is adopted, his blood parents stipulate with those who adopt as to the property settlement that will be made on the child.

58. *Servants and slaves as inheritors.*—Retainers have no rights whatever as to the property of their masters. Frequently, however, a small field is settled on them.

59. *Wills and testaments.*—There are no wills or testaments among the Ifugaos. If a man desires to make a settlement of his property that is out of the ordinary, he must do it before he dies. Even then he would have to get the family's consent to the unusual features. Ifugao parents are singularly impartial in the allotment of the family property to their children. That some children are not loved more than others is unbelievable; but it is exceedingly rare that any child is favored above another in property settlements, except by the law of primogeniture. There is always a lot of talk in connection with the assignment or inheritance of family property—in the matter of

talk the Ifugao is not different from other Malays. But it is not often that permanent ill feeling is engendered in such settlements. The laws of the descent of property are, as has been said, the clearest and most concise of all Ifugao laws.

SETTLEMENT OF DEBTS OF THE AGED AND DECEASED

60. *When the debtor has children.*—At the same time that the wealth of the family is apportioned to the children, account is taken of the debts owed by the family. The debts may or may not be individually apportioned among the children. *If the eldest child inherits or receives any property,* the obligation of primogeniture holds as to the debts; that is to say, he is responsible for the payment of a greater proportion of them. Otherwise all the children are equally responsible. There are many cases in which the debts that are handed down by an Ifugao's parents greatly exceed the property handed down.

Children who receive no family property are not responsible for the payment of the debts of the parents, *provided there be a child or children that do receive family property.* The apportionment of the debts of the deceased must be in proportion to the amount of property received. If none receive family property, all are responsible for payment.

61. *When the debtor is childless but leaves a spouse.*—A spouse is responsible only for those debts incurred in behalf of the couple's mutual interests: for example, debts incurred in obtaining animals for sacrifice in case of sickness of the children of the couple, or for sacrifice at the funeral feasts of the children, or for the purchase of rice fields or other joint possessions of the spouses. A spouse may not be held for debts incurred in the purchase of animals for sacrifice at the funeral feast of a member of the other's family (except for the pig and death blanket due from her family in such cases), nor for debts incurred in paying fines or indemnities levied as a result of the other's misdoing. A spouse may not even be held for debts incurred in providing sacrifices to secure the recovery of her husband from sickness (except for the pig due as stated under section 13; however, this pig is really her own obligation).

62. *Debts for which the kin of the deceased are held.*—When a debtor dies childless, the kin who inherit, if there be such, must pay debts that were incurred on behalf of their family. They are, too, jointly responsible with the wife, for these debts incurred on behalf

of the debtor's descendants. If there be nothing inherited, all the kin are responsible for these debts in proportion to nearness of the kinship.

It is a matter of doubt as to whether a man's kin or his spouse can be held for his gambling debts. Such debts are purely personal, and are about the only debts that an Ifugao contracts in his own selfish interest. The Ifugaos did not gamble heavily, at least not before the coming of the Spaniards; since their coming, custom in this matter has not had time to crystallize.

63. *Attitude toward debts.*—A debt is a sacred thing to an Ifugao. The non-payment of a debt is disgraceful. The non-collection is still more disgraceful, for the presumption is that a man who does not collect from his creditors cannot do so. If he cannot collect his debts, it must be because he is a coward. In the babbling that prevails about the rice-wine jar when tongues are loosened, one who has debts long outstanding that other men would collect, hears things not calculated to tickle his pride.

BORROWING AND LENDING

To a far greater proportionate extent is borrowing and lending carried on among the Ifugaos than in our own country. Almost any event that carries with it a large payment or expenditure carries with it as a corollary a large amount of borrowing. The things usually borrowed are death blankets, animals for sacrifice, and rice.

64. *Lupe, or interest.*—Interest on things borrowed is exceedingly high. But where borrower and lender are brothers, no interest is charged; where they are kin of somewhat remoter degree, a low interest, as a rule, is charged. In any case a special agreement may be made by which the interest is not as high as usual. It may be stated as a general principle that a thing borrowed must be repaid by twice its value if paid soon—that is within a year or even two years. But if repayment be made after a long time, three perhaps, four times the value must be repaid. The Ifugao does not hold to the calendar very severely in reckoning interest. But where full interest is charged, the rule is that a thing borrowed must be repaid by twice its value, even if it be paid within two weeks. Thus rice borrowed two weeks before harvest time must be repaid by double the quantity immediately after harvest.

65. *Patang, or interest paid in advance.*—This is the Ifugao form of bank discount. It is interest paid in advance for one year. On a

carabao (worth usually about eighty pesos) this amounts to thirty
pesos a year. At the end of the year if the carabao be not paid back,
the *patang* must be followed by a second payment of the same quantity,
called *unud,* "following," for the next year. If it be intended to repay
the carabao within three months, the interest in advance is ten pesos,
and is called *baloblad.*

66. *Another form of patang.*—Somewhat similar is the fee or interest paid to the owner of anything seized by a man of a different district
or village to cover an unpaid indebtedness owed the latter by a neighbor or co-villager of the former. It is the amount of interest usually
paid for one year; but there is no *unud* or further payment, since it
is presumed that by the end of the year the delinquent neighbor ought
to have been compelled to pay.

Thus A of one village owes C of another village a debt. After several fruitless attempts to collect, C seizes a carabao belonging to B,
a co-villager of A. C sends a go-between to pay B thirty pesos, telling
him of A's debt, and informing him that he must get his carabao back
from A.

GO-BETWEENS

67. *The go-between.*—No transaction of importance of any sort
between persons of different families is consummated without the inter-
vention of a middle man, or go-between, called *monbaga* (bespeaker)
in civil transactions; and *monkalun* (admonisher) in criminal cases.

Go-betweens are used commonly in (*a*) buying and selling of family
property of whatever kind or value; (*b*) buying and selling of animals
and the more valuable personal property, except chickens, and in some
cases pigs; (*c*) the borrowing of money or other wealth; (*d*) marriage
proposals and the negotiating of marriage contracts; (*e*) collection of
debts; (*f*) all steps connected with the *balal,* such as pawn of rice fields,
or their redemption; (*g*) demands for damages to property or persons;
(*h*) the buying back of heads lost in war, the ransoming of the kidnapped, or the making of peace.

The go-between is the principal witness to a transaction. For his
services he receives pay which is fixed to a fair degree of exactness
for a particular service. This pay ranges from a piece of meat to a
fee of twenty or twenty-five pesos.

68. *Responsibility of go-betweens.*—Go-betweens are responsible to
both parties to a transaction, for the correct rendering of tenders,
offers, and payments. Their word binds only themselves, however—

not their principals. Go-betweens are not agents of one party more than another. They are supposed to be impartial, and interested only in consummating the transaction involved in order to get their fee.

Thus, suppose that A sends B as a go-between to sell a field to C, a man of another district. B finds that he cannot sell the field for the price A asked for it, and, anxious to consummate a sale and so collect his fee, he agrees to sell the field to C for a lower price than that asked by A.

In such a case as this, B is responsible to C in case A refuses to abide by C's agreement to sell. C has the right to collect damages.

The oriental propensity to "squeeze" is proverbial. It is condoned in law—one might almost say legitimized, provided it be not found out. Thus:

A sends B to Nueva Vizcaya to buy a carabao. The regular commission for this service is ten pesos, the agent to deliver a living carabao to the principal, and to be responsible for the value if the carabao die on the route. This, the usual agreement, holds between them. A furnishes B with eighty pesos with which to purchase the animal. B returns with the animal, representing that he paid seventy pesos for it, when, as a matter of fact, he paid out sixty pesos, thus gaining ten pesos "squeeze."

If A finds out that B paid only sixty pesos for the carabao, the only thing he can do is to collect the ten pesos difference between what A paid and what he said he paid. He cannot assess punitive damages.

68. *Conditions relieving a go-between of responsibility.*—An act of God or the acts of a public enemy relieve a go-between or an agent from responsibility. Thus an agent sent to purchase an animal in *baliwan* (the stranger country) is under obligation to deliver it alive. But if it be struck by lightning, or if the carabao be taken away from him by enemies, and he has a wound to bear witness that he offered due resistance to them; or, in case he has no wound, if he has witnesses or good proof of the fact that the enemy was so superior in force as to make resistance foolhardy, he cannot be held for payment of the animal.

70. *Payment due those who find the body of one dead by violence.* —An Ifugao who finds the body of one dead by violence or drowning, and not an inhabitant of the same district as himself, must perform a general welfare feast to remove the liability to misfortune that is likely to result from such an incident. Consequently, he is entitled to a payment, varying from one to ten pesos, according to the rank of the dead person. If there be more than one who encounter the dead body, all are entitled to the same payment. This payment is called *halat.*

CONTRACTS FOR THE SALE OF PROPERTY

71. *On whom binding.*—Contracts for the transfer of property for consideration are binding on the seller only. Rarely, if ever, is there a payment to bind the bargain. The simple promise to sell is sufficient to constitute a contract to sell. The breaking of a contract to sell renders the breaker of the contract liable for damages *only in case he took the initiative* in making the contract.

Damages paid for the breaking of a contract to sell, are called *hogop*. In case an agreement to sell a rice field is broken, the damages are usually one large pig (fifteen or twenty pesos). In the case of questions of this sort over minor property, the *hogop* may be a death blanket, a small pig, or a chicken.

The following examples will serve to illustrate:

A sends B as a go-between to sell a rice field. B first contracts to sell the field to C. Later, knowing the terms of the sale offered by A to be very advantageous, he sells the field to a kinsman D.

In this case B is liable for the *hogop* to C.

In the above case B, after contracting to sell the field to C, duly reports to A that C has accepted the terms offered, and that he is raising the amount required for the first payment; that he will go again by agreement with C to receive this first payment on such and such a day. A sells the field to somebody else.

In this case A is liable to C for the *hogop*, and to B for his fee as go-between.

It becomes a matter of common knowledge that A has a gold neck-ornament for sale. C agrees to purchase at the stated price and A agrees to sell to him. A sells the ornament to somebody else.

A is not liable for the *hogop*, for the reason that C made the first advances.

In no case can one who makes a contract *to buy* be held for any payment of damages for breaking his contract.

IRRIGATION LAW

72. *The law as to new fields.*—If all the land below a spring or small stream located on ownerless land, be common land—that is, land without an owner—he who makes the first rice field below the source of the water supply is entitled to all the water needed for his rice field. Another man, making a rice field between the field of the first comer and the source of the water supply, may not use the spring or stream to the detriment of the first comer.

But should a man make a field, be it on common or on owned land, below a spring or stream, and should another man make a field between the first field and the source of the water supply on *owned land,* the second comer would have the right to whatever water might be useful to him.

73. *The law as to water.*—Water which has been flowing to an area of irrigated land may under no circumstances be *diverted* to irrigate a different area, even though that area be nearer the source of the water.

A person who acquires rice fields, one of which is near the source of the water supply and the other at a considerable distance from it, may not pipe or trough the water from the upper field to the lower one if the water has meantime been irrigating an intervening area. Thus:

Manghe of Ambabag, having a field near Baay, acquires a field near Ambabag, about a quarter of a mile upstream from the first. He threatens to put a line of troughs from one field to another so as to supply sufficient water to the lower field. This action would rob intervening fields of their accustomed water supply, and would be illegal.

A spring belongs to him on whose land it is situated, and so also does all the water issuing from the spring. The owner may sell the surplus water to whom he pleases. The water rights so sold are *perpetual.* Thus:

A has a rice field in which there is a spring. He sells the water to B, whose field is to one side—perhaps at a considerable distance from A's. C has a field immediately below A's. He purchases A's field and unites it with his own. But he may not divert the water from A's original field to his own original field, unless he buy the water right from B.

74. *The law as to irrigation ditches.*—Constructors of an irrigation ditch may sell interest in the ditch. The ditch thus shared with others becomes an equal burden as to upkeep on all the owners.

The constructors of an irrigation ditch who have sold part of the water from their ditch, must share the water in time of water scarcity with those to whom they have sold, in proportion to the respective areas of the rice fields. That is, every owner of an irrigation ditch is entitled to a share proportionate to the area of his rice land, of the water diverted by means of the ditch.

Repetition of the malicious destruction of an irrigation ditch, or the turning of the water from it or out of it, is an offense punishable by fine or even in some cases by death. The first offense, when the culprit is discovered, is not punished; but there is a warning against repetition.

Diversion of water from an irrigation ditch in which the diverter has no interest is not a very serious offense. On the first offense the diverter is warned. If he repeats it, all the water is drained from his field or he is given a beating.

PENAL LAW

The Ifugaos have two punishments for crime: the death penalty and fine. These punishments are inflicted and executed by the offended person and his kin.

75. *Nature and reckoning of fines.*—Fines are of two sorts: fines of "tens," *bakid*, and fines of "sixes," *na-onom*, each unit of the ten or six being a portion of the whole fine. The different parts of the fine go to different people. Oftentimes sticks, knots, or notches are used to assist in calculation. In Banaue and neighboring districts these aids to calculation are also kept as a record. The unit payments grow successively smaller from the first to the last.

The first unit of any series is called *pu-u,* meaning "base." It is of the greatest value, and goes to the injured individual. The second payment, sometimes, goes to the go-between. In that case, the kin of the injured man take all the rest. If the fee of the go-between be provided for outside of the fine, the kin of the injured man take all except the *pu-u,* the first unit. This is but just, since they have backed their kinsman in his action against the offender, have perchance risked their lives in his cause, and also stand ready at all times to help pay any fines that others may assess against him.

The second, and sometimes the third and fourth units, are called *haynub di pu-u,* meaning "followers of the base." They are of less value than the *pu-u.* Then follow units consisting, each, of four irons (spear-heads, axes, knives). These units are called *natauwinan.* Then come units of three irons each, called *natuku;* then units of two irons each, called *nunbadi;* then units of one iron each, called *na-oha.* In the case of fines composed of six units, there is usually no *haynub.*

The Malay does nothing without first thoroughly talking it over. After a payment has been tentatively consented to by the offender and his family, there yet remain many conferences with the go-between before everything is arranged. An uninitiated white man on seeing a group of these people, squatted in a circle, moving little sticks about, and in heated discussion, might think they were playing some primitive but absorbing native game. And, I am not sure that the attitude of their minds is very different!

The following tables of fines assessed for the four degrees of adultery illustrate the manner of reckoning fines, their amounts, the value of the units, as well as the fines proper to the three classes of society in the Kiangan district.

TABULATION SHOWING THE PAYMENT EXACTED FOR ADULTERY IN ITS VARIOUS DEGREES AND FOR INDIVIDUALS OF DIFFERENT RANK

For adultery committed after the *mommon* (first ceremony) and before the *bango* (second ceremony)

FOR THE WEALTHY
Na-onom or "six" fine

Divisions of the fine	Article exacted	Appraisal
1. *Pu-u*	1 death blanket	₱8.00
2. *Haynab*	1 kettle	5.00
3. *Natauwinan*	4 irons	1.00
4. *Natauwinan*	4 irons	1.00
5. *Natuku*	3 irons	.50
6. *Natuku*	3 irons	.50
Liwa (fee of the go-between)	1 ceremonial clout	2.00

Total, ₱18.00

FOR THE MIDDLE CLASS
Na-onom or "six" fine

Divisions of the fine	Article exacted	Appraisal
1. *Pu-u*	1 kettle	₱5.00
2. *Natauwinan*	1 kettle	1.00
3. *Natauwinan*	1 kettle	1.00
4. *Natuku*	1 kettle	.50
5. *Natuku*	1 kettle	.50
6. *Na-oha*	1 kettle	.20
Liwa (fee of the go-between)	1 *natauwinan*	1.00

Total, ₱9.20

FOR THE POOR
Na-onom or "six" fine

Divisions of the fine	Article exacted	Appraisal
1. *Pu-u*	1 kettle	₱2.00
2. *Natauwinan*	1 kettle	1.00
3. *Natuku*	1 kettle	.50
4. *Natuku*	1 kettle	.50
5. *Nunbadi*	2 irons	.40
6. *Na-oha*	2 irons	.20

The go-between takes the first *natuku* listed above

Total, ₱4.60

For adultery committed after the *bango* (second ceremony) and before the *bubun* (final ceremony)

FOR THE WEALTHY
Hin-bakid or "ten" fine

Divisions of the fine	Article exacted	Appraisal
1. *Pu-u*	2 death blankets	₱16.00
2. *Haynab*	1 death blanket	8.00
3. *Haynab*	1 death blanket	4.00
4. *Haynab*	1 death blanket	4.00
5. *Haynab*	1 kettle	4.00
6. *Haynab*	1 kettle	2.00
7. *Natauwinan*	1 kettle	1.00
8. *Natauwinan*	1 kettle	1.00
9. *Natauwinan*	1 kettle	1.00
10. *Natauwinan*	1 kettle	1.00
Liwa (fee of the go-between)	1 kettle	5.00

Total, ₱47.00

FOR THE MIDDLE CLASS
Hin-bakid or "ten" fine

Divisions of the fine	Article exacted	Appraisal
1. *Pu-u*	1 death blanket	₱8.00
2. *Haynab*	1 kettle	5.00
3. *Haynab*	1 kettle	2.00
4. *Natauwinan*	1 kettle	1.00
5. *Natauwinan*	1 kettle	1.00
6. *Natauwinan*	1 kettle	1.00
7. *Natauwinan*	1 kettle	1.00
8. *Natuku*	1 kettle	.50
9. *Natuku*	1 kettle	.50
10. *Na-oha*	1 kettle	.20
Liwa (fee of the go-between)	1 kettle	4.00

Total, ₱24.20

FOR THE POOR
Na-onom or "six" fine

Divisions of the fine	Article exacted	Appraisal
1. *Pu-u*	1 kettle	₱5.00
2. *Haynab*	1 kettle	2.00
3. *Natauwinan*	1 kettle	1.00
4. *Natauwinan*	1 kettle	1.00
5. *Natuku*	1 kettle	.50
6. *Nunbadi*	1 kettle	.40
Liwa (fee of the go-between)	1 kettle	2.00

Total, ₱11.90

For adultery committed after the *bubun* (final ceremony) the penalty is doubled for the higher classes, and increased to a fine of "ten" for persons of the lower class. That is, a poor man pays for adultery after the *bubun* what a middle-class man would pay for adultery before the *bubun*.

For adultery in the aggravated degree known as *hokwit* (see sec. 94) the fines just mentioned are doubled; so that a wealthy man would pay 188 pesos, a middle-class man 96.80 pesos, and a poor man 48.40 pesos.

CIRCUMSTANCES WHICH AFFECT PENALTY

Certain circumstances, namely, criminal responsibility, alienship, kinship, confession, and the relative rank of offender and offended, affect penalty, either as to its severity or as to the likelihood of its being inflicted at all.

76. *Moral turpitude not a factor.*—Moral turpitude, which plays no small part in our own law in determining punishment, seems not to enter into the consideration of Ifugao law. Thus, such crimes as incest between brother and sister, parricide, matricide, fraticide, and treason against one's family, all go unpunished. Even the betrayal of a co-villager into the hands of the enemy subjects the offender to only a third degree of likelihood of being punished (see sec. 80). These crimes probably go unpunished in accordance with the following correlated fundaments of Ifugao society: Legal procedure is conducted by and between families; the family unit is the most precious thing in Ifugao social life; *family unity must, at all hazards, be preserved.* In the case of a murder accomplished by treachery, as for example, the killing of a guest, the moral turpitude involved might perhaps hasten punishment—it might even increase its severity in that the kin of the murdered person might retaliate on a greater number of those concerned in the murder. But such an abuse of hospitality appears never to have occurred.

Another reason why what we consider moral turpitude does not enter into punishment is that treachery, ambush, and accomplishment by superior force are the rule, not only in commission of crime, but also in perfectly legal capital executions and seizures of property.

PENAL RESPONSIBILITY

As between principals and their accomplices and accessories, Ifugao law recognizes only gradations in likelihood of punishment. The penalty is the same for all of them; but very frequently the offense is considered as having been expiated by the punishment of those whose responsibility for it is greatest, and the rest go free.

77. *The nungolat, or principal.*—The *nungolat* (he who was strong) is the conceiver, planner, and director of an offense. He may or may not take an active part in its commission. Whether or not he does so, he is considered to be responsible for it in the highest degree. He is, of all who take part in the offense, the most likely to be punished.

The following example, continued through several succeeding sections, shows the various degrees of criminal responsibility, and the corresponding degrees of likelihood of punishment:

A decides to avenge the death of a kinsman. He consequently calls a number of his kinsmen and proposes a war expedition to take the head of Z, an enemy concerned in the death of the murdered kinsman, in another village. They agree. A calls the family priests to his house to perform the necessary religious preliminaries to setting out on a head-hunting expedition. The ceremonies are performed, and the omen of the bile sac promises well. But, just before starting, some accident happens to A, which the priests attribute to the sorcery of the enemy. A consequently does not accompany the expedition. He is, notwithstanding, the *nungolat,* and is more likely to be the object of vengeance than any other, should the crime be accomplished.

78. *The tombok, or "thrower."*—In offenses in which a spear is thrown, he who throws the effective spear is called the *tombok.* His responsibility for the crime is second to that of the *nungolat,* as is also his likelihood of being punished.

79. *Iba'n di nungolat, the "companions of the one who was strong."*—Those who assist in the commission of a crime by reinforcing, accompanying, assisting, backing, giving aid and comfort to the committer thereof, or furnishing anything needful to the consummation of the crime incur the next lesser degree of criminal responsibility and of likelihood of being punished to those of the conceiver and committer of the crime.

80. *The montudol, "shower," or informer.*—One who gives a person in the act of committing a crime information necessary to the successful carrying out of his intent, is guilty in the same degree as are persons of the preceding paragraph.

Thus, continuing the illustration started above, suppose that B, C, D, E, F, G, H, and I go to take the head of A's enemy and theirs. They meet O, a co-villager of Z, the man whose head they want to take, and ask him regarding Z's whereabouts. The fact could not be otherwise than patent to O, that a head-hunting party was addressing him. He answers truthfully that Z is in his sweet-potato field, and that the party may reach the field by such and such by-path without their being seen by Z's kin or co-villagers. The party follows O's directions. B spears Z.

B is the *tombok;* C, D, E, F, G, H, and I are the "companions of the one who was strong," and O is the *montudol.*

81. *Servants who commit crimes at the bidding of their masters.* —Retainers incur a lesser degree of criminal responsibility than does the master. They will be punished if the master cannot be punished. Sometimes both are punished.

82. *Likelihood of punishment.*—

(Continuation of illustration given above.) Z's kinsmen of course decide to avenge his death. It is a general rule that all debts must be paid with liberal interest, the interest being at least equal to the debt. The debt of life is no exception to this rule. The kinsmen, whom we will call Q, R, S, T, and U, decide that, at least, they will kill A, the *nungolat,* and B, the *tombok,* and that if opportunity offers they will kill one or two of the others. They go to the vicinity of the village of A and B and lie in wait for them. They may do this a number of times. Finally we will suppose that they kill A. Their thirst for blood is somewhat appeased, and they may not pursue their first intention. But it would be the part of wisdom for B to be extremely cautious. Z's kinsmen are likely to make an expedition or two to take his head.

On the other hand, suppose that A dies a natural death or falls in some other feud. The full likelihood of punishment now falls on B.

Suppose that B, H, and O walk past the place of ambush of the avengers. The latter will try to make sure of B, but will also try to kill the other two.

Suppose that B, like A, meets death in some other way than at the hands of Z's avengers. C, D, E, F, G, H, I, and O are now equally likely to be punished.

In case several unsuccessful expeditions are made to secure the head of A and B, the avengers are likely to take a head or heads from some of the others rather than continually to place themselves in jeopardy by their expeditions into an enemy region. Especially is this true if the enemy's village be distant. If the villages be near, it is probable that C, D, E, F, G, H, I, or O might walk past the ambush of the avengers at first with impunity, since the avengers are desirous of taking the heads of the principals, and do not want to put the principals on their guard by slaying those whose guilt is less.

83. *Drunkenness and insanity in relation to criminal responsibility.*—Except in the case of murder, drunkenness mitigates the severity of punishment, provided there be no evidence to show that the culprit became intoxicated with the intent to commit the crime, and provided he sincerely repents on becoming sober. Even insanity is not an alleviating circumstance in the case of murder; but it is one in all other crimes.

84. *The relation of intent to criminal responsibility.*—Gulad or intent, is probably the greatest single factor in determining penal responsibility. Thus:

A deed committed without intent, and without carelessness, is excused. One has not, usually, even to make restitution for the injury done. Thus, in the case of a bolo flying out of a man's hand, and putting out the eye of another, no damages were assessed. An enormous number of men, every year, are injured in the free-for-all scrambles over sacrificed carabaos. Many of these injuries result in stiff joints; some of them in deaths. In no case, not even in the case of death, is a payment demanded. Suppose that in the chase a number of hunters have surrounded a wild boar. The boar charges one of them. This man leaps backward, and, at the same time, draws back his spear to throw it at the boar. In so doing, he stabs a companion behind him with the shod end of the spear handle. This is not an uncommon accident. The others of the party are witnesses that the killing was purely accidental (*naloktat*). No fine is assessed; but the killer, to show. that he is sorry, usually assists in the funeral feast. Of course, if there were no witnesses, and if there were a possible motive to complicate matters, the ending of the case might not be so happy.

Suppose that a number of men are throwing at a target with their spears. A child runs in the way, and is killed. One-half the usual fine for manslaughter is assessed on the ground that the thrower was careless in that he did not make sure before he threw the spear that such an accident could not occur. In this case there was an absence of intent; but carelessness was present.

A man kills a neighbor at night, acting under the impression that he is killing an enemy seeking his life. He is subjected to a much heavier fine.than if he had killed him through carelessness, since there is present both the intent to kill, although not criminal, and carelessness in that he did not make sure at whom he was casting his spear.[13]

OTHER FACTORS AFFECTING LIABILITY

85. *Alienship.*—If the culprit be of a foreign village, the fact that he is a foreigner is a strong aggravating circumstance. If found *in delicto,* he is almost sure to be killed, in cases of theft or the more serious crimes. In such crimes as insult, the same fine might be demanded of the foreigner as of a co-villager, but not so much effort would be made to arrange matters peaceably. If the fine demanded be not paid and paid quickly, a kidnapping would ensue, or the culprit would be killed. A man committing a minor crime in a foreign village if not killed would be caught, tied, and held prisoner until redeemed.

86. *Confession.*—Confession before steps have been taken to inflict punishment alleviates to a considerable degree except in murder and adultery. In the latter case, if the adulterer made a voluntary confession of guilt to the offended spouse, without having been confronted with the evidence, it would be taken as brazen boasting, and of the nature of an insult.

---

[13] In one case, to be hereafter considered, the absence of both intent and carelessness do not excuse (see sec. 105).

87. *Kinship.*—Kinship is so strong a mitigating circumstance as often to excuse crime altogether. It has already been stated that crimes of one brother or sister against another are not punished. Inasmuch as all procedure is conducted by and between families, and since the family of the two brothers is identical, procedure in such cases is impossible. In the case of relatives of remoter degree, kinship is a strong extenuating circumstance in the event of the more serious crimes. In minor crimes, while the usual amount of the fine might be demanded, it would very frequently not be collected; especially, if the offender were very poor.

It has previously been said that the family is the only organization, political or social, that the Ifugao has, and that, in proportion as it is precious and necessary to him, he cherishes it; that Ifugao law, consequently looks with the greatest disfavor upon anything that would divide a family or destroy its unity.

In case a man steals from his cousin, who is married, restitution is usually demanded, together with half the usual fine, which half goes to the cousin's spouse—not to himself. Insults on the part of one cousin to another are rare and are more rarely prosecuted.

88. *Rank and standing in the community.*—This is probably the greatest single factor in determining the severity of punishment in cases where a crime is punishable by fine. But the aggressiveness and the war footing of the two parties to the controversy enter even here to an astounding degree.

In the Kiangan-Maggok area, there are three grades of fines—the highest for the punishment of crimes of one *kadangyang* or rich man, against another; a medium grade for crimes of persons of the *tumok,* or middle class, against each other; and a third and lowest grade for the *nawatwat,* the poverty stricken.[14] Each lower grade of fine is a little more than half the next higher one.

In the Kababuyan area, there are five grades of fines—one for the very rich, one for the fairly rich, one for the middle class, one for the poor, one for the poverty stricken. In Sapao and in Asin, there are four grades.

So long as both offender and offended are of the same class, there is no trouble about determining the fine proper in a given case. But when they are of different classes, the case is not so simple, and the factors of fighting strength and personality enter.

---

[14] *Kadangyang:* an upper-class person. In most parts of Ifugao persons must give expensive feasts to attain this rank. *Tumok:* persons who have enough rice to last them throughout the year, but who do not sell rice. *Nawatwat:* persons who are poverty stricken.

Suppose that R, a rich man, commits adultery against P, a poor man. P sends a go-between to demand the highest grade of fine for this crime—that is, the grade which *kadangyang* pay. R does not deny the crime, but states that he considers the payment of the fine that is due one rich man from another preposterous. He states that he is willing to pay the fine proper to the poorer class. To this P replies that he did not begin this action for the purpose of getting money, but for the purpose of so punishing R as to make a repetition of the crime improbable. There are three possible endings in such a case:

(*a*) P's kin represent to him that they cannot afford to have war with R; that R's people hold a lot of debts over their heads; that should R prove obdurate, and should the affair end in a lance throwing, R's people would wipe them off the earth. They advise P to be satisfied with the lowest grade of fine. He agrees.

(*b*) P and R compromise on the grade of fine that is midway between their stations; that is, the fine of the middle class. In Kiangan this is the usual settlement.

(*c*) P shows such *bungot* (wrath and ferocity) that R's kin advise him to pay the larger fine. They point out that the fine is a small matter as compared with the loss of life, and state that there is no telling what this poverty-stricken but rampant dog will do. This settlement is not uncommon in the Kiangan area, where the poor people have a great deal of pride and bravery, but rare in other parts of Ifugao.

Aside from other matters, the diplomacy and tact of the go-between would have a great deal to do toward determining which of these contingencies would result.

It is extremely hard to make a general statement as to fines when offender and offended are of different classes. It may safely be said that the fines assessed average the amount midway between the fines proper to the two classes concerned. Thus, when a poor man offends a rich man, and when a rich man offends a poor man, the average of the fines assessed equals approximately the fine assessed for injuries within the middle class. In questions in which rich and middle class persons are involved, the fines approximate an amount half way between the fines of the rich and of the middle classes.

89. *Importance of influential position and personality.*—The fact has already been mentioned (see sec. 4) that Ifugao administration of justice is remarkably personal in nature. We have just seen, in the example given in section 88, to what an extent personality and war-footing enter into the infliction of fines when offender and offended are of different classes. Nowhere can a man of magnetism and force reap greater benefit from these qualities, relatively speaking, than in an Ifugao controversy. The fact stares us in the face in every phase of Ifugao law, especially in procedure.

89a. *Cripples and unfortunates.*—Cripples and those afflicted by disfigurements or disfiguring diseases are often in a desperate mood for the reason that life is not at all precious to them. They are likely to be erratic and to constitute exceptions in punishment of crimes and procedure. I remember a case that happened in Baay District a few years ago which illustrates to what extent determination and absolute abandon to a single purpose are valuable in carrying a point in Ifugao procedure. I did not make note of the names but shall designate the rich man as R and the poor man as P. P was afflicted with the disease *hiphip*—probably ichthyosis—a skin disease in which the skin becomes white, rough, and scaly. R met P one day and sneered at him, saying, "Although you have neither fields, gongs, nor jewelry, I see that you have become a *kadongyang*, for you are wearing a white coat" (referring to the skin disease). P became violently angry but restrained himself from assaulting R. He calmly informed R that for this insult he fined him a large and valuable field, R's property in Dayukong; that life meant little to himself, and that if R resisted and interfered with his taking possession of the field, he would certainly kill him. P further stated that he knew that R's kin would retaliate and that he would lose his own life but that he did not care since he was miserable anyway. None of the women would deign him their favors and being poor—well, what was the use of living! P carried his point and maintains possession of the field to this day. Having the field, he managed to get a wife, who, although homely, has borne him two or three children who are not afflicted with his disease.

Another case in point is the following: Piklud, a fairly wealthy man of Kurug, was paralyzed from the knees down and in his locomotion he had to crawl on all fours. He loaned a neighbor a chicken. There was a quarrel over the repayment of this which left ill feeling between the two. A little while after the quarrel, the neighbor met Piklud crawling along the path through the village, and called to him as to a dog, "Doa! doa! dé-dé-dé!" Piklud pretended not to notice and even feigned amiability. He gossiped a little about the drought which was parching the rice fields. Finally he said, "Let me see your spear." He felt the edge and then with the words, "It is pretty sharp, isn't it?" he thrust it upward into the other's abdomen.

THE PRINCIPAL CRIMES AND THEIR FREQUENCY

90. *List of offenses.*—In the Kiangan-Nagakaran-Maggok area, the principal crimes, in order of their probable frequency, are: sorcery; adultery; theft; murder (or in the case of women and children, kidnapping); the putting of an innocent person in the position of being considered an accessory to crime; manslaughter; rape of a married woman; arson; incest. Minor crimes are: insult; slander; false accusation; rape of a girl.

SORCERY

91. *The ayak* (soul-stealing) is a series of religious ceremonies in which the sorcerer calls to a feast the ancestral spirits of some man whose death he desires to encompass, together with many maleficent spirits and deities, and bribes them to bring to him, incarnated as a blue-bottle fly, a dragon fly, or a bee, the soul of the man whose death he desires. When one of the insects mentioned comes to drink of the rice wine in front of the sorcerer, it is imprisoned and put into a bamboo joint tightly corked. The enemy, being thus deprived of his soul, will die.

This form of sorcery cannot be practiced unless the sorcerer knows the names of the ancestral spirits of his victim-to-be. For this reason, when the Lamot people, who are famous sorcerers, come to Kiangan and approach a religious feast, the Kiangan people do not invoke their ancestral spirits until after the visitors have gone. Needless to say, sorcery is always practiced in secret. It sometimes happens that it is practiced by a man against his kin. In such a case, kinship does not extenuate his punishment, since the preservation of the family necessitates the extirpation of the sorcerer within its gates. This is the only exception I know of to the general rule that a family may not proceed against one of its members.

92. *Other forms of sorcery.*—Certain persons have an evil "cut" of the eye, which, whether they wish it or not, brings misfortune or sickness on whomsoever or whatsoever they see. Injury by means of the "evil eye" may be effected intentionally or entirely unintentionally.

The words of certain persons even though innocent and unconnected with evil, and though spoken as they usually are without malicious intent, have the quality of bringing whatever is spoken to an evil end.

Thus A, afflicted with the "blasting word," goes to the house of B, and, seeing a sow with a litter of handsome pigs, remarks, "That's a fine litter of pigs you have!" If A be truly afflicted with the blasting word, the pigs will die, even though A was without intent to do injury, and was even ignorant of his affliction.

The evil eye and the blasting word are frequent afflictions—afflictions that their possessor is the last to learn about. They may be cured by the possessor's offering sacrifices of the proper sort. In the event of injury unintentionally being done by evil eye or blasting word, no punishment is meted out, although in some cases restitution is demanded.

Curses are of two kinds: directly by word, and indirectly by curses laid on food, drink, or betels. Kiangan people are afraid to purchase rice from the Lamot people to the south of them through fear of being affected by curses that may have been laid on the rice.

93. *Punishment of sorcery.*—Sorcerers are not punished hysterically. To his credit, it must be said that the Ifugao proceeds slowly in condemning a person for this crime. Before he takes action, he demands not merely strong grounds for suspicion, but proof beyond a reasonable doubt that the suspected person is a sorcerer. Proof that one has performed the *ayak* ceremony against a person is sufficient ground for the infliction of the death penalty. But in the case of the evil eye and the blasting word, it must be proved that the death of the pigs, the betel vine, or whatever it be that dies, was due to the glance or words of the bewitched, and that both glance and words were used with evil intent. This would obviously be hard to do; but for the purpose of justifying an injured person in killing such a sorcerer or bewitched one, a record of previous misdeeds of the kind, and a general conviction, in which a portion, at least, of the man's kin concurred, that the suspect was a malicious sorcerer, would be sufficient.

A curse, by one who has no reputation for supernatural powers, is punishable by the following fine:

KADANGYANG *Hin-bakid* (One ten)		MIDDLE CLASS *Hin-bakid* (One ten)		NAWATWAT *Na-onom* (Six)	
Pu-u (2 death blankets)	₱16.00	*Pu-u* (death blanket)	₱8.00	*Pu-u* (*dili*)	₱8.00
Haynub palyuk	5.00	*Haynub palyuk*	5.00	*Natauwinan*	1.00
Haynub palyuk	2.00	*Haynub palyuk*	2.00	*Nuntuku*	.50
Natauwinan	1.00	*Natauwinan*	1.00	*Natuku*	.50
Natauwinan	1.00	*Natauwinan*	1.00	*Na-oha*	.20
Natauwinan	1.00	*Natauwinan*	.50	*Liwa* comes out of the *No-onom*	
Natauwinan	.50	*Nuntuku*	.50		
Nuntuku (3 each)	.50	*Nuntuku*	.40		
Nuntuku	.50	*Nunbadi*	.40		
		Na-oha	.20		
	₱27.50	*Liwa* comes out of the *Hin-bakid*			
Liwa or fee of go-between (1 death blanket)	₱8.00				
Total, ₱35.50		Total, ₱19.00		Total, ₱10.20	

A curse by one who had a reputation of being a sorcerer might possibly lead to the death of the sorcerer on the spot. In case he were not killed, and the person or thing cursed died, the death penalty would be inflicted later.

The following instances will be of value as illustrations. Some are recent, others historical:

Before the coming of the Spaniards, Atiwan of Longa acquired a reputation as a sorcerer. He killed several of his kinsmen in Baay. Even his relatives in Longa admitted that he was a sorcerer, and said that he ought to be killed. Ginnid of Baay and several companions went to Longa one night, and called to Atiwan that they had come to see him. He opened the house and put down the ladder. The party ascended, and set upon Atiwan with their war knives and killed him. In trying to protect him, his wife, Dinaon, was wounded. The killing was universally approved.

Kimudwe (alias Dulnuan) of Tupplak is a famous, or rather an infamous, sorcerer. Owing to a quarrel with one of his nephews, Butlong, over a debt, he performed an *ayak* to cause the latter's death. Butlong was informed of the fact by one who, eavesdropping below Kimudwe's house, heard the prayers and incantations. On a certain day on which there was a feast in Ambabag, to which Kimudwe was nearly certain to come, Butlong waylaid him, firing a rifle at him from cover near Ambabag. His marksmanship was atrocious. Before he could reload women rushed out from the village and covered Kimudwe with their bodies, interceding, and stating that there was not sufficient certainty that Kimudwe was guilty to justify his nephew in killing him. (This occurred in the interval between Spanish and American rule.)

Kimudwe is reputed to have killed by means of sorcery several of his kinsmen. Recently a child died in Tupplak whose death was attributed to him. He killed, it is said, the son of Bahni, another of his nephews. Bahni sent Dulinayan of Ambabag as a go-between to Kimudwe to challenge him to an ordeal, saying that he had no intention of killing him, even if guilty, owing to the peculiar prejudice of the Americans against such doings, but for his own satisfaction he wanted to know if Kimudwe were the sorcerer. He stated that in case Kimudwe won in the ordeal, he (Bahni) would pay a fine of a gold bead for having accused him falsely. This was an unusually large fine. Kimudwe refused, or rather evaded, saying: "If I am a sorcerer, it is a case of the entire family, including Bahni, being guilty." In other words, he took refuge behind the Ifugao doctrine of collective responsibility (see sec. 4).

In cases of strong suspicion, a supposed sorcerer was often openly accused and challenged to an ordeal. The ordeal was usually more in the nature of a duel, the two exchanging spears at twenty steps (20 meters) distance. If the ordeal showed the suspect guilty, he was killed if he stayed in the region. He was not, however, killed on the field of duel—unless killed in the duel or ordeal itself—because such an execution might precipitate a battle with this kin.

ADULTERY

94. *Forms of adultery.*—In its unaggravated form, adultery is called *luktap*. *Luktap* signifies sexual intercourse between a spouse and some person other than the one to whom he (or she) be married, uncomplicated by insults and scandalous behavior flaunted in the face of the injured spouse. The intention to abandon the spouse is either not present, or is concealed.

The aggravated form of adultery is called *hokwit*. It consists of openly and scandalously bestowing one's love and body upon some other person than the spouse; of insulting the injured spouse; or of repeatedly, while living under the same roof with the spouse, meeting the third person and having sexual intercourse. The intention is present of separating (or effecting a separation) from the injured spouse. The following is an illustration:

> Maxima, a girl of Umbul, was married to Ananayo of Pindungan. But Ananayo had not yet reached the age of puberty, while Maxima herself had reached that age. Sergeant Dominong, of the constabulary company at Kiangan, began paying attentions to Maxima, while Maxima was living in the house of Ananayo's father. During the season of watching the rice fields against theft of water these two continually cohabited, the sergeant going to where Maxima was watching the fields at night. Ananayo attaining the age of puberty in the meantime, Maxima refused to have anything to do with him. Both Maxima and Dominong were guilty of *hokwit* in this case. Maxima's conduct was considered especially reprehensible, since she was a *binawit* in the house of Ananayo's father (see sec. 14).

95. *Punishment of adultery.*—In both *luktap* and *hokwit*, the offending spouse and the lover (or mistress) are equally guilty. Each is equally liable to punishment. However, the offended spouse may, if he chooses, forgive the offending spouse without forgiving the partner in crime. This frequently happens. A wife is more likely to forgive than is a husband.

The adulterer when taken *in delicto* is sometimes punished by death. The offended spouse is justified by public opinion in administering this punishment to a considerably greater degree than our laws in the United States would justify him. Several stories are told of persons caught in the commission of this crime who were impaled by a single spear thrust. It should be stated that the kin of those killed for this crime rarely look upon the killing as justified, and often avenge it. They take the stand that the offended spouse ought to have demanded the usual fine; that if this had not been immediately forthcoming, no one would have questioned the propriety of the killing. On the other hand, the kin of the offended spouse take the ground, and it may be said that in general public opinion backs them in it, that a self-respecting man could not well do otherwise than kill the offender, and that the holding off and demanding money would savor too much of the mercenary.

It is to be noted that a sexual offense committed after the *mommon* ceremony is punished by a small fine; that an offense committed after the *imbango* or *hingot* ceremonies is punished by a larger fine, and that an offense committed after the *bubun* ceremony is punished by what to the Ifugao is a very large fine. These fines are diagramed Ifugao fashion in sec. 75. *Hokwit,* aggravated adultery, is punished by twice the greatest fine demanded in the case of simple adultery, *luktap.*

Adultery being a very hard crime to prove, the Ifugao takes as proof: (1) the confession of either party; (2) evidence that the accused wilfully and intentionally placed themselves in such a position or circumstances that the crime would be presumed by any reasonable person to have been consummated. Thus, the sleeping of the accused together at night in the absence of the spouse would be sufficient evidence.

Both offenders must pay the fine demanded by the circumstances to the offended party or parties. Thus, if both the offenders be married, each must pay a fine to (*a*) his own offended spouse, and (*b*) to the offended spouse of the partner in the crime. The *pu-u* of the fine goes to the offended spouse—the rest to the kin of the offended spouse. In addition to paying the fine, should the offender desire to continue the marriage relation with his offended spouse, he must provide animals and other perquisites for a *honga* (general welfare feast) in which the kin of both parties take part, and which is supposed to start the spouses anew in domestic harmony and felicity, and in all that the Ifugao considers prosperity, namely, abundance of pigs, chickens, rice, and children.

96. *Sex in relation to punishment for adultery.*—Although the punishment for adultery is the same for either sex, the likelihood of the adulterer's being punished is much greater if the offender be a woman than if he be a man. This is for the reason that men are more jealous than women and less attached to their spouses, usually. A great deal of adultery on the part of men goes unpunished. Most women would rather not hear about the peccadillos of their husbands. They do not want to take action unless it be forced upon them. But once the matter is brought to their "official attention," they have to take action in order to "save face." Women sometimes tell their husbands "It would be all right for you to have a mistress if you could only do so without my hearing of it." And when they learn of some such offense on the part of their husbands, they sometimes upbraid them, saying: "Oh, why didn't you do this thing in such a way that I would not hear of it?"

The husband, on the other hand, usually punishes, and often divorces his offending wife.

Once an offense is known, it *must* be acted on. Otherwise, the offended spouse is considered to be lacking in self respect. And indeed I believe that the insult involved in adultery is more serious than any other phase of the crime. The Malay's "face" is exceedingly dear to him.

THE TAKING OF LIFE

97. *General considerations.*—It is extremely difficult to unravel the law, if there be a law, with respect to murder, executions, and war. The Ifugao has no tribunals to sentence, and no government to execute. He makes no declarations of war. Doubtless no two nations or tribes of the world ever engaged in a warfare in which each did not consider the other the aggressor, or at least, the offender. The same is true with respect to feuds between families, which were almost as numerous as the families themselves. In spite of the years of American occupation during which comparative peace has prevailed, these feuds still exist. We must substitute, however, for patriotism, fraternal and filial love; the sense of duty to the unavenged dead, love of vengeance, and intense hatred engendered and justified by a well learned catalogue of wrongs and assassinations inflicted on the family by the enemy family. Once started, a blood feud was well nigh eternal (unless ended by a fusion of the families by means of marriage), for the reason that what was a righteous execution to one family was a murder (usually treacherous) to the other.

Outside of manslaughter, to be treated of later, it may be stated as a general tenet of Ifugao practice that the taking of a life must be paid by a life. Considering, too, that a member of an Ifugao family rarely if ever effected or accomplished any except the most ordinary and elemental acts without previous consultation with his family, and that nearly all killings were effected pursuant to a decision of a family council, it was not without a fair show of reason that Ifugao law held that a murder might be punished almost as well by the execution of some member of the murderer's family as by the execution of the murderer himself. For, if not principals in the commission of the crime, other members of the family were at least accomplices or accessories. Indeed Ifugao law held the whole family guilty, looking upon the crime, quite correctly, as an offense for which the whole family was responsible.

War, murder, and the death penalty exacted in execution of justice, in the Ifugao's society are so near each other as to be almost synonymous terms. We have already seen that a capital execution for crime is nearly always looked upon by the kin of the executed as being a murder; it is retaliated by them, by what to them is a justifiable execution; but by what, to the killers, is considered as a murder to be punished by another execution, and so on *ad infinitum*.

The Ifugao has one general law, which with a few notable exceptions he applies to killings, be they killings in war, murders, or executions, which public opinion would pronounce justifiable and legal. That law is: *A life must be paid by a life.* Let us pass now to a consideration of various classes of the takings of human life.

98. *Executions justifiable by Ifugao law.*—Public opinion or custom, or both, justify the taking of a life in punishment for the following crimes: sorcery; murder; persistent and wilful refusal to pay a debt when there is the ability to pay; adultery discovered *in flagrante;* theft by one of a foreign district; refusal to pay a fine assessed for crime or for injury suffered. But even though custom and public opinion justify the administration of the extreme penalty in these cases, the kin of the murdered man do not, in most cases, consider the killing justified. There are innumerable circumstances that complicate a given case. Was the sorcery proven or only suspected? Was it a murder that the man committed; or was he justified in the killing? Would not the debtor have come to his right mind had his creditor waited a little longer; and did the creditor approach him in the right way with reference to the debt? Did not the woman make advances in the adultery case that no self-respecting male could turn down? Was not the indemnity assessed too large or otherwise improper; or did the injured party wait long enough for the payment? These and a thousand other questions may arise with respect to the various cases.

If the death penalty be inflicted by persons of a foreign district, it is sure to be looked upon as a murder.

At feasts and gatherings about the "bowl that cheers" and especially in drunken brawls, an unavenged killing, no matter what the circumstances, is likely to be brought up as a reflection upon the bravery or manhood of the living kin, and so urge them to the avenging of what was really a justified execution.

Murder, sorcery, and a refusal to pay the fine for adultery justify the infliction of the death penalty even on a kinsman if he is not too close a relative. An execution of one kinsman by another is not so likely to be avenged as is justifiable execution by one outside the family. This is in accordance with the principle of Ifugao law: *The family must at all hazards be preserved.*

99. *Feuds.*—A feud is a series of takings of human life as vengeance, in which the heads may or may not be taken. There are some hundreds of ways in which feuds may start. As a rule they begin with a taking of life that is not justified in the eyes of the kin of him whose life was taken. They may begin from a retaliation for a kidnapping or even from an accidental killing. Feuds exist between neighboring districts, or districts not far distant between which to a certain extent ties of blood and marriage exist. It is exceedingly rare—if it ever occurs—that entire villages or districts are involved. The feud is an affair between families only. It consists of a series of vengeances and "returning of vengeances." Feuds may even start within the district; but as a rule, they are short lived, being stopped by the counsel of the influential. Feuds between districts are well nigh interminable usually, but may come to an end by means of intermarriage or when one or two of the leaders of each family are afflicted by certain diseases[15] thought to be inflicted by certain deities that desire the peace ceremony. As has been hitherto stated, each killing in a feud is considered by the killers to be an entirely justifiable execution in punishment of crime. The deities of war and justice are called to witness that the debt is not yet paid. Contemporaneously, the kin of the slain are calling on the same deities to witness that their family is sorely afflicted; that no debt was owed the others; that no chickens or pigs, or rice had been borrowed; that no theft or other crime had been committed, and so on; yet, that innocent, they are being slaughtered.

100. *War.*—Before the American occupation, districts that were far distant might be said to be continually at war with each other. The war was carried on as a series of head-takings. There was no formal declaration of war. As a rule there were no large expeditions to the enemy country, and heads were taken from ambush, on the outskirts of an enemy village or along much traveled paths. Women's heads were taken in these exploits; but not as a rule, in feuds. To avenge lives taken in war, while no doubt the life of the actual head-taker was preferable, the life of any person of the enemy village might be taken; just as in feuds, the life of any member of the enemy family might be taken.

---

[15] Tuberculosis and persistent cough (see sec. 141).

101. *Head-taking.*—Heads were not taken in the case of executions for injury. In feuds within a district, heads were not taken. In feuds between families of different districts, heads might or might not be taken. Usually they were taken if there were no ties of kinship between the districts. It should be emphasized, however, that there was no definite boundary between districts, and consequently, no well-defined line beyond which heads might be taken. Families from the southern part of a district would take heads in territory from which those in the northern part of the district would not take them. Heads were always taken in the case of those killed in war, if circumstances permitted.

102. *Hibul or homicide.*—The Ifugao law clearly recognizes several grades of homicide.

(*a*) The taking of life when there is an entire absence of both intent and carelessness. As for example, in the case already cited (see sec. 84), when a party of hunters have a wild boar at bay. The boar, as there stated, charges the most advanced of the hunters, and in retreating backwards, the latter jabs one of his companions with the shod point of his spear handle. There is no penalty for such a taking of life.

(*b*) The taking of life when there is clearly an absence of intent, but a degree of carelessness. For example, a number of men are throwing spears at a mark. A child runs in the way, and is killed. The penalty is a fine varying from one-third to two-thirds the amount of the full fine for homicide according to the degree of carelessness.

(*c*) Intentional taking of the life of another, under the impression that he is an enemy when in reality he is a co-villager or a companion. In case the killer can make the family of the slain understand the circumstances, only a fine is assessed. This fine is called *labod*. (See sec. 106.) If the killer be unrelated to the slain, the full amount of the *labod* is demanded; if related, the amount is usually lessened.

Example: Dumauwat of Baay was irrigating his fields at night. Some of his companions told him that there were some head-hunters from an enemy village near. In the darkness, Dumauwat encountered another man, Likyayu, the betrothed of his daughter. He asked him who was there. On account of the noise of water falling from the rice fields, Likyayu did not hear the inquiry, and said nothing. Dumauwat speared him. Likyayu cried out. Dumauwat recognized his voice, and carried him home. He furnished animals for sacrifice to secure Likyayu's recovery. Likyayu recovered. Had he died, Dumauwat would have been called on for the full amount of the fine; but had Likyayu been *firmly* engaged to Dumauwat's daughter, that is, had the *bango* ceremony been performed the full amount of the *labod* fine would not have been demanded, since the relationship would have been an extenuating circumstance.

(*d*) The taking of life by persons in a brawl or by an intoxicated or insane person. In case the slain died before his slayer could agree to provide animals for sacrifice, the latter would probably be killed by the kin of the slain if he were of a foreign district. He might be killed if a non-related co-villager. He would be fined the *labod* if a kinsman. He would probably go scot free if a brother or uncle.

Example: A of Longa became insanely drunk at a feast at the house of his brother Gimbungan. He attempted to embrace the comely daughter of Gimbungan, his niece. Gimbungan tried to quiet him, and in so doing aroused his ire. He drew back his spear menacingly, and in so doing pierced the girl—who was at his back—with the shod point at the end. She died. A was properly penitent when he sobered, and furnished animals for sacrifice. The fine *labod* was not, however, demanded of him. This was about thirty-five or forty years ago. Considerable feeling exists between the two branches of the family to this day, owing to this occurrence.

The burden rests upon the slayer in the above cases to show that the killing was accidental or that he was so drunk as to have utterly lost his reason. The absence of a motive is a great help to him in this. If he has ever had a serious altercation with the slain, in the absence of controverting evidence, the presumption is likely to be that the killing was intentional, and that he has been "feigning friendship in order to kill by *ugâ* (treachery)."

103. *Attempts to murder.*—An attempt on the part of an enemy of another district on the life of a person is punishable by death. An attempt by one of the same district may or may not be punished by death; in most cases peace would be arranged by mutual friends and kinsmen. In such a case, he who made the attempt would be required to furnish animals for a peace feast.

104. *Wounding.*—Wounds inflicted accidentally and without intent or carelessness are not punished. In case the element of intent or carelessness be present, he who inflicts the wounds must furnish animals for sacrifice, pay the wounded man and his kin a fine, and stand the expense of a feast to make peace. The following is a typical list, for the *kadangyang* (wealthy) class, of the expenses of animals for sacrifice and fine:

(*a*) First feast for the recovery of the wounded man, sacrifices to the war deities: 3 pigs at 15 pesos; 10 chickens at 1 peso; total 55 pesos.

(*b*) Second feast for recovery, the *pinochla*, or feast to cure wounds and infections: 1 pig at 10 pesos; 2 chickens at 1 peso; 8 spear heads as fees of priests at 25c; total 14 pesos.

In case the wounded man lives, the following fine is paid him and his kin:

(*c*) Fine of two *bakid* (two tens) amounting to 72 pesos; fee of the *monkalun*, 10 pesos; total 82 pesos.

(*d*) Peace-making ceremony: 1 pig at 15 pesos; other appurtenances of feast, 2 pesos; total 17 pesos.

105. *Special liability of the givers of certain feasts.*—The givers of *uyauwe* or *hagabi* feasts (glorified general welfare feasts to which

great numbers of people come) are responsible for wounds or deaths that occur at these feasts. When a man decides to initiate himself and his wife into the ranks of the *kadangyang* by giving one of these feasts, he appoints one of the old priests of his family to perform the *tikman* ceremonies. These ceremonies are sacrifices to the various classes of deities whose special function is the "tying up" of men's stomachs and passions. Prayers are addressed to these deities that a little food satisfy the guest that attends the feast, to the end that the giver be not eaten out of house and home; that a little rice wine suffice to intoxicate the people; that the passions of men be tied up to the end that no quarrels or frays occur; that no rice-wine jars or gongs be broken; that no accidents occur—in short, that the whole feast pass off smoothly. The duties of the *manikam* (the priest who performs these ceremonies) are rather arduous. To say nothing of the ceremonies he conducts, he must fast for a number of days and must observe a number of taboos. He receives rather a large fee for these services. And, indeed, their importance, in the eyes of the Ifugaos, and the legal responsibility he incurs, certainly justify a large fee.

The *manikam* priests are jointly responsible with the giver of the feast for accidents or violence that may occur. This liability of the giver of the feast for wounds or loss of life is based on the supposition that if he had not given the feast the wound would not have occurred; and possibly that he gave the feast with the motive of bringing about such an occurrence. The liability of the *manikam* is based on the supposition that there must have been a remissness on his part in his religious duties, else the accident or loss would never have occurred. The following is an actual instance that would indicate that this provision of the law is an incipient employer's liability provision.

Malingan of Pindungan, many years ago, gathered together his kin and friends, performed the preliminary feasts, and went to Payauan to make a *hagabi* (lounging bench, the insignium of the *kadangyang* class). They made a very large *hagabi* that weighed nearly a ton. In helping to carry it across the river two men were carried downstream by the current and drowned. Demand was made on Malingan and the *manikam* of the feast for the *labod* fine (see sec. 106). It was paid, and that is the reason Malingan's descendants are not wealthier today, for formerly Malingan was one of the wealthiest men of the district.

It should be stated that brawls and accidents are much more common in feasts of this character given in parts of Ifugao other than the Kiangan-Nagakaran-Maggok area. This is due to the fact that in the area named above only relatives and persons invited by relatives attend, while in other regions the event is not so exclusive. There is the further consideration that in this area, on the night before the general drink-fest begins, an old man makes a speech in which he tries to put the crowd assembled in a good humor, and in which he warns each and every one to seize and hold any person who begins to disgrace hospitality by unseemly brawling.

106. *The labod, fine assessed for homicide.*—This fine is paid to the family of the slain. For the *kadangyang,* or wealthy class, the full fine consists of ten portions or divisions, totaling 975 pesos in the case tabulated below. These divisions may be briefly described as follows:

THE LABOD FINE

1. Outlay for a *honga* (general welfare feast):
   - (1) carabao .... ₱80.00
   - (2) 3 pigs 60.00

   Total .... ₱140.00

The *honga* is performed by the man's kin as a means of preventing the recurrence of such misfortunes in the family. The animals are sacrificed to all the deities.

2. *Dangale* (sacrifices at funeral feast):
   - (1) 2 carabaos .... ₱160.00
   - (2) 5 pigs 80.00

   Total .... ₱240.00

The animals of this part of the fine are killed at the funeral feast of the slain.

3. *Gagaom* (funeral shrouds):
   - (1) 8 death blankets ...... ₱64.00
   - (2) 4 clouts 4.00
   - (3) 1 ceremonial clout 1.00

   Total .... ₱69.00

The clouts are to tie the dead man in the death chair: one about the chest; one about the head; one about the shoulders; and one to tie on the head and beak of the hornbill worn as a mark of rank. The ceremonial clout is worn on the breech of the corpse.

The corpse is wrapped and entombed in the eight death blankets.

4. *Habalag* (hangings at funeral feast):
   - (1) 2 death blankets as fee of the *monkalun* ₱16.00
   - (2) 9 *maginlotan* (cheap death blankets) 36.00

   Total .... ₱52.00

The nine cheap blankets are distributed among the man's kin.

5. *Mata-na* (his eyes):
   - (1) 1 gold neck-ornament for left eye .... ₱80.00
   - (2) 1 gold neck-ornament for right eye 80.00

   Total .... ₱160.00

6. *Putu-na* (his belly):
  (1) 1 *pango* (string of
    beads) .... ₱120.00
7. *Puhu-na* (his heart):
  (1) 1 *guling* (rice-wine
    jar, small) .... ₱80.00
8. *Ubuna-na* (his seat):
  (1) 1 gong .... ₱80.00
9. *Nunlidludagan* (his place to lie):
  (1) 2 death blankets .... ₱16.00
10. *Hidit* (peace-making):
  (1) 1 pig and other essen-
    tials of feast .... ₱18.00

     Total ....₱314.00

Articles listed under numbers 5 to 9 inclusive, go to the dead man's heirs and kin.

For making peace with the family of the slain.

The rank of the slain has something to do with the amount of the *labod*. The amounts given above are those that would be collected in the case of the killing of a Kiangan man of the *kadangyang* class. If the slain were a middle class or poor man the amounts would not be so great.[16] If the slayer were a middle class, or poor man, the amounts above might be lessened somewhat, but not very much. If the slayer be unable to pay, he is saddled with the rest as a debt. If he cannot pay the debt during his lifetime, his children must pay it.

107. *Accidental killing of animals.*—The accidental killing of an animal is not a crime. Sometimes even the value of the animal is not demanded or accepted if tendered.

If a dog runs out threatening to bite a passer-by, and the latter kills it, he is required to pay the value of the dog. If a dog bites a passer-by, the latter may kill the dog and need not pay a fine. If the dog bites him, and he does not kill it, he may demand a payment from the owner. It was a provision of primitive Roman law that "If an injury were done by a slave, the person injured had the right to exact vengeance against the slave personally, thus injuring the master's property; and the master or owner was consequently allowed to prevent this vengeance by making compensation for the injury done."[17]

Should a pig, at that period of the year when rice is stacked below the granary to dry out, enter through the fence and eat of the rice, it may be killed by the owner of the granary; but he must give the owner another pig in place of it. Such a killing is not considered

[16] Compare the practice of our Saxon forefathers among whom the "life of a king's thane was worth 1200 shillings, while that of a common free man was valued only a sixth as high," and that of a slave at only his property valuation.

[17] R. R. Cherry, *The Growth of Criminal Law in Ancient Communities* (London, 1890). Dr. Cherry shows how masters' liability for injuries done by their employees has arisen from this principle (pp. 4 ff.).

malicious, for the pig was spoiling the "miraculous increase" of the year's harvest.

A pig that enters a rice field and eats of the unharvested rice is usually returned to the owner with the request that he tie the pig up. Should it again enter the field, the damage it does must be paid for. Should the owner refuse to pay this indemnity, and should the pig again enter the field, the owner of the field would be likely to kill the animal. The owner of the pig might consider such a killing malicious and improper. Public opinion would sustain the owner of the field.

108. *Malicious killing of animals.*—This is a serious crime. Its seriousness is due partly to the fact that domestic animals are to a great extent considered members of the household and as such loved and protected, and further to the fact that the intentional and malicious killing of such a member of a household would have a tendency to bring a like fate on the human members thereof, owing to the mystic power and force of analogy.

A *labod* fine is demanded for the malicious killing of a pig. The fine, in case a wealthy family is concerned, is as follows:

LABOD FINE FOR MALICIOUS KILLING OF A PIG

1. The corpse of the dead pig is surrounded by living pigs, one on each side, i.e., four pigs are exacted in return.

2. *Dangale* (see sec. 106): 1 carabao. This animal is simply handed over, not killed for a funeral as is the case when a human being is concerned.

3. *Gagaom* (see sec. 106): 6 death blankets; 1 *bayaó* (fancy blanket); 1 *tinunwe* (ceremonial clout); 4 clouts.

4. *Habalag* (see sec. 106): precisely as in the case of a homicide.

5. *Liwa,* fee of the *monkalun,* or go-between: 1 death blanket,

PUTTING ANOTHER IN THE POSITION OF AN ACCOMPLICE

109. *The tokom, or fine for compromising another.*—He who, voluntarily or involuntarily, puts another in the position of an accomplice, or in such a light that he might be regarded as being an accomplice in the commission of a crime, and so be liable to punishment as such, must pay the person so injured a fine, called *tokom*. It may almost be said that he who causes another person's name to be prominently mentioned or bandied in connection with a crime must pay this fine.

The following are instances in which a *tokom* would be demanded:

A of another district comes to the house of B, and is received by B as a guest. While he is going home and while he is in the outskirts of the district he is speared by C, a neighbor of B's or a resident of the same district. B must force C to pay a *tokom*.

B steals or illegally confiscates property belonging to A. C sees B in the act. He demands a *tokom*—in this case it may be the bolo or spear that B is carrying—and so puts himself ''on record'' as not having been an accomplice. But he says nothing about the crime unless it come to light that he was a witness of it. In this case he proves by the *tokom* that he received that he had no connection with it. As a matter of practice it would seem that a gift received from the thief would tend to lead the witness to conceal the crime.

A gives an *uyauwe* feast. At the attendant drink feast B in a drunken brawl kills C. A and the *manikam* D must demand a *tokom* from B in order to clear their reputations.

The following is the amount of the *tokom* usually demanded in the case of murder, head-hunting, or slaughter:

In case of the death of a kadangyang Honga	In case of the death of a middle-class man Honga	in case of the death of a poor man Honga
1 carabao ...... ₱80.00	8 pigs .... ₱80.00	4 pigs .... ₱40.00
2 pigs 30.00	1 *bakid* 25.00	1 *bakid* 15.00
1 *bakid* 44.00		
Total .... ₱154.00	Total .... ₱105.00	Total .... ₱55.00

One who is put in a position in which a *tokom* is due him must collect the *tokom*. It is not sufficient that he demand the payment of it—he must enforce the payment. Otherwise he will be considered by the kin of the injured as having been an accomplice, and liable to punishment accordingly.

Should the culprit refuse to pay the *tokom*, the obligation rests on those to whom the *tokom* is due to take the leading part in the punishment of the crime. Thus, in the first example given above, if C does not pay the *tokom* to B, the obligation rests on B more heavily even than it rests on A's relatives to kill C, and so avenge A's death. Should he not do this, he would be held liable to punishment by A's relatives along with C.

Visitors came to the house of Timbuluy of Ambabag from the district of Maggok. It was suggested that a contract of friendship and alliance be accomplished between Timbuluy and his Maggok visitors by means of the feast called *monbiyao*. A day was appointed for this feast, and Binwag of Bolog was named as the go-between in matters pertaining to the feast. These preliminaries having been finished, the Maggok people started home. On the road they were killed by some people from Wingian.

The following persons were under obligation to demand a *tokom*: Timbuluy, whose guests they had been, and Binwag, the go-between. But the murderers were poor people, while the murdered were wealthy. It would have been impossible for the murderers to have paid the *tokom* proper for having killed a *kadangyang*. Consequently without any ado, Binwag killed one of the murderers, and Timbuluy kidnapped one of the women folk of another.

Timbuluy sold this woman to slavery in Nueva Vizcaya, receiving four carabaos. He gave one carabao to each of the four villages Pindungan, Ambabag, Bango, and Baay—all in Kiangan valley—on the consideration that if the people of Wingian retaliated by capturing a Kiangan woman in the open territory surrounding or adjacent to one of these villages, the people of that village would collect the necessary sum and redeem the woman.

THEFT

110. *Of theft in general.*—There is a considerable degree of difference in the severity with which theft is punished in different parts of Ifugao. The following is the general law with respect to the theft of articles of medium or slight value:

Kadangyang class: It is a general principle that true *kadangyang* do not steal. However, it sometimes occurs, especially in the Kiangan-Maggok area, that persons who have the right to claim this rank become needy. The rule for the punishment of members of this class is: The *kadangyang* must return the stolen thing, or, if it shall have been consumed, its equivalent in value, and must entirely surround it with like things of equivalent value. This rule merely amounts to the paying of five times the value of the stolen thing. He must also pay a fee to the go-between.

Middle class: A thief of this class must return the stolen thing and *ulpitan* it, i.e., place a like thing, or an equivalent value, on either side of it. He must also pay a *liwa* fee to the go-between of the case.

Very poor: A thief of this class must repay the stolen article or its equivalent value, *tokopna,* and pay a fee to the go-between in the case.

In the case of the theft of heirlooms of great value, such as ricewine jars, or *gansas,* the thief must repay, besides the stolen articles, their *tokop,* or equal, and in addition must furnish a certain number of pigs or other articles of medium value. The following shows how the Ifugao visualizes a payment of this sort.

The stolen article.
Its equal or equivalent.
Honga, a full-grown pig.
Yubyub, a full-grown chicken.

Theft should not be confused with improper or illegal confiscation. This latter is commonly effected by members of the *kadangyang* class. It is punished in much the same way as theft, but is not so disgraceful.

A thief discovered *in delicto* is likely to be punished by death if the thief be of a different district. If not punished by death, the culprit is caught and tied and kept prisoner until his kin in the other district pay the fine demanded. This fine, needless to say, is somewhat larger than would ordinarily be assessed for the crime. If a member of the home district be caught in an unaccomplished theft, the case is not altered in any way from an ordinary, consummated theft.

111. *Theft of rice from a granary.*—The theft of rice is considerably more serious than would be theft of any other article of equal value, because it ruins the miraculous increase of the rice that the Ifugao as well as all other Malay tribes in these islands so thoroughly believe in. If the thief confesses and shows himself docile, he may wipe out his guilt with the following payment:

> *Hulul-na,* 1 large pig, payment of the stolen rice.
> *Honga,* 1 large pig and 1 large chicken, for granary feast to secure return of the miraculous increase.

If, however, the accused persistently deny his guilt, he is challenged to an ordeal. If by this he is proven guilty, he is fined one *bakid* or one "ten"—in Kiangan about thirty pesos—in addition to the payment above. If he refuse to submit to the ordeal, he is adjudged guilty, and has to make the same payments as if he had submitted to the ordeal and had been adjudged guilty. The fee of the *monkalun* is included in, and is not additional to, the *bakid* in this case.

112. *Theft of unharvested rice.*—In a case of this sort, the amount of rice stolen can be determined by estimating it from the number of headless stalks. The punishment is:

> The return of the stolen rice or its equivalent value.
> A full-grown pig for the owner's harvest feast.
> The fee for the *monkalun.*

113. *Illegal confiscation.*—What the Ifugao recognizes as legal confiscation is treated below under Procedure, sections 134 to 138. The following is a case of illegal confiscation in the district of Banaue.

A owes B a debt, which he persistently refuses to pay. Both men are of the *kadangyang* class. B is somewhat afraid of A, or for some reason cannot or does not dare collect the debt according to the ordinary mode of procedure. He accordingly runs away with a valuable rice-wine jar belonging to A, *leaving nothing behind to show who took it.*

B finds out who ran away with his jar. He pays the debt he owes B, if it be truly owed, and demands the following from him for his improper procedure:

> The return of the stolen jar.
> Another one like it, or an equivalent of some sort.
> A gong as a *dalag* (fine for illegal confiscation).
> A large pig for a *honga* (general welfare feast).
> A kettle worth five pesos called *habale* (pegs on which house charms are hung).

4 yards of brass wire. This payment is called *nundopa,* referring to the jumping down of the culprit when he carried off the jar.

Death blanket with which to carry jar home.

If B, when he ran away with the jar, had left behind his scabbard or bolo or some other of his belongings to show his identity, the above would have been a case of legal confiscation, and not punishable.

Illegal confiscation lacks the elements of disgrace that theft carries with it, and, in the mind of the confiscator and his relatives at least, is justifiable. It may be that it is for this very reason that this crime is punished more severely than ordinary theft.

ARSON

114. *Fines assessed for goba or arson.*—One caught in the act of setting fire to a house or granary would be likely to be killed on the spot. Should he consummate the act and escape, demand would probably be made upon him and his kin for *two* granaries full of rice and for the animals necessary to consecrate them by the usual feasts. This would be the *probable* punishment. The crime of arson is rare, and consequently there is no penalty or restitution well defined by law. The punishment might be death, or the kidnapping and selling into slavery of a member of the culprit's family, or a fine as above. Which of these it would be would depend very much on the personality of the injured party.

KIDNAPPING

115. *Circumstances under which kidnapping may occur.*—If performed to cover a debt for which payment had been repeatedly demanded, or to cover an injury for which a proper fine had been repeatedly demanded in due form,' kidnapping was a legal seizure, although the victim and his kindred might not consider it so.

But there were a good many cases in which the kidnapper's motive was utterly different. He might wish, for example, to display his valor, or to profit financially by the sale of his captives. Sometimes, too, a head-hunting party, failing to get a head, would capture a woman and carry her back with them to their village. In some parts of Ifugao the woman was ravished for a period of five days by the party of head-hunters. She was then sold into slavery.

The penalty inflicted by the kin of the kidnapper was either death or retaliation by kidnapping.

INCEST

116. *Rarity of such offenses.*—Incest is a very rare crime in Ifugao. It seems to be becoming more frequent, for there has undoubtedly been a growing laxity in morality ever since the establishment of foreign government. A case recently occurred in Mongayan, in which a father, on humane grounds as he put the matter to her, deflowered his own daughter. This case was not punished.

RAPE

117. *Both parties being unmarried.*—The unmarried Ifugaos, from earliest childhood, are accustomed to collect in certain houses, using them as dormitories. Usually both sexes sleep together in these dormitories. Naturally, too, there is a great deal of sexual intercourse each night, for sexual intercourse takes the same place among the Ifugaos that embraces and kisses do in the courtship of some other peoples. The nature of the female human being, says the Ifugao, is to resist the advances of the male. He naïvely points out that the hens, the cows, and, in fact, the females of any species resist the male in this respect, notwithstanding they may be quite as anxious for the sexual act as the male himself. It is so with women, he says. It is considered shocking in some sections of Ifugao for a girl to yield herself to her lover the first time without resistance. This idiosyncracy of feminine nature being a fact, it is sometimes difficult to be certain as to whether the resistance offered by a girl is *bona fide* or not—as to whether she is willing for the sexual act to occur, half willing, or entirely opposed to it. There may or may not be doubt in the mind of the male—usually there is none—but friends of the girl, by distorting or by putting a slightly different interpretation on what occurred, could make a case of rape in the white man's courts out of almost any of these common events. Furthermore, a girl on the advice of her parents, were such a rape punishable by fine, might and frequently would, entice some youth into forcing her, in order that her family might benefit financially.

Consequently if a girl be "caught" in a sleeping house by a youth who habitually sleeps there, the Ifugaos do not look upon it as a case of rape, even though force be used. By following this principle a great many questions and "put-up-jobs" are avoided. If a girl be seized and raped by one who does not habitually sleep in or frequent the girl's dormitory, and the evidence establishes a case of *bona fide* resistance on the part of the girl, a fine of "six" is assessed against the raptor as follows:

Kadangyang class		*Middle class*		*Very poor*	
Death blanket	₱8.00	Cooking pot	₱2.00	Cooking pot	₱2.00
Cooking pot	2.00	*Natauwinan*	1.00	*Na-oha*	.25
Natauwinan	1.00	*Natauwinan*	1.00	*Na-oha*	.25
Natauwinan	1.00	*Nunbadi*	.40	*Na-oha*	.25
Natuku	.50	*Nunbadi*	.40	*Na-oha*	.25
Natuku	.50	*Na-oha*	.25	*Na-oha*	.25
Total, ₱13.00		Total, ₱5.05		Total, ₱3.25	

It will be noted that the above are very light fines. In some parts of Ifugao they would be considerably higher—notably in the Silipan country.

The committing of the crime of rape in broad daylight, as, for example, the "catching" of a woman in a *camote* field, constitutes an aggravating circumstance. Such a rape as that punishable by a fine of "six" above would be punishable by a fine of "ten" of a value for the three classes respectively of about thirty-two pesos, sixteen pesos, and eight pesos, if committed in broad daylight. This is owing to the greater "shame" which the woman feels on account of the unwonted hour.

118. *Rape of a married woman by an unmarried man.*—This is a serious offense. It is punishable by a fine equivalent to twice the fine assessed for *luktap*, or unaggravated adultery. One-half of this fine goes to the husband of the outraged woman and his kin and one-half to the woman and her kin.

119. *Rape of a married woman by a married man.*—This is a case still more serious for the offender, since in addition to paying the afore-mentioned fine, he must pay to his own wife an additional fine as penalty for *luktap*.

MA-HAILYU OR MINOR OFFENSES

Minor fines are punishable by fines called *hailyu*. The rape of an unmarried woman by an unmarried man, considered in the preceding section in connection with the more serious forms of rape, is a minor crime.

120. *False accusation.*—He who accuses another falsely or he who, accusing another of crime, challenges him to an ordeal, which ordeal proves the accused to be innocent, must pay the following fine:

Hailyu Paid by the Accuser to the Falsely Accused

Kadangyang class One *bakid* (ten)		*Middle* class One *bakid* (ten)		*Very poor* One *onom* (six)	
2 death blan- kets	₱16.00	1 death blanket	₱8.00	1 death blanket	₱8.00
Cooking pot	5.00	1 cooking pot	5.00	*Natauwinan*	1.00
Cooking pot	2.00	1 cooking pot	2.00	*Natauwinan*	1.00
Natauwinan	1.00	*Natauwinan*	1.00	*Natuku*	.60
Natauwinan	1.00	*Natauwinan*	1.00	*Natuku*	.60
Natauwinan	1.00	*Natauwinan*	.60	*Na-oha*	.40
Natauwinan	1.00	*Nuntuku*	.60		
Nuntuku	.60	*Nunbadi*	.40	Total, ₱11.60	
Nunbadi	.40	*Na-oha*	.25		
	₱28.00		Total, ₱18.85		

Fee of go-between:
1 death blanket   8.00

Total, ₱36.00

Fee of go-between:
iron pot of value of
₱5 included above.

Fee of go-between:
one *natauwinan* in-
cluded above.

The amount of the fine depends to a great extent on the seriousness of the offense of which one is accused.

121. *Baag or slander.*—This offense is punishable by a somewhat smaller fine than that above. The following is an instance to illustrate what trivial statements may be considered as slanders. At an *uyauwe* feast Bahni of Tupplak made remarks derogatory to Bumidang of Palao, the principal of which was to the effect that Bumidang would never have been a *kadangyang* had it not been for the fees that he received from the Palao people for acting as go-between in buying back the heads of their slain from their Silepan enemies. Bumidang considered this as slander, and seized a carabao belonging to Bahni, holding it until payment of the fine assessed for insult was made.

122. *Threats of violence.*—*Ongot*, or threat, is punished by about the same fine as slander.

123. *Insult.*—The saying to another person of anything reflecting on his honor, prestige, or rank; the use of abusive language to an equal or superior; insinuations as to improper relations with kins-women; improper language and behavior in the presence of people of opposite sexes who are related to each other within the forbidden degrees; breaking of various taboos—all of these constitute insults, and are punishable by a fine varying in size from the fine for slander to that for false accusation.

There exist a considerable number of taboos, for breaking of which a penalty is exacted.

First. There are taboos relating to exogamy. In the presence of male and female kin that are of the degrees within which marriage is forbidden it is taboo: (*a*) to look fixedly at the woman's breasts or hips; (*b*) to speak of the dormitory of the unmarried; (*c*) to mention the love affairs of an unmarried couple except most guardedly; (*d*) to break wind; (*e*) to blackguard; (*f*) to play the *bikong,* lover's harp. Matters connected with sex must not be referred to unnecessarily; whenever it is necessary to refer to them, the most delicately veiled euphemisms must be used. Thus an unborn babe must be called "the friend"; the placenta must be termed a "blanket"; the short plank that constitutes the Ifugao's bed must be designated as a "level"; even an egg must be referred to as a "soft stone" or "stone of the chickens." It is a very grave insult, knowing two people to be of the forbidden degrees of kinship, to ask them if they are married. Even if asked in ignorance of the kinship, such a question is considered to show exceeding ill breeding. On my first arrival among the Ifugaos I was several times made to feel like a boorish lout by having asked the question of the wrong people. I then hit upon the scheme of asking two people if they were brother and sister before asking if they were married. This, however, was equally a *faux pas* in case the two were husband and wife, since to the Ifugao it amounted to asking a man if he had married his sister. I then learned to do as a well-bred Ifugao does in such cases: to observe and deduce from the conduct of the two what their relationship might be. This was never a difficult matter.

Second. Acts which savor of adultery are tabooed. Among such are the intentional touching of the body of a married woman. If a man meets a married woman on a rice-field dike, the proper thing for him to do is to step off into the mud and water and let her pass. He may not grasp her body in order to squeeze past her and thus avoid stepping into the water. It is forbidden, too, to enter a house in which a married woman is alone.

Third. It is taboo, knowing a person to be dead, to ask his sons or near kin if he is dead.

Fourth. Certain acts are believed to be injurious to others because they are bad in their magic influence. Thus trying to collect a debt when a member of the debtor's household is ill is taboo. The penalty for this act is the loss of the debt, be it large or small. It is believed that any subtraction from the sick person's or his family's possessions is bound to react injuriously on his health.

Passing near or through a field of rice in a foreign district during harvest is taboo, because it is a disturbing factor and interferes with the miraculous increase.

PROCEDURE

124. *Family unity and coöperation.*—The mutual duty of kinsfolk and relatives, each individual to every other of the same family, regardless of sex, is to aid, advise, assist, and support in all controversies and altercations with members of other groups or families. The degree of obligation of the various members of a family group to assist and back any particular individual of that group is in direct proportion: *first,* to the kinship or the relationship by marriage; *second,* to the loyalty the individual in question has himself manifested toward the family group, that is, the extent to which he discharges his obligations to that group.

The family is without any political organization whatever. It is a little democracy in which each member is measured for what he is worth, and has a voice accordingly in the family policy. It is a different body for every married individual of the whole Ifugao tribe.[18] There are a great many relationships that complicate matters. An Ifugao's family is his nation. The family is an executive and a judicial body. Its councils are informal, but its decisions are none the less effective. The following rules and principles apply to the family and to individuals in the matter of procedure.

Brothers of the blood can never be arrayed against each other. They may fall out and quarrel, but they can never proceed against each other. This is for the reason that their family is identical (before marriage at least), and a family cannot proceed against itself.

Cousins and brothers of the half-blood ought never to be arrayed against each other in legal procedure. In case they should be so arrayed, the mutual kin try to arrange peace. Only in the event of serious injuries may a cousin with good grace and with the approval of public opinion collect a fine from another cousin, and even then he should not demand as much as from a non-related person. In the case of minor injuries he should forego punishing his kindred. The following is an example:

[18] Thus A and B, two brothers, are members of the same family until they marry. After marriage A's family consists of his blood kin and of his relatives by marriage, and the same holds of B's family. Thus after marriage only half the individuals of the families of the two brothers are identical. The families of two cousins are identical as to one-half the component individuals before their marriage and as to one-fourth of the component individuals after their marriage.

A steals some rice from his cousin B. Theft and thief become known. A takes no steps against the thief; but A's wife cannot overlook it—and the injury was an injury to her as much as to A. Her kin take the matter up. They collect half the usual indemnity for their kinswoman. A foregoes his half of the indemnity.

In cases of minor injury, procedure against more distant kin is frowned on, but sometimes occurs.

It is the duty of mutual, equally related relatives and kin to try to arrange peace between opposing kin or relatives.

In the event of procedure on the part of one kinsman against another, those who are related to both take sides with him to whom they are more closely related. Besides blood relationship, there is marriage relationship oftentimes to make it a very complex and difficult problem for a man to decide to which opponent his obligation binds him. This is most frequently the case among the remoter kin. A man who finds himself in such a position, and who knows that on whichever side he may array himself he will be severely criticized by the other, becomes a strong advocate of compromise and peaceful settlement.

In case a kinsman to whom one owes loyalty in an altercation is in the wrong and has a poor case, one may secretly advise him to compromise; one must never openly advise such a measure. One may secretly refuse him assistance and backing—one must never oppose him.

One owes no obligation in the matter of procedure to another merely because he is a co-villager or inhabitant of the same district.

The obligation to aid and assist kinsmen beyond the third or fourth degree is problematic, and a question into which elements of personal interest enter to a great extent. One of the greatest sources of the power of the principal *kadangyang* lies in their ability to command the aid of their remote kin on account of their prestige and wealth and ability to dispense aid and favor.

There is also a class, small in number, corresponding somewhat to the "clients" of the chiefs of the ancient Gauls. This body is composed of servants who have grown up in the service and household of a master, and who have been well treated, and in times of need sustained and furnished with the things needful to Ifugao welfare; another division consists of those who habitually borrow or habitually rent from one who stands in the nature of an overlord to them. This class is most numerous in districts where most of the lands are in the hands of a few men. The duty of the clients to their lord and of their lord to them seems to be about the same as those duties have always been in a feudal society; that is to say, the duty of rendering mutual aid and assistance.

The first step in any legal procedure is to consult with one's kin and relatives. In initiating steps to assess a fine or collect an indemnity, the next step is the selection of a *monkalun*.

THE MONKALUN OR GO-BETWEEN

125. *Nature of his duties.*—The office of the *monkalun* is the most important one to be found in Ifugao society. The *monkalun* is a whole court, completely equipped, in embryo. He is judge, prosecuting and defending counsel, and the court record.[19] His duty and his interest are for a peaceful settlement. He receives a fee, called *lukba* or *liwa*. To the end of peaceful settlement he exhausts every art of Ifugao diplomacy. He wheedles, coaxes, flatters, threatens, drives, scolds, insinuates. He beats down the demands of the plaintiffs or prosecution, and bolsters up the proposals of the defendants until a point be reached at which the two parties may compromise. If the culprit or accused be not disposed to listen to reason and runs away or "shows fight" when approached, the *monkalun* waits till the former ascends into his house, follows him, and, *war-knife in hand,* sits in front of him and compels him to listen.

The *monkalun* should not be closely related to either party in a controversy. He may be a distant relative of either one of them. The *monkalun* has no authority. All that he can do is to act as a peace making go-between. His only power is in his art of persuasion, his tact and his skillful playing on human emotions and motives. Were he closely related to the plaintiff, he would have no influence with the defendant, and *mutatis mutandis* the opposite would be true.

Ultimately in any state the last appeal is to a death-dealing weapon. For example, in our own society a man owes a debt which he does not pay. Action is brought to sell his property to pay the debt. If he resists, he is in danger of death at the hands of an agent of the law. Much more is he in danger if he resists punishment for crime. The same is true in the Ifugao society. The lance is back of every demand of importance, and sometimes it seems hungry.

---

[19] The word *monkalun* comes from the root *kalun,* meaning *advise.* The Ifugao word has the double sense, too, of our word *advise,* as used in the following sentences, "I have the honor to advise you of your appointment" and "I advise you not to do that."

An Ifugao's pride as well as his self-interest—one might almost say his self-preservation—demands that he shall collect debts that are owed him, and that he shall punish injuries or crimes against himself. Did he not do so he would become the prey of his fellows. No one would respect him. Let there be but one debt owed him which he makes no effort to collect; let there be but one insult offered him that goes unpunished, and in the drunken babbling attendant on every feast or social occasion, he will hear himself accused of cowardice and called a woman.

On the other hand, self-interest and self-respect demand that the accused shall not accept punishment too tamely or with undue haste, and that he shall not pay an exorbitant fine. If he can manage to beat the demands of the complainant down below those usually met in like cases, he even gains in prestige. But the *monkalun* never lets him forget that the lance has been scoured and sharpened for him, and that he walks and lives in daily danger of it.

The accuser is usually not over anxious to kill the accused. Should he do so, the probabilities are that the kin of the accused would avenge the death, in which case he, the slayer, would be also slain. The kin of each party are anxious for a peaceable settlement, if such can be honorably brought about. They have feuds a-plenty on their hands already. Neighbors and co-villagers do not want to see their neighborhood torn by internal dissension and thus weakened as to the conduct of warfare against enemies. All these forces make for a peaceful settlement.

It is the part of the accused to dally with danger for a time, however, and at last to accede to the best terms he can get, if they be within reason.

TESTIMONY

126. *Litigants do not confront each other.*—From the time at which a controversy is formally entered into, the principals and their kin are on a basis of theoretical—perhaps I ought to say religious—enmity. A great number of taboos keep them apart. Diplomatic relations between the two parties have been broken off and all business pertaining to the case is transacted through the third party, the *monkalun*. He hears the testimony that each side brings forward to support its contention. Through him each controversant is confronted with the testimony of the other. It is greatly to the interest of the *monkalun* to arrange a peaceful settlement, not only because he usually receives

a somewhat larger fee in such case, but because the peaceful settlement of cases in which he is mediator builds up a reputation for him, so that he is frequently called and so can earn many fees. To the end of arranging this peaceful settlement, the *monkalun* reports to each party to the controversy the strong points of the testimony in favor of the other party, and oftentimes neglects the weaknesses.

There are no oaths or formalities in the giving of testimony.

ORDEALS

127. *Cases in which employed.*—In criminal cases in which the accused persistently denies his guilt, and sometimes in case of disputes over property the ownership of which is doubtful, and in cases of disputes over the division line between fields, ordeals or trials are resorted to. The challenge to an ordeal may come from either the accuser or the accused. Refusal to accept a challenge means a loss of the case, and the challenger proceeds as if he had won the case.

If the accused comes unscathed from the ordeal, he has the right to collect from his accuser the fine for false accusation.

If two people mutually accuse each other, *panuyu*, they are both tried by ordeal. If both be scathed, they are mutually responsible for the indemnity to the injured person. If only one be scathed, he is responsible for the indemnity to the injured person and for a payment of the fine for false accusation to the one whom he accused.[20]

128. *The hot water ordeal.*—A pot, a foot or more in depth, is filled with water and heated to a furious boiling. A pebble is dropped into it. The accused must reach his hand into the water without undue haste, extract the pebble, and then replace it. Undue haste is interpreted as a confession of guilt. This ordeal is used in certain sections of Ifugao, while in others the hot bolo test is used. It is interesting to note that neither of them is efficacious in determining accusations of adultery. This is for the reason that the gods of animal fertility and growth do not permit an accused to receive an injury

---

[20] When a crime such as theft has been committed, and it cannot be determined from any evidence at hand who was the culprit, the injured person frequently resorts to the *hapud*. One form of this ceremony consists in placing an egg or areca nut on the edge of a knife or the bevel of a spear and repeating the prayers necessary to make the egg or areca nut balance and stand on end at the mention of the guilty person. Another form consists in spanning an *agba* stick. At the mention of the guilty person the stick grows longer, as revealed by its length in relation to the span of the priest. These sticks are kept for generations. Many of them are over a hundred years old. These ceremonies are not of virtue as evidence and are entirely without the pale of Ifugao procedure. They are of value only to the injured person in assisting him to determine who has committed the crime.

for that act which is so eminently useful in their particular sphere of activity. Thus, Ifugao religion looks with the greatest disfavor upon things which tend to restrict population, just as our law frowns upon statutes in restriction of marriage.

129. *The hot bolo ordeal.*—In this, if two persons mutually accuse each other, their hands are placed side by side. The *monkalun* lowers a hot knife on their hands. The knife burns the guilty person much more seriously than the guiltless one. If only one person be put to the test, it is said that the knife bends away from the hands of an innocent person. The *monkalun*, with all his might, it is said, cannot put the knife down on the hand: the gods of war and justice will not permit it. But if the person be guilty, the knife grips the hand in its eagerness. If the accused show fear and try to withdraw, the kin of the accuser may catch him and burn him well. I know a man whose fingers were burned off in this way, the thumb adhering to and coalescing with the palm.

130. *The alao or duel.*—Eggs, *runo* stalks, or spears are used in trials, the accused facing each other and, at the word of the *monkalun*, hurling their missiles. The duel is not without its dangers. Even though eggs or *runos* be used, the one struck is likely to return a stone; and from throwing stones to throwing spears is an easy step. The two parties of kin are likely to take a hand. How much more likely are they to take a hand and avenge their kinsman if spears be the missiles and he be wounded!

The duel is used in cases of adultery, sorcery, and in some disputes over rice fields, everywhere in Ifugao. In adultery cases, only eggs are used in the duel.

131. *Trial by bultong or wrestling.*—This ordeal is used throughout Ifugao, preëminently to settle cases of disputed rice-field boundaries.

The Ifugao clearly recognizes that the processes of nature—landslides, the erosion of rainfall in wet weather, and caking and crumbling in dry weather—tend to wear away a terrace not maintained by a stone wall. A terrace maintained by a stone wall is a rarity in the Kiangan district. Should the boundary not be well marked by *paghok* (see sec. 43) a dispute is nearly sure to result sooner or later. These disputes are usually settled by wrestling matches. The wrestling matches are usually friendly. The Ifugao believes that the ancestral spirits of the controversants know which party is in the right, that they know just where the true boundary is, and that they see to it that he who is right shall win, provided always that they be invoked with the proper sacrifices; and that they "hold up" even the weaker of the wrestlers, and cause him to win, provided his cause be just. Notwithstanding this belief, the people are sufficiently practical to demand that the wrestlers be approximately evenly matched. The owners of the adjacent fields may themselves wrestle, or they may choose champions to represent them. Between kinsmen these matches are presumably friendly; and only sacrifices of dried meat are offered the ancestral spirits. But between those not related, there is often a great deal of unfriendly feeling. In this latter case numerous chickens and two or three pigs are sacrificed, and ceremonies like those against enemies are performed.

On the appointed day the two parties meet at the disputed boundary and occupy opposite ends of the disputed land. A party of mutual kin follows along and occupies a position midway between the adversaries. With each party is one of the family priests. Taking betels and dried meat (presuming the contest to be a friendly one) from a head-basket, the priest prays very much as follows: "Come, Grandfather Eagle, Grandfather Red Ant, Grandfather Strong Wind, Grandfather Pangalina; come, Grandmother Cicada, Grandmother Made Happy, Grandmother Ortagon; come, Grandfather Gold, etc. [throughout a list of perhaps a hundred ancestors]. Here are betels and meat; they are trying to take our field away from us. And was it here, Grandmother Grasshopper, that the boundary of the field was? No, you know that it was a double arm's length to the right. Hold us up, you ancestors, in order that *we* may be the wearers of gold neck-ornaments; in order that *we* may be the ones who give expensive feasts. Exhort [here the priest names over the gods of war and justice] to hold us up. Was it here, Grandfather Brave, that the boundary was when you bought the field? Do not let them take our land away from us, for we are to be pitied. We are sorely tried!"

After the prayers of the priests, each champion is led by one of his kinsman to the place where the first wrestling is to occur. This leading is very ceremoniously done, and suggests the heralding of the champions in feudal days. The dike of the upper terrace has been cleaned off at intervals of fifteen to twenty-five feet in order that the owner of the upper field may have no advantage. The champions frequently work themselves down half-thigh deep in rice-field mud, water, and slime. Catching fair and even holds, they begin to wrestle, encouraged each by the shouts and cries of his kinsmen and by the calling of the old men and old women on the spirits of the ancestors.

Each wrestler tries to push his opponent into the territory that that opponent is defending and to down him there. If A throws B in B's·field, ten feet from the line on which they wrestle, A wins ten feet of the rice field at that point. Finally, there is a fall that more than likely capsizes one or both of them in the black mud. One point in the boundary is determined. Frequently the lower terrace is eight or ten feet lower than the upper one, but there are no injuries for the reason that the mud is at least two feet deep and is a soft place in which to fall.

At every fifteen or twenty feet along the disputed boundary there is another wrestling match. Sometimes the champions are changed. The new boundary runs through every point at which there has been a fall.

132. *The umpire and the decision.*—The *monkalun* is the umpire in trials by ordeal. He interprets undue haste or a faulty performance as a confession of guilt. On the day following the trial by fire or hot water he goes to the house of the accused and examines the hand and forearm. If he finds white inflamed 'blisters, he pronounces him guilty. In the case of a duel, he pronounces the one struck by the missile guilty. The Ifugaos believe that the gods of war and justice turn missiles aside from the innocent in these duels. For the umpire to be manifestly unfair, would be for him seriously to imperil his own life.

As a matter of fact, a person whose skin is rough, dry, and horny has a great advantage in these ordeals. Since sword climbing and the walking on hot stones and live coals have occurred in other parts of the world, it would seem that a question might be raised whether *state of mind,* or other factors as yet unexplained, may not enter these affairs.

EXECUTION OF JUSTICE

133. *Retaliation.*—In the case of lives lost in feuds, sorcery, murders, and head-hunting, capital punishment inevitably follows, provided the kin of the slain be sufficiently daring to execute it.

Capital punishment is the rule, and is almost invariably inflicted in cases of the refusal to pay proper fines, for which demand has been made in correct form, and after a reasonable length of time has been given in which to raise the sum demanded, in punishment of adultery, manslaughter, the putting of another in the position of an accomplice in case of murder or death in feud, or for wounds, provided the culprit be not a kinsman or person closely related by marriage. Rarely would there be much trifling in the infliction of this penalty. Seizure of something of sufficient value to cover the fine assessed might sometimes be made, except in the cases of adultery and manslaughter. To practice seizure in the case of adultery—except when a kinsman were the offender—would have the aspect of anxiety to profit by the pollution of the wife's body and might give rise to suspicion of conspiracy on the part of husband and wife to bring about the crime in order to profit financially. In the same way, a self-respecting family would disdain to accept payment for the life of a kinsman except as a matter of forbearance and mercy to the taker thereof. We have seen before that unless the *tokom* be collected the injured person is in danger of losing his own life should he not slay him from whom the *tomok* is due.

The crime of arson undoubtedly justifies the death penalty; but it is so rare a crime that it is impossible to say what is the usual Ifugao practice in punishing it.

The non-payment of a debt when there is the ability to pay it, and after many and repeated demands have been made in the proper manner for it, justifies the infliction of the death penalty.

Capital punishment is administered by the injured person and his kin. In all cases it is fraught with the greatest danger to the inflicters. Usually it is inflicted from ambush, although it may be a sudden slaying in the heat of passion. The culprit is never notified that he has been sentenced to death. The withdrawal of a go-between from a serious case is, however, a pretty good warning. It has about the same significance as the withdrawal of an embassy in an international complication.

The infliction of a death penalty has been the starting point of many an interminable feud between families. For this reason the injured person exhausts every effort to effect a punishment in some other way if any other punishment be consistent with his dignity and respectability.

134. *Seizure of chattels.*—If a kinsman of remoter kinship than that existing between brothers commit a crime punishable by death, except sorcery or murder, and obstinately refuse to pay the fine assessed, seizure of his property or part of it is made.

Seizures are made from unrelated persons to cover fines due in punishment of theft, malicious killing of animals, arson, and the minor crimes, also to secure payment of a debt.

The following is a list of the things usually seized: gongs, rice-wine jars, carabaos, gold beads, rice fields, children, wives.

A seizure may be made by fraud or deceit, or it may be made in the absence of the owner of his household, or it may be made by superior force. Considering only the manner of the seizure, there is but one law to be followed: the seizure must be made in such a manner as to leave no doubt as to the identity of him who seizes. Thus if B persistently refuses to pay a fine owed to A, A may go to B's house when there is nobody at home and may run away with a gong. If he leaves his bolo, his scabbard, his blanket or some other personal effect in the house as a sort of a visiting card, his seizure is legal. Or A may go to B's house and, pretending friendship, borrow the gong, representing that he wants to play it at a feast and, having secured possession of it, refuse to return it till the fine be paid. Or suppose that an agent of B's is bringing a carabao up from Nueva Vizcaya, and that the agent has to travel through A's village. A and his friends stop the agent and take the carabao away from him, telling him to inform B that the carabao will be delivered to him when the fine is paid.

There is a second kind of seizure, a seizure of the property of some relative or kinsman of the culprit. The property of a wealthy kinsman may be seized to cover a fine due from a poor kinsman who has no property. This kind of seizure is more likely to lead to a lance throwing than a seizure from the culprit himself. The danger of such an ending increases with the remoteness of the kinship between the culprit and the person from whom the seizure is made.

A third kind of seizure is practiced against neighbors of delinquents who live in another district. Suppose a man B in one of the districts to the west of Kiangan to have gone to Nueva Vizcaya (east of Kiangan) and there to have purchased a carabao. He owes no debts, nor have any fines been levied against him. He returns through Kiangan, however, and his carabao is seized by A, a Kianganite. B is informed that C, a resident of the same district as he, stole a pig a year or two ago from A. The evidence against C is placed before him in the minutest details. He is given thirty pesos as *patang* (interest in advance) and told to collect from C the payment proper to the case, and in addition the thirty pesos advanced as *patang*. When he makes these collections, and delivers them to A, he gets back his carabao. If C is innocent of the crime charged, he may kill A for this, or he may do so even if guilty. More likely he kidnaps A's wife or child and sells them for a ransom sufficiently great to repay B, and leave a substantial surplus for himself. A may or may not retaliate with the lance.

In quarrels between *kadangyang* (for their dignity is very dear to them) and between persons of different districts or contrary parties, it is more frequently than not the case that the thing seized is not returned. Powerful individuals in a district are rather glad to have a seizure made of their property, since they can nearly always manage to come out winner in the finish. Thus in the case above, B, if a powerful individual, probably collects two or even three carabaos or their equivalent value from C, and besides he receives thirty pesos *patang*. It would seem that the obligation rests on every Ifugao—notwithstanding there is no political government—so to conduct himself as not to involve his neighbors in trouble with individuals of inimical or semi-inimical districts; and that should he so involve them, he is liable to whatever punishment circumstance metes out to him.

In the case of altercations between individuals of different districts, seizure of animals was generally practiced by persons of those districts through which the road led to the region from which the animals were imported. Of all districts, Kiangan was most advantageously situated in respect to this matter; since, for the greater part of Ifugao-land, the road to Nueva Vizcaya (whence most of the animals imported into Ifugao came) led through it.

135. *Seizure of rice fields.*—The seizure of rice fields is practicable only in case the fields are near the village of him who seizes them. For if located in a distant district, the working of the field would be extremely hazardous, and its protection and continuous holding impossible.

Fields may properly be seized for collection of debt or for refusal to pay fines or indemnities. Portions of fields are seized sometimes in disputes as to ownership or boundaries.

Disputes over ownership and boundary come to a head during spading time. One party begins to spade for the next year's crop the land claimed by the other. The other party sticks up *runos*, tied "ethics lock" fashion (*alpud*), along the line which he claims to be the true boundary. The first party then pulls up these *runos*, and sticks down others along the line claimed by it as the true boundary. The issue is joined. The defendant has made his "rejoinder." A *monkalun* is now selected by the plaintiff party, and tries to arrange— and in case of disputed boundaries nearly always does arrange—a means of peaceful settlement, either by compromise or through trial by wrestling. Sometimes the ownership of a field itself is in question. Usually the question is one of inheritance; although there are a num-

ber of other causes that may give rise to dispute.[21]   Ownership is
usually peaceably settled by means of a wrestling match.

We come now to those cases in which a field is seized for debt
as payment of a fine or indemnity.   The plaintiff or prosecutor seizes
the field at spading time by planting *runo* stalks, *alpud,* in it.   The
defendant probably pulls up these stalks and throws them away.[22]
An attempt may be made by mutual friends and relatives to recure a
peaceful settlement of the trouble.   A rice field is a thing so dear to
the Ifugao, and so necessary and useful to him, that such attempts are
extremely likely, however, to come to naught.

If the matter be not arranged otherwise, the seizer of the field
sends a body of men to spade it, holding in reserve an armed force of
kinsmen and relatives to protect and maintain the spaders if they be
attacked.   The other party emerges with an armed force to drive
the spaders away.   The two parties meet.   If one be greatly superior
in strength, the other usually retires, and surrenders the field.   If they
be fairly evenly matched, a battle is likely to ensue.   If the first wound
be a slight one, the party receiving it is likely to withdraw; but if it
be serious, or if one of their number be killed, they fight to avenge
him.   Sometimes four or five men are killed in one of these frays.

But in the meantime, and often before actual fighting begins, a
body of mutual relatives, friends, and neighbors emerges and tries to
make peace and secure an amicable settlement.

136. *Enforced hospitality.*—Sometimes a creditor and a numerous
and ·powerful following of kinsmen descend upon a debtor's house as
unwelcome guests, consume his stores of food, and force his hospitality
until appeased by the payment of the debt.

This form of collection can only be used in the case of debts, for
in all other controversies, taboos forbid the eating of the adversary's
food, drinking his water, chewing his betels, etc.   Even in the case of
debt, if a go-between has been sent to the debtor, this means may not
be used.   It can only be used in a case where "diplomatic relations"
have not been ruptured.

---

[21] The very day that I wrote this, the ownership of a field was settled by
a wrestling match.   An Ifugao some time before pawned a field to a christianized
Ifugao.   This worthy had the temerity to sell the field.   Although the pawner
would have surely been sustained in his right had he appealed to the lieutenant-
governor, nevertheless, he was so confident, being in the right, that he would
not lose, that he consented to settle the ownership by a wrestling match.   He
won.   The christianized Ifugao may possibly now have more faith in the tenet
of his former religion that the ancestral spirits uphold him who is in the right.

[22] He may gratuitously add an insult by implanting a few of them in a pile
of fecal matter.

137. *Kidnapping or seizure of persons.*—Interior districts had no opportunity to seize animals from those districts nearer than they to the region whence animals were imported. Of necessity, then, they kidnapped and sold or held for ransom women and children from those districts.

138. *Cases illustrating seizure and kidnapping.*—The following instances actually occurred in times past. They are excellent and veritable illustrations of this phase of Ifugao administration of justice:

Bahni of Tupplak spoke scornfully of Bumidang of Palao. Some time subsequently he sent a man to buy carabaos in Nueva Vizcaya. The man bought two, and returned on the homeward journey, travelling through Palao. Bumidang took one of the carabaos away from him there, and with his kin, killed it and ate it. Bahni with his kin shortly afterward went to the house of Dulauwan of Bangauwan, a neighboring village, and stole away with Dulauwan's carabao. Dulauwan followed after them, hotfoot, and was given as *patang* three pigs, and told to collect his carabao from Bumidang. Dulauwan gathered together a great host of kinsmen and neighbors, descended on Bumidang's house, and camped there demanding three carabaos. To show that they meant to get them, they helped themselves to rice needed for their daily food from Bumidang's granary. Bumidang was unable to get together a sufficient force to frighten away his guests, and accordingly he paid the three carabaos.

Ginnid of Umbul presented a demand to Guade for the payment of a long-outstanding debt. Guade denied that the debt was owed. Ginnid seized Guade's field. Each party led a force of kinsmen to the field. There they fought with spears and shields. The first man wounded was Tului of Pingungan, a kinsman of Guade. He received a slight wound. Guade's party then withdrew. Guade paid the debt, and got his field back.

Gumangan of Ambabag when a youth, sent án advocate to ask for the hand of the daughter of M of Umbul. He was accepted. But he changed his mind about the girl, and went to Baininan, where he engaged himself to a girl of that village without assuaging the mental agony of his jilted fiancée by paying the *hudhud* indemnity. M seized a carabao belonging to Gumangan. Gumangan gathered together his kin and went to Umbul—only a quarter of a mile distant—to prevent the slaughter of his animal. But M's party was so much more powerful that Gumangan's kin ran away. M's party then killed and ate the carabao.

Gumangan married in Baininan, and bearing in mind his former humiliation, decided to do something that would restore his prestige and at the same time assure him a sufficiently large body of followers to make him strong to demand and to resist demands. He consequently gave a great *uyauwe* feast at which the unheard of number of six carabaos was slaughtered, to say nothing of innumerable pigs. And later, he gave the *hagabi* feast—an even more expensive operation.

Dumalilon of Tupplak borrowed a carabao of Gumangan. Five years elapsed, yet he made no move to repay the debt, notwithstanding repeated demands of Gumangan. Gumangan seized Dumalilon's field, which had already been spaded, and threw his seed-bed away. Both men led armed parties to the field, but this time Gumangan was careful to have a sufficient number of backers on hand. Dumalilon's party took to flight.

In Burnai, a fight occurred over the seizure of a rice field that resulted in the killing of four men.

Kodamon of Pindungan and Katiling of Ambabag[23] had a dispute over the boundary of a field. There were *paghok* to mark the boundary, but Kodamon contended that all memory of the planting of the *paghok* was absent, and that they were, consequently, without significance in the matter of dispute. They wrestled, and Kodamon lost a little ground, but Katiling tried to take more than was due him according to the verdict of the wrestling matches. Katiling sent men to spade the disputed territory, and led an armed force out to support them. Kodamon led an armed force to the field. At the same time and at a safe distance, the mutual kin of the two parties and a goodly number of neighbors gathered. Kodamon was armed with a Remington rifle whose trigger was broken; Dulinayan, a kinsman of Katiling, with a revolver for which he had no ammunition. The other members of each force however were substantially, if less spectacularly, armed with spears which they well knew how to use. Women rushed in between the two parties, and catching the warriors by the waist tried to lead them away. One can well believe that the air was riven by curses, threats, accusations, upbraidings, imprecations, invocations. The male neutral kin shouted from their safe distance that if Kodamon killed Katiling, they would kill Kodamon (as a vengeance for the death of their kinsman) while if Katiling killed Kodamon, they would avenge their kinsman's death by killing Katiling. ''What kind of a way is this for co-villagers to settle a dispute,'' they shouted. ''Go back home and beget some children, and marry them to each other, giving them the two fields, and then it will make no difference where the division line is!'' There was an exchange of spears in which Buaya, a kinsman of Kodamon's, was wounded slightly. The matter was then left in abeyance with the understanding that as soon as possible, the two families be united by a marriage, and the two fields given the married couple.

It happened, however, that on account, of the sexes of the unmarried children of the families, a union between them was impossible. Accordingly, Kodamon gave his field to his son Dulnuan, and Katiling traded his field to Pingkihan, his brother. Both of these young men had pregnant wives. Pingkihan's wife gave birth first, the child being a girl. Shortly afterward, Dulnuan's wife gave birth. I met Dulnuan, and not knowing of the event, and noticing that he seemed downcast, asked him why he was so sad. ''My wife has given birth to a *girl* baby,'' he said. The quarrel over the boundary is as yet unsettled.

Kuyapi of Nagakaran, before the Spanish occupation, sent a slave child to Guminigin of Baay, to be sold in Baliwan (Nueva Vizcaya), stipulating that the child must bring at least five carabaos. Guminigin sold the child for seven carabaos, delivering five to Kuyapi, and kept two.

The Spaniards came. They were exceedingly partial to the people of Kiangan district in which the village of Baay is located. They paid little or no attention to complaints of people of other districts against people of Kiangan district. Many debts owed by Kiangan people were unpaid, for the Kian-

---

[23] The villages of Pindungan and Ambabag are less than a mile distant from each other.

ganites took advantage of the protection given them by the Spaniards. And yet the Nagakaranites and Kianganites were very closely united by marriage and by blood. Indeed Kuyapi and Guminigin were second or third cousins.

Owing to the difficulty the Nagakaran people had in collecting debts owed them by the Kianganites, they conceived for the latter and for the Spaniards a most violent hatred, and began to make reprisals. The Spaniards punished these reprisals by making an expedition to Nagakaran in which they came off second best.[24] They sent another and stronger expedition, which killed a number of people and which burned all the houses in the district. To this day the Nagakaran people have not been able to rebuild their houses—the large trees having long since been cut from nearby forests—and live in wretched shacks built on the ground. They blame the Kiangan people, saying that the latter invited the Spaniards into Ifugao.

Kuyapi claimed that the terms on which he sent the slave to Guminigin were that Guminigin was to receive only one carabao for having effected a sale, and that all the rest were to be delivered to him, and that there was consequently a carabao still due him. It seems likely that the claim was false, and that it was advanced merely as an excuse for making a reprisal.

Pagadut, the son of Guminigin, to whom demand was presented for the payment of the carabao claimed to be yet due, refused to pay this debt. The Nagakaran people made an expedition into Kiangan district (about two miles distant) and captured Ormaya, the daughter of Pagadut, a very comely girl of sixteen or seventeen. In order to make her walk, and in order that she should not continually offer resistance, they took her skirt off so that she would have to cover her shame with her hands and would also hurry to arrive at the journey's end.[24a] But the Baay people managed to cut off Lubbut the son of Kuyapi, and imprison him. They took him to a granary in Baay, intending to keep him as a hostage for the return of Ormaya. But word was carried to the ears of the Spanish *commandante* of this capture. He had Lubbut brought before him. He struck Lubbut, tied although he was, twice in the face, and would have continued, had not Alangwauwi the husband of Ormaya seized and held his arm and beseeched him not to use Lubbut harshly. The *commandante* promised not to take his life. But a soldier called attention to the fact that a gun had been captured with Lubbut, which gun, it was claimed, was that of a Spanish corporal whom the Nagakaran people had killed. Alangwauwi and his companions started back to their homes in Baay. But on the road, they saw, across the valley, Lubbut with his back turned to a firing squad, saw a puff of white smoke, and saw Lubbut fall into a rice field. Alangwauwi says he burst into tears for he realized that this meant serious trouble for him and his relatives, and placed Ormaya's life in the greatest peril.

When the Nagakaranites heard of Lubbut's death, they at first blamed the people of Baay for it. Inasmuch as it is against the ethics of people of the Kiangan-Nagakaran-Maggok area to kill women, or at least to kill any but Silipan women, they considered walling Ormaya up in a sepulchre and leaving her to die for want of food and drink. The women relatives of Lubbut wanted very much to kill Ormaya, and pointed out that while it would not be permissible for the men to kill her, there would be no disgrace in their doing

---

[24] The Nagakaran people claim that only five out of forty of the first expedition returned.

[24a] This was the usual method of treating kidnapped persons. It is interesting to note an almost parallel practice on the part of the Allies in the present war. When prisoners are taken, the buttons are cut off their clothing, in order to keep their hands engaged during the march to the rear.

so. But Kuyapi would have none of it. He himself guarded his prisoner two or three nights to see that her life was not taken.

Soon a *monkalun* was sent to ascertain the true details of Lubbut's death. His report exonerated the Baay people. The Nagakaran people held Ormaya's ransom considerably higher, however, because of that death. They received five carabaos, twenty pigs, two gold beads, and a great number of spears and bolos, and death blankets. It was five months before the Baay people could raise the amount of this ransom. During this time, Ormaya was well treated— for was she not a kinswoman?—but she was carefully guarded.

THE PAOWA OR TRUCE

139. *The usual sense of the term "paowa".*—The word *paowa* means literally prohibition. As most commonly used, it denotes a period of truce imposed by the *monkalun* in cases that cannot be peaceably arranged. It is a period that gives both sides to a controversy a chance to cool off. It avoids that rash and ill-considered action that would be likely to follow the breaking off of diplomatic relations between the two parties.

I say the *paowa* serves these purposes. However, it is imposed by the *monkalun* in order to allow him to withdraw with dignity from the case, and without loss of reputation. A lance throwing or a seizure made while he is acting as *monkalun* or occurring soon after he has severed his connection with the case is an insult to him. People say to him: *Dinalan-da tolban-mo*, "they went over your head." Such an occurrence is exceedingly hurtful to his reputation. People will not employ him as *monkalun* for the reason that his cases do not end in peaceable settlements. He thus loses many fat fees.

Assuming that the Ifugao's culture would some day, if left alone, develop courts somewhat after the fashion of the courts of civilized nations, have we not here the embryo of "contempt of court"?

The period usually set by the *monkalun*, as truce, is fourteen days. During this time, should one of the parties to the controversy commit any act hostile to the other, the *monkalun* must avenge or punish it. At the conclusion of this period of truce, the two parties may fight out the dispute to suit themselves, kidnapping, seizing property, or hurling lances, without injuring the dignity of the *monkalun;* or the aggressive party may employ another *monkalun.*

140. *Another sense of the term "paowa".*—Should a wife have committed a crime against the marital relation, and should her husband be unable for any reason to collect the *gibu* due him in the case, he may put a prohibition on her marrying any other man until the *gibu* be paid.

TERMINATION OF CONTROVERSIES: PEACE-MAKING

141. *The hidit or religious aspects of peace-making.*—The word *hidit* has three senses: It refers to a class of deities, the offspring of one of the principal deities of war; it refers to sacrifices to these deities; it refers to peace-making. Deities, sacrifice, and peace may seem widely distinct, but a glance into the Ifugao's religion will show the connection.

The *hidit* (deities) desire peace: but the peace must be made in the proper manner, and accompanied by sacrifice to themselves. The *hidit* have established the taboo that those who are involved in a controversy or enmity must not chew betels with an adversary, nor be in the same house or gathering or feast with him, nor drink with him, nor receive gifts or hospitality from him. The penalty for breaking this taboo is the affliction by the *hidit* with diseases of the lungs, throat, voice; the condition known as "big belly," *leukaemia,* short wind, swelling of the feet, dropsy, etc. This may be said to be the punishment for making peace without ceremonies. But sometimes the *hidit* punish the prolongation of a feud, enmity or controversy, by afflicting one or both of the parties as set forth above. Those who are involved in long enmities sacrifice continually to the *hidit* in order to offstand such affliction.

The *hidit* or peace-making ceremony is performed in the following cases:

(*a*) At the termination of the funeral of a married person. It is performed between the kin of the dead spouse and between those of the living spouse.

(*b*) Between adversaries in case of adultery, rape of married woman, sorcery, murder, manslaughter, malicious killing of animals, false accusation, disputes over rice fields, theft (sometimes), or other serious controversy, *provided* the controversy terminate peaceably.

(*c*) At the peaceful termination of all ordeals and trials.

(*d*) Between the kin of a dead spouse and the widow or widower on occasion of remarriage of the latter.

(*e*) Between parties to a controversy ending in payment of the *tokom* fine.

(*f*) At the termination of a feud, between the families involved in the feud. A feud was rarely—my belief is that it was never—terminated except by a marriage or on request of one of the members of the family afflicted by the *hidit* deities. In the latter case, peace might or might not be purchased. At any rate, the family suing for peace furnished the animals for sacrifice.

In most parts—I believe all—of Ifugao, peace was never made between *districts* or *villages*. Peace was always made between *families;* but peace between the principal families of two villages or districts was sometimes *in effect* a peace between the districts or villages involved—I say *sometimes* because such a peace was uncertain and undependable.

When peace was made between families of different districts, or between families of the same district in cases of serious controversy, two men were chosen, one by each party to the peace, and with appropriate prayers and ceremonies, were given good spears. It was understood always that these spears were for the purpose of killing the first one of either party who reopened the feud, war, or controversy. After this ceremony, other spears were broken and tied together as a symbol of the breaking and tying up of all enmity; as a symbol, too, that spears were no longer needed.

AN INTER-VILLAGE LAW

142. *Neutrality.*—When a war expedition or party passed through a village *en route* against another village, the intermediate village might signify its neutrality by casting a spear at the party. The spear never struck a member of the party, of course, nor was its casting taken as an unfriendly act. It was merely a declaration of neutrality. Should a village fail to cast a spear in these circumstances at such a party, the people of it would be held as enemies and accomplices of the members of the war party.

APPENDIXES

All Ifugao words denoting relationships except the words for father and mother are common in gender.

To any individual of any generation:

1. All his kin of his own generation are *tulang* (brothers, sisters).

2. All children of his kin of his own generation are *anak* (sons, daughters).

3. All grandchildren, great-grandchildren, etc., of his kin of his own generation are *apo* (grandsons, granddaughters).

4. All kin of the same generation as his father and mother are *ama* or *ina* (father or mother).

5. All kin of the same generation as his grandparents, great-grandparents, etc., are *apo* (grandparents).

6. All relatives by marriage who are the husbands and wives of the kin of the same generation are *aidu* (brother-in-law, sister-in-law).

7. All relatives by marriage, the husbands and wives of the kin of the generation of his father and mother, are *amaon* or *inaon*.

8. The father or mother of his wife are *ama* or *ina* (father or mother), by courtesy.

9. The kin of the father or mother of his wife are *tulang di ama* (or *ina*) *'n di inay-ak* (kin of the father, or mother, of my wife).

In the Benaue district, the kin of one's father or mother, in addition to being called father or mother, are also called *ulitao* (uncle or aunt), and the husbands or wives of the *ulitao* are called *ulitaon* (uncles-in-law, aunts-in-law). The son or daughter of a kinsman or a kinswoman of the same generation in addition to being called son or daughter of one's self is called *amanaon*.

An Ifugao myth.—Partly because of its connection with the Ifugao marriage ceremony, partly because it illustrates so well the use to which the Ifugao puts his myths—rarely telling them for amusement, but reciting them in religious ceremonies as a means to magic—and partly because it is so characteristically Ifugao, I have decided to append the following myth, despite the fact that it might more properly appear in a work on religion.

Most of the Ifugao's myths have either been invented or if not invented, changed, for the purpose of affording an analogy to the solution of the difficulties or misfortunes that confront men today. The Ifugaos have a myth telling of a great flood, whose only survivors were a brother and sister—Balitok and Bugan. In chagrin and shame because her brother has gotten her with child, Bugan flees into the East Region to seek destruction from the terrors there. They refuse to destroy her, but teach her how to take the curse off marriages between kindred by the sacrifice of two pigs, a male and female of the same litter. Notice how a flood myth—an element in the mythology of nearly every people under the sun—has been modified and made to serve a magic purpose.

The myth given below is a further and utterly inconsistent modification of this flood myth. In the myth above, Balitok and Bugan are represented as having a child and not wanting it—in the myth below, they have no child but want one.

The ceremony of using a myth to serve a religious end consists of two parts. The first is the recitation of the myth by the priest. This is called *bukad*. In affords an analogy to the condition of sickness, war, famine, harvest, union in marriage, or what not, in which the performers of the ceremony find themselves, and the happy solution of the problem. It is terminated by what I term the *fiat*. This is an expression of the priest's will that the happy solution related in the myth shall be existent in the present situation. It is not, I think, the fact of the priest's will that is thought to bring about the solution so much as the compelling and magic power of his spoken word to that end.

Up to this stage, the ceremony is sympathetic magic. In the second stage it becomes witchcraft, and is called *tulud*, "pushing." In it the priest "pushes" the deities of the myth over the route from their habitations in the Skyworld, the Underworld, the East Region, the West Region, or wheresoever they may abide, step by step to the village of the Ifugaos performing the ceremony. He may recite their passage through as many as thirty or forty localities, and as the priest drones: "They climb the steep at Nunbalabog; they descend at Baat, they wade at Monkilkalney," etc., the compelling power of his spoken word "pushes" the deities along. Finally the deities arrive and declare through the priest that they will confer the benefits requested.

This myth is employed in all of the final ceremonies of marriage, and in all ceremonies of married persons that have the obtaining of children as their object. The translation is absolutely literal and without embellishment.

How Balitok and Bugan obtained children.—And it is said that Bugan and Balitok of Kiangan were childless. "What is the use [of living]?" said Bugan. "Stay here, Balitok. I am going to go to the East Country. I will see Ngilin, Umbumabakal, Dauwak, Pinyuhan, Bolang, and the Gods of Animal Fertility of the East." She got betels together and packed them. Bugan and Balitok ate. After finishing, they chewed betels.

Bugan put her pack on her head and started. She came to Baladong [Ligaue Gap]. She went on to Kituman. Went eastward to Ulu. Forded at Agwatan. Encountered the Fire at Bayukan. He [the Fire] asked, "Where are you going, Bugan?"

"I am going into the East Region," said Bugan, "because we are childless, Balitok and I. I am going to find some one to devour me, because we are very lonely." Fire laughed. "Do not feel so, Bugan," he said, " keep going eastward until you come to Ngilin, Umbumabakal, and the deities of the East Region."

Bugan put her pack on her head and continued to Balahiang. She came to the lake [or ocean(?)] at Balahiang. She aroused the Crocodile.

"Who are you, human?" said the Crocodile.

"I am Bugan of Kiangan."

"And why is it," said the Crocodile, "although the Flood of the East Region and the Flood of the West Region came upon me and fear to arouse me, that you, Bugan, a [mere] human, [presume to] molest me?"

"Yes," said Bugan, "that was my intention; for I am searching for someone to devour me."

"Why?" said the Crocodile.

"Yes, for I have become very lonely; for Balitok and I have no children."

The Crocodile chuckled. "Oh, I will not devour you, Bugan," he said. "I would shame to devour one so beautiful. Continue on eastward, and arrive at the dwelling of the Shark. Wake him up, in order that he shall be the one to devour you."

Bugan thought well of it. She put her pack on her head. She went on eastward and came to the waters where dwells the Shark. It was fear-inspiring, and caused her to exclaim "*Inay!*" She was terrified, but she conquered her fear. She reached for betels, and threw them between her teeth. She crushed them. They became like blood. Bugan spat into the waters. She beheld a great wave circle. The Shark came into sight. He grunted.

"Who are you, human?" he said.

"I am Bugan, the wife of Balitok at Kiangan," she said.

"And why is it that you arouse me, human? And there come the Strong Wind of the East and the Strong Wind of the West, and they arouse me not; for I am ferocious here in the East Region. Yet you, Bugan, the wife of Balitok at Kiangan, you arouse me?"

"Yes, that is what I purpose," said Bugan, "for I am looking for someone to devour me."

The Shark chuckled. "Why?" he said.

"Yes, for I want to be devoured because Balitok and I have no children."

"I would shame to do so, for you are a beautiful woman. Come into my house in the Waters in order that we may eat."

Bugan entered . They ate.

"Continue," said the Shark, "into the East Region. Go unto the dwellings of Umbumabakal and the Gods of Animal Fertility."

Bugan rose to the surface of the waters, and on the beach again put her pack on her head. She continued the journey. She came to Lumbut, to the house of Umbumabakal. The house was covered with enormous ferns. It terrified her. She threw betels between her teeth, and put down her fear. She passed through the gate of the enclosure about the house, and sat down on the rice mortar. In the evening of the day Umbumabakal came down. He was looking for something to eat. He passed through the gate. Bugan hid herself in a large wooden bucket. Umbumabakal kept sniffing the air.

"Why is it that there is something human here now," he said, "yet nothing of the kind has ever happened before?"

He sought for Bugan. He found her in the bucket.

"Why, human, are you here?" he said.

"I am Bugan, the wife of Balitok."

"Why do you come here, Bugan, wife of Balitok?" he said.

"Because I want to be devoured."

"Why?"

"Yes, for we are childless at Kiangan."

"Umbumabakal laughed. "Well," said he, "tomorrow we will go to the dwelling of Ngilin and the other Gods of Animal Fertility."

On the morrow they visited the various Gods of Animal Fertility. They gathered pigs and chickens as gifts to Balitok and Bugan. "Return to Kiangan," they said. "We will go with you."

[At this point, some priests change the myth into a *tulud*, while some continue it as a myth. We will here insert the method of this change.]

[*Fiat* by the priest, *i.e.*, a statement of the priest's will:] It is not formerly, but now; not to Kiangan that they come but here to our village of X, in order that they relieve A and B of childlessness; in order that they increase the life here in our village of X. They bring children and pigs and chickens and miraculous increase of rice to A and B here in our village of X.

They return to Lumbut. They come west to Agab. They continue to X. [Here follows a detailed "pushing" of the party from the East Region to the village in which the priest is performing the invocation, and to the house of the childless couple.] They look up. "Why, it is our children in X," they say.

"Yes," [says the priest,] "for they are childless. Give them children. Let some be male and some be female. Let there be a myriad of shields [figuratively: men] and a myriad of *tudong* [women's sweet potato baskets; figuratively: women] here in our village of X. Let the pigs and the chickens become many. May the rice be miraculously increased. Bring us much life here in our village of X.

[If the priest does not change the myth to a *tulud* at the point above, he continues it as follows:]

They continued with Bugan to Kiangan. They gathered together the "sitters" [priests] at Kiangan. They sacrificed the pigs and the chickens. The Gods of Animal Fertility taught them how to perform the bubun ceremony. They divided [as a tribute] the meat with Ambahing [who takes semen from the womb of women and carries it off in his hip-bag] and with Komiwa [who stirs up semen in the womb so that conception is prevented].

Bugan and Balitok multipied at Kiangan. There came to be a myriad of shields [men] and a myriad of sweet-potato baskets [women] in Kiangan. The pigs and the chickens became many. Their children scattered throughout the hills of Pugao [the Ifugao's earth]. The rice dikes climbed up the mountains. The hills smoked day by day [from the burning off of clearings for sweet-potatoes]. Life was miraculously increased.

[*Fiat by the priests:*] It is not then but now; not in Kiangan, but here in our village of X. It shall be the same with these children, A and B. Their children will be many. Let some be male and some female. Let their pigs and the chickens, etc., etc.

[*Tulud.*] "We will go now," said Umbumabakal. "All right," said Bugan. "There is a calling above," said Ngilin.

"Have you kin yonder?" said Umbumabakal.

"Yes," said Bugan, "we have kin in the village of X."

"Let us thither," say the Gods of Animal Fertility. They come westward to Tulbung. They continue to X. [The priest "pushes" the deities step by step on the way to the village in which he is performing the invocation. When they arrive, the same occurs as shown in the *tulud* inserted above.]

The halupe feast.—The *halupe* are a class of deities that keep an idea constantly before the mind of one whom they are sent to harass. They are most frequently used against debtors; but they may be sent to soften the wrath of an enemy or the stubbornness of a pretty girl, or for other purposes. They are induced to serve the end of him who invokes them by the sacrifice of a pig or chicken and by offerings of betels and rice wine. There are about a hundred of these deities.

After the ancestral spirits have been invoked, and beseeched to intercede with the *halupe* for the purpose desired, the *halupe* themselves are invoked, in some such words as the following:

"Ye *halupe* of the Skyworld, of the Underworld, of the West Region, and of the East Region, are beseeched to attend. It is prayed ye that ye go and harass (name) so that he will not sleep for thinking of his debt to me. If he goes to get water, go with him; if he goes to get wood, go with him; if he goes on a trading trip, go with him. Harass him to the extent that he will give me his pigs, his rice, his chickens, his death blankets, his money, his rice fields, his "irons," his house furnishings: [There is no danger of asking too much of a deity or a white man!] May the speech of the go-between make him ashamed to refuse! Do not let him sleep till he pays the debt."

A subclass of the *halupe* deities have, for their especial function, the soothing of obstinate debtors so that they may not get angry at the words of the go-between, nor run away from him when they see him coming. These are also invoked.

The priest then is possessed by the *halupe* one by one, and through him, each of the *halupe* takes a sip of rice wine, and states that he will harass the debtor and that he will not allow him to sleep till he pays.

After this ceremony, a fowl or pig is sacrificed and given the *halupe*. The meat is cooked and spread out on some cooked rice.

Myths relating how some ancestor successfully invoked the *halupe,* are then recited for the magic power that lies in the recital, and are followed by *tulud,* ceremonies of witchcraft in which the deities are "pushed along" by the compelling power of the word of the priest to do his bidding. More frequently than not, the myth changes abruptly into the *tulud.* The following instance is taken verbatim from a series of ceremonies that I had a priest perform against a delinquent debtor who owed me a sum of money. I regret to say that the ceremonies were not efficacious.

Bukad (Myth).—Oadda kano da Tumayaban ud Kakunian ke da Panubok ke da Binantawan ke da Banaban ke da Dimpuyu. Kon-da takon da monnigi, dola-da 'd Kabunian. Panganun-da amaiyu da. Ahi-da peman padapadan. Inhungal di amaiyu. Bohwagon-da hagiit. Punayaman 'd Kabunian, ya nunudnud-da ud Pangagauwan. Unudun di halupe ya dimatong ud Pangagauwan. Agan-da ya domatong-da amaiyo. Mondaiyo-da ud Baladong ya hidi peman kano balobgon-da. Buyangon-da ta dauutan-da. Oadda Halupe Binantawan ya ihaga-na banting. "Maid banting-ko," konan Tumayaban. Oadda kano Bugan da nak Tadona ud Kiangan ya monbuliwong, te "Eak," kano, "monbaga di mangigamal ke haoy ta kaliwak di gimauwat an haoy, an adi-da umidet di guwat-da." Pitaowan-na paiyo ud Kiangan. Oadda, kano, Binantawan ya inanang-na Bugan, an "Eka, Tumayaban," konana, "ta tumutung-ka 'n Bugan! Ime Tumayaban hi kadwan Bugan ya Konana Tutung-ok nihbo! Bugan" Kimali Bugan, ya konana "Kon manahauliu-ka? "Antipi?" konan Tumayaban. "Ya te monbuliwong te eak manila mangigamal ke haoy," "Antipi?" konan Tumayaban. "Om te maato-ak an mangibaga di gimauwat an haoy." "Antipi, tuali adi-da mitugun?" konan Tumayaban. "Ibangad mo hi balei-yo, ta itugun-mo dakami 'n halupe."

Bimangad Bugan, ya patayon-na manok ya ayago-na halupe. "Umetako," konan Banaban, "te intugan ditako di nak Tadona 'd Kiangan. Higupan-mi dola-da ud Kiangan. Ibaga-da punbagaan da. Badangan-mi tulang-mi ud Kiangan." Ime-da halupe, ya halupaiyan-da punbagaan an gimauwat di babui 'n di tulang-da ud Kiangan, ya ununud Bugan, ya monbaga, ya inala-na babui-da ya peho-da ya gumok-da ya manok-da ya page-da ya paiyo-da. [Then he waves his hand.]

[The priest blows, in the direction of his debtor.]

Bokun ud Kiangan, te hitu, ta ume-ak hi bigat ta alak di babui Kodamon ya gamong-na ya paiyo-na peho-na ya manok-na. Balinan di hapihapito-ko. Kai-ak halupe, kai-ak Banaban, ta idet-na ta magibu ta maid di pangidoh-dohana.

[Here the myth changes into a *tulud,* "pushing."]

Oadda, kano, halupe, ya monbaga-da ya "Monbangad,-tako" konana dola-tako ud Kakunian. "Oadda tugun," konan Tumayaban. "Tipi oadda tugun ud tapâ? Dehidi iba-yo?" "Om," konan Bugan. "Dehidi iba-mi 'd tapâ."

Oadda halupe, ya tikidan da ud Tataowang. Agan ud Kulab. Ladangon ud Gitigit. Ladangon ud Pangibauutan. Tikidan ud Nunbalabog. Itanglig-da tungun ud Baay ya Pindungan ya maid. "Aha! ud Ablatan di montugun" kalion-da. Mondotal ud Panaangan. Mondayu ud Iwakal. Paadan ud Upupan. Agan-da ya ladangan ud Tobal. Buduan-da ud Uhat. Agwatan ud Nungimil. Abatan ud Boko. Agan-da ud Pugu. Montikid ud Takada g. Humabiat ud

D
omok. Mondotal ud Palatog. Dongolon-da tugun. Mihidol ud Palatog.
Monbanong ud Kabonwang. Agwatan ud Tudunwe. Ladangon ud Umbul.
Domatong ya belibelion-da, ya "Kon da Barton ya Patikwal" konan
Tumayaban. "Daan di punbagaan-yo?" konana. Dehidi hi Kodamon an adi-
na idèt di gauwat-mi. Ume-kayo ta mipong alitaangan-na ta halhalupayan-yo
ta nemnemon-na gauwat-na; ta takon di adi mahuyop hi tonga 'n di labi.
Balinan-yo. Banabanan-yo. Halupayan-yo ta maid di udum an nemenemon-na,
ta gibuan-na gauwat-na, ta igatang-na paiyo-na, ta idetan-na peho-na ya manok-
na ya babui-na ya page-na ya gumok-na.

[The priest blows and waves his hand in the direction of Kodamon's house].
Ooo-of! Hadon-yo, ta umeak hi bigat!

Translation.—And it is said that Tumayaban and Panubok and Binantawan and
Banaban and Dimpuyu of the Skyworld decided to go hunting there in their region
of the Skyworld. They fed their dogs. And then, indeed, they sent them on the
chase. The dogs found a trail. They started up a wild boar. They chased it
about the Skyworld, and followed down to Pangagauwan [the mountain that
towers over Kiangan]. The *halupe* [the deities above named] followed after.
They came up with their dogs, and t ...re, it is said, they speared the quarry.
They spread grass on the earth and cut it up. And *Halupe* Binantawan asked
for fire.

"I have no flint and steel," said Tumayaban.

And it is said that Bugan, the daughter of Tadona of Kiangan, was sick of
life; for she said, "I will beg some one to eat me up in order that I may forget
my debtors who will not pay the debt they owe me." She set out across the
rice fields at Kiangan. Binantawan saw her and said: "Go, Tumayaban; get
fire from Bugan." Tumayaban got up and went to where Bugan was.

"Let me have fire, Bugan."

"Are you in a hurry?" said Bugan.

"Why?" said Tumayaban.

"For I am tired of life, and am hunting for somebody to eat me up," said
Bugan.

"Why?" said Tumayaban.

"Yes, for I am tired of beseeching my debtors to pay their debts."

"Why, indeed, will they not listen to reason?" said Tumayaban. "Go back
to your house and call upon us *halupe*."

Bugan returned, and sacrificed chickens, and called upon the *halupe*. "Let
us go, for the daughter of Tadona has called upon us at Kiangan," said
Banaban. [The old Kiangan about four miles below the village now called
Kiangan by American officials.] "They have gathered together in Kiangan.
Let us assist our kinsfolk there." The *halupe* went and they harassed those
of whom it was asked [the debtors], those who had borrowed pigs of the kin
in Kiangan. And Bugan followed after and took their pigs and their "irons"
and their money and their chickens and their rice and their rice fields and their
death blankets.

[The priest blows and waves his hand in the direction of his debtor's house.]

Let it be so, not at Kiangan, but here, so that I may go in the morning and
take Kodamon's pigs, death blankets, rice fields, money, chickens. May my
words carry shame to him. May I be like a harasser and like a soother, in
order that he pay, in order that it may be finished, in order that there come no
serious result of the controversy.

[Here the myth changes into a *tulud*, "pushing".]

The *halupe* speak, saying, "Let us return to our village in the Skyworld."

"There is a calling," said Tumayaban. "Whence comes this call from above? Have you kin there?"

"Yes," said Bugan, "we have kindred above."

And the *halupe* ascend at Tataowang. They come on to Kulab. They continue to Gitigit. They continue to Pangibautan. They climb up to Nunbalabog. They listen for a calling at Baay and Pindungan. [These are villages in the vicinity of Umbul, the village where the priest was performing the ceremony.] "Aha! the calling is at Umbul!" they say. They walk on the level at Panaangan. They descend at Iwakal. They come to Upupan. They continue to Tobal. They come out at Uhat. They wade at Nungimel. They go around the hill to Boko. They continue to Pugu. They climb at Takadang. They ascend to Domok. They walk on the level at Palatog. They listen for the calling. They hear it there. They travel on the rice dikes at Kabonwang. They wade at Tudunwe. They come round the hill at Umbul. They arrive and, "Why, it is Barton and Patikwal," says Tumayaban. "Where are your refractory debtors?"

"There is Kodamon. He does not pay his debts to us. Go and disperse yourselves in the vicinity of his house, and harass him continually with the remembrance of his debt, so that he may not sleep, even in the middle of the night. Make him ashamed. Soothe him (so that he will not be angry). Harass him so that he may think of nothing else than his debt; so that he will finish with it; so that he will sell his rice fields (in order to pay); so that he will give us his pigs, his money, his irons, his rice, and his rice fields."

[The priest blows and waves his hand in the direction of Kodamon's house.] "Ooo-of! Wait there till I come in the morning."

The collector of a large fine performs an unpretentious series of ceremonies directed to the gods of animal fertility and growth. The fact that he has won out in collecting the fine shows that his star is in the ascendancy and that a more pretentious feast is not needed.

Peace-making ceremonies.—A full account of these ceremonies would be too extended to give here. The following are two of the myths that are recited in the course of these ceremonies:

(1) And it is said that the father of Amtalao of the Skyworld spoke to his son, saying: "Go down and cause the enemies of earth to make peace, in order that there be no longer coughings, and shortness of breath, and bleedings from the nose, and quick fatigue among them."

Amtalao packed his betels, put on his hip-bag, and took his spear in hand. He descended to Habiatan. [Here the myth goes into a detailed account of the places passed in the journey.] He arrived in Kiangan. He went to the house of Balitok [the hero ancestor of the people of Kiangan culture area]. He thrust the shod point of his spear handle into the flat stone used as a seat in front of the house. It crackled like a dry leaf.

"You have spoiled the flat stone," said Balitok. Amtalao kicked the pieces of stone with his foot. They all joined together as if never broken apart. "I did not spoil it," said Amtalao.

"Why is it, Balitok, that you do not make peace with your enemies? Is it that you wish to be afflicted by the *hidit?*"

"I do not know how," said Balitok. Amtalao went to the sons of Imbalitayan. "Make peace with Balitok, in order that ye be not afflicted with coughings and snorings and bleedings from the nose and shortness of the breath," said he.

And they caught their pigs and chickens, the sons of Imbalitayan, and the people of Kiangan, and Amtalao taught them to make peace. And when they had finished, Amtalao ascended into the Skyworld.

"How many did you cause to make peace?" said his father.

"There are no more enemies on earth," said Amtalao. Even though the Ifugao travel far, they are safe. Even though spears be thrown, they do not scathe. No longer is there shortness of the breath, and labored breathing, bleeding from the nose, and coughings and quick fatigue. The people are like unto gold, which tarnishes not, like unto the waters of the river, which never become small, and like unto the dancing plumes of the *cogon and runo* grass. They talk and talk, and talk straight. They ask for what they want and get it."

Let it be so, not at Kiangan, but here; not then, but now; in order that there be no more shortness of breath and coughing and labored breathing [the priest's will being that the benefits mentioned by Amtalao in the paragraph immediately preceding become existent].

(2) The Thunderer of the Skyworld was sitting on his lounging bench in the Skyworld. "Alas! why do the people keep fighting all the time?" he said. He took his spear in hand. He descended unto Kiangan. He went to the house of Balitok. "Why do you not make peace with the sons of Imbaluog?" said he.

"I desire to make peace, but they will not," said Balitok.

"Come with me," said the Thunderer. They went to the village of the sons of Imbaluog. The Thunderer shouted to them. They came down out of their houses, spears in hand, and carrying their shields. They advanced toward Balitok. The Thunderer was angry.

"Why did the people of Kiangan offer to make peace, and ye would not?" shouted he. The Thunderer snorted. The branches fell from the trees. The sons of Imbaluog were blown to pieces. Their limbs were torn from their trunks and went hurtling hither and thither.

And below every house was heard the wailing of the old women. And every woman's head was encircled by mourning bands.

Let it be so, not then, but now, with those that do not keep the peace! Let them be blown to pieces and scattered hither and thither, and may there be none to avenge them.

The chewing of betels together by the reconciled enemies is the essential part of the peace-making ceremony. Three constituents are used in betel chewing: the betel leaf, the areca nut, and the lime. The priest takes position between the two (as yet) enemies. One of the enemies then gives the other an areca nut, and his courtesy is returned by his enemy giving him a betel leaf. Both are then supplied by the priest with lime. They proceed to chew betels then, and the priest prays as follows:

"Ye are chewed, Betel Leaf, Areca Nut, and Lime. Let not them who were enemies be afflicted with coughings, shortness of breath, quick-coming fatigue, bleeding from the nose, nor labored breathing. Let them, instead, be like gold, which tarnishes not; like the tail feathers of the full-grown cock, which never touch the earth; like the waters of the river, which never cease coming; like Talal of Ambuaya, who ate his own children, yet was not afflicted by the *hidit*. Let them be as active as the waters of Inude (a cataract) or the feathery plumes of the *cogon* and *runo* grass. Let them be like the rising sun, like the Cobra of the White Mountain, like the Full-grown Cock of Dotal, like the Hard Stone of Huduan.[25] May their enemies stand aside from them in fear. May their valor be heard of in all the hills.''

Ceremonies connected with the payment of large fines.—At the termination of a controversy in which a large fine is paid, the two parties perform the *hidit,* peace-making ceremonies, as a matter of self-interest. To leave them unperformed would be to subject themselves to the wrath of the *hidit* deities who would afflict them with tuberculosis, shortness of breath, etc. The peace so made is theoretical, oftentimes, rather than actual. Usually there is a great deal of ill feeling smoldering in the breasts of the controversants.

He who pays any large fine invariably performs a general welfare feast soon afterward. To this feast he invites all the deities of the Skyworld, the Underworld, the Fabulous Region of the East and the Fabulous Region of the West. In addition, if he feels great resentment against the fine collector, he secretly performs the following ceremony:

Tulud (Pushing).—''The Ender of the East Region sits on his lounging bench there. He hears a call. He arises and puts betels in his hip-bag and takes his spear in hand. He hesitates, and then starts westward. He comes on to Payya. [The priest ''pushes'' him, as in the preceding *tulud,* stage by stage through the following places: Ulikon, Hapid, Ulalahi, Lana, Kudug, Lingay, Balahiang, Lau, Bayukan, Ula, Tuktukbayahan, Kituman, Kiangan. From Kiangan onward the route is variable, depending on the village of the priest.]

He arrives at [village]. He receives the chicken. He chops off its head. [The priest at this stage chops off the chicken's head.] Even so [he says] I chop off the life of the fine collector. [The priest blows and swings his arm in the direction of the fine-collector's house.] Travel thither, Ender, to the house of him who took from us the death blankets. Stay with him. If he goes to get wood, turn the axe into his body. If he travels, push him off the steep. If he sleeps, sleep with him. In the middle of the night stab him, and we will hear about it with the rising sun. For we are poverty stricken. We owed them no debt, yet they have taken our pigs and our chickens and our death blankets and our rice [etc.]. We are to be pitied, alas!''

Other deities that may be sent against the fine collector are the Spider-webbed One, the Smotherer, Dysentery, the Short-winded One, the Trapper, the Twister.

---

[25] Myths relate how the Full-Grown Cock overcame the Half-Grown Cock, how the Cobra overcame the Python, how the Hard Stone overcame the Soft Stone.

APPENDIX 3: PARRICIDE

A rather startling case was called before the Court of First Instance in Kiangan in December, 1913. Limitit of Ayangan was charged with having murdered his father. The phrase "Are you guilty or not guilty?" translated into Ifugao changes significance slightly, and stands "Are you at fault or not at fault?" With a candor almost pitiable, Limitit admitted the facts in the case, but pleaded "not at fault." "He was my father," he said. "I had a right to kill him. I am blameless, for I provided a generous funeral feast for him."

Interrogation developed that Dilagan, the father, was a spend-thrift. He had raised a sum of money—possibly for the purpose of gambling—by pawning, *balal*, his son's rice field. The son was angry, but Dilagan promised faithfully to redeem the field by planting time. But planting time came round, and Dilagan was unable to keep his promise and redeem the field. In a quarrel over this matter, the son lost patience and killed his father. So far as I am able to ascertain, his act is justified, or at the very least, condoned by his co-villagers. They excuse him on two grounds:

First, the old man was worthless, and deserved killing for having wronged his son. Even though the damage done was not irremediable, it was probable that it would be repeated, and that he would impoverish his son for life.

Second, the old man was Limitit's father, and Limitit had the right on that account to kill him if he wanted to; at least *it was the business of nobody else.*

The American court, if I remember aright, sentenced Limitit to life imprisonment. He died shortly after being incarcerated.

Another case of parricide was that of Bayungubung of Kurug. He killed his father for the same reason that Limitit killed Dilagan: that is, for the wrongful pawning of a field.

The essence of the attitude of the people in both these cases seemed to be that the son had the right to kill his father if the latter imperiled the family livelihood or position in society. It seems to us an inhuman doctrine. But remember that the be-all and the end-all of Ifugao existence is the family, and *not* the individual. With us, the opposite is true: the rights of the individual supersede those of the family. The fields in question had been handed down from past generations. The son in each case was responsible at the time of the parricide for the welfare of future generations of the family. The old man in each case was a traitor to the welfare of the family. He had had his day, and was worse than useless. Remember that in a country where a living must be eked from a tough, stony mountain-side with a wooden spade, the means to life handed down from the sweat of former generations is a thing as sacred, as it is precious.

Besides these considerations, there is the principle on which Ifugao society is based: The family exists principally for the youthful and future generations of it.

APPENDIX 4: CONCUBINAGE AMONG THE KALINGAS

The Kalingas are a tribe having a culture remarkably similar to the Ifugao. In respect of warfare, head-hunting, and social organization, it is an even more dazzling example of a barbarian culture, I believe. Concubinage is universally practiced by the wealthy. The concubine has a legal status. A man must secure his wife's consent to take a concubine, but the consent is universally forthcoming.

During a six months' residence in Kalinga I became quite well acquainted with the unusually intelligent wife of a Kalinga headman. I asked her one day why the women permitted their men to take unto themselves additional wives.

"Oh, that's the custom of us Kalingas."

"I know it's the custom. But I think it's a poor one for you women who are so unfortunate as to be married to men who practice it."

"Why are we unfortunate? Their children can inherit none of his wealth. Our children get it all."

"Yes, but doesn't it hurt you to see your husband running after other women?"

"I never see it. The other women never come here. Or if they do come to the house it is as if they were perfect strangers. They have their own house."

"But you must know that your husband does leave you to go to these other women."

"Oh yes! But I don't see it. Besides their children are subject to my children. If my children suffer injury, they fight to avenge them. If my children demand, they stand back of them. It is good to have a large family."

The logic of concubinage is embraced in this last reply, I think. It is an institution to render the family "strong to demand, and strong to resist demands."

A strong healthy Kalinga chief has usually two, often more concubines. He gives them rather limited material support: now and then a suckling pig to rear, a little rice to help out the year, work at good wages, yarn to keep them busy at the loom, a little capital for trading trips, and the like. He may *help* them a great deal, but they rarely cost him much. As indicated above, their children have no inheritance rights.

GLOSSARY*

adi, term of negation.

agamang, dormitory of the unmarried. In some sections of northern Ifugao a special building is constructed for this purpose. Among the Ifugaos generally a vacant house or the house of a widow is used.

agba, a magic stick used for the purpose of determining the cause of illness, or the answering of other difficult questions. The stick is believed to grow longer when it desires to make an affirmation.

aiyag, call, name. A ceremony to recall the soul of a sick or dead person.

alaag, a cooking pot of Chinese origin.

alao, duel with lances.

alauwin, a gourd carried as a water jug by women working in the rice fields.

alpud, runo stalks with blades tied in a loop. It is an "ethics lock," and denotes private property. Used by placing near or on whatever it is desired shall remain unmolested; as, for example, a sugar-cane thicket, cord of wood, house in the absence of owners, rice field in dispute, and so forth.

ama, father (see Appendix 1).

amana-on, father-in-law (see Appendix 1).

amaon, aunt's husband, etc. (see Appendix 1).

anak, son or daughter (see Appendix 1).

apo, grandparent (see Appendix 1).

*areca, a slender graceful palm which produces the areca nut, erroneously called the betel-nut, which, with the leaf of the betel pepper and lime, are universally chewed by the Ifugaos. The physiologic effect is similar to that of coffee.

ayak, sorcery.

baag, facetious or uncalled-for remarks.

baal, a hand servant; a household servant.

bakid, a "ten"; a half-score.

balal, a form of pawning of family property, in which a sum is loaned, the property passing into the hands of the lender, and remaining so until the sum is repaid. The use of the property constitutes the interest on the loan.

baloblad, interest paid in advance at the time a loan is made.

banga, a pot or tobacco pipe.

bango, a back-basket used for carrying necessities on a journey. It affords a considerable protection against rain.

banting, flint and steel for fire making. Even applied sometimes, though improperly, to modern methods of fire drawing by means of matches. Never applied to fire making by means of sticks or fire syringe.

---

* Starred words are not Ifugao.

bayaó, a kind of fancy blanket.

binangwa, anything that has been cut in two; halved. Sometimes used to denote the half of anything.

binawit, a child spouse that lives in the home of his or her parents-in-law.

binokbok, a ceremony performed three days after a burial. The soul of the deceased is brought back to the village and interviewed.

bobod, a tie, a knot.

*bolo, a heavy knife about 14 to 16 inches long, whose shape varies among the different tribes. It serves a multitude of purposes, answering now for an axe, now for a spade or hoe, now for a weapon, now for the ordinary uses of knives.

bubun, the final ceremony of marriage. Its main purpose is to secure offspring for the couple.

budut, one of the principal payments in the Benaue district in the purchase of a rice field.

bukad, a religious ceremony in which a myth is recited for its magic effect.

bultong, a wrestling match; trial by wrestling.

bungol, jewel, specifically, ancient agate beads.

bungot, ferocity; the nearest approach in the Ifugao language perhaps to ''bravery''. The Ifugao's ideal of bravery seems to be an aggressive and relentless, boastful, angry assertiveness. *Mahui*, a synonym, has the sense of relentless boldness.

*camote, a tropical sweet potato, of which there are numerous varieties.

dalag, offering to the soul of a deceased person.

dangale, funeral feast.

datok, offering to the soul of a deceased person.

di, the article, ''of the.''

dotag, flesh; meat.

duyu, a wooden dish.

*fiat, a term which I use to denote those phrases in religious ceremonies in which the priest clinches or compels the magic effect of an analogy by means of the spoken word.

gagaom, funeral shrouds.

*gansa, or *gangha*, a gong made of copper alloyed with zinc, tin, or silver. Many are very old. Some have been made in Igorot-land, others imported from China.

gatang, purchase price; business transaction, the main payment.

gibu, fine for marital or postmarital delinquency.

goba, arson, burn.

gogod, cut, bisect.

gulad, intent.

guling, a small but valuable, and usually artistic, rice-wine jar.

habalag, a peg on which articles are hung up. One of the payments in the fine for illegal confiscation.

habale, peg or bracket upon which articles are hung.

hablal, flood; flooding of fields with water.

hagabi, a lounge cut out of a lare tree trunk. It is the insignia of the upper class Ifugao. Its carving out of the trunk, and its bringing in from the forest, is an affair in which many villages participate, and is accompanied by pretentious ceremonies and feasts.

hagaphap, cleaning of terrace wall; chopping off grass and weeds.

hailiyu, a lesser fine.

hakba, gifts to kindred of bride from kindred of bridegroom.

hakit, hurt, anguish.

halat, payment due persons of a foreign village who find the body of one dead by violence.

halupe, a class of deities somewhat corresponding to the Greek Furies; suggesting and harassing deities.

hapud, blowing, or breathing on.

haynub, follower; succeeding units of a series.

hibul, treachery.

hidit, peace ceremony; peace deities; sickness inflicted by peace deities because of delayed peace ceremony.

hin, a form of the word *oha,* meaning ''one''.

hingot, the third of the marriage ceremonies.

hogop, damages due the injured party in case of breach of contract.

hokwit, scandalous adultery, accompanied by insults to the offended spouse.

honga, a general welfare ceremony.

hudhud, fine for offense against engagement or for breaking off engagement.

hukup, lid.

hulul, exchange.

iba, companions; sometimes, kindred.

ibuy, ceremony at transfer of ownership of rice field.

iho, evil, bad.

imbango, sacrifice at second ceremony of marriage.

ina, mother (see Appendix 1).

inagagong, a kind of Ifugao blanket.

inagamid, adopted; taken to oneself.

inaon, uncle's wife, etc. (see Appendix 1).

inay, exclamation of pain or awe.

inhida, eaten; one of the payments at the *ibuy* ceremony.

inipit, something held with pincers or pliers; also something grasped between the toes. In eating meat the Ifugao holds his knife between the toes and, grasping the meat with his hands, cuts it by sawing it back and forth on the knife.

inlaglaga, bastard.

iyao, form of *iho.*

iyu, a form of *iho.*

kadangyang, a wealthy person; person of the upper class. Some observers have interpreted *kadangyang* as ''noble''; others as ''chieftain''. Correctly speaking, there are neither chieftains nor nobles among the Ifugaos. The more powerful *kadangyang* rise to the dignity of headmen—no further.

kalakal, an edible water beetle found in the rice fields.

kalun, advice.

kindut, carried under the arm.

kinta, surplus; portion of food left after appetite has been satisfied.

kolating, harvest feast.

kulpe, feast at time rice fields are planted.

kumadangyang, to become wealthy.

labod, blood payment; indemnity for homicide or severe wounds.

lanad, commission of go-between. Also called *liwa.*

linutu, cooked.

liwa, fee of go-between. See *lanad.*

lukbu, commission; fee paid an agent.

luktap, unaggravated adultery; adultery unaccompanied by great scandal and by insults to offended spouse.

lupe, interest; increase.

maginlotan, death blanket, usually imported. Of less value than the *dili.*

ma-ibuy, property for whose transfer the *ibuy* ceremony is necessary.

mangdad, pig or chicken, given by kindred of bride to kindred of groom as a return for pig given the former by the latter in the *hango* and *hingot* ceremonies.

manikam, priest who performs certain ceremonies preliminary to the *uyauwe* feast (see *tikman*).

mata-na, his eyes.

mommon, preliminary marriage ceremony.

monbaga, asker, requester.

monbiyao, an alliance between families of different districts. Celebrated by very pretentious ceremonies.

mongatang, seller.

monkalun, advocate, adviser. Specifically, in law, the go-between in a penal or civil case.

montudol, a ''shower''; specifically, a traitor to his village; a betrayer.

nabungol, jeweled.

nadulpig, in addition to; accompanying.

na-imbalbalayen (lit., ''made one's child''), adopted child.

na-oha, single; one only; one alone.

na-onom, six at a time; a unit consisting of six subunits, or parts.

natauwinan, four at a time.

nate, dead.

natuku, consisting of three subunits, or parts.

nawatwat, poverty-stricken; term applied to the lowest class of Ifugao society.

nemnem, mind, feeling, thought, emotion, worry, intention. The term is of very broad meaning and applies to the mind or any act thereof.

nikkop (lit., ''taken to one's self''), adopted child, or a servant that is treated as one of the family.

nunbadi, a pair; consisting of two subunits or parts; two together.

nundopa, the ''jumping down from.''

nungolat (lit., ''he who was strong''), the conceiver, or originator, of a plot; he who assembles others to himself, and leads them in committing an injury or offense.

nunlidludagan, place where it was laid, or had fallen.

nunókop, a payment of two units of a series by means of a single article. The Ifugao prefers to divide all sales into ten subpayments. If the sale be comparatively small, two subpayments may be paid by one article, as by a death blanket.

oban, a blanket, about eight feet long and two feet wide, with which a baby is carried on the back of an elder. It is of great religious and poetic significance.

ohok, sticks or trellis for climbing vines.

om, yes; affirmative.

ongot, menace; threat.

otak, a large knife, universally carried by the Ifugaos. It is used in war or in work; commonly called throughout the Philippines ''*bolo*'' in both English and Spanish.

paduldul, comfort; causing consolation.

paghok, landmark; usually chunks of wood or stone buried at a boundary line.

pakimáan, "causing to chew betels together."

pango, jewels, usually agate beads.

paniyu, taboo.

panuyu, mutual accusation, false accusation.

paowa, prohibition, truce.

patang, interest paid in advance on something borrowed.

piduan, repetition.

pinokla, a ceremony to cure wounds.

pinohat, carried under the arm.

ponga, ceremony to remove the prohibition on marriage of cousins. Full cousins may not marry.

pugug, finish; termination.

puhu-na, his heart.

putu-na, his belly.

pu-u, base.

*runo, a tall reed that covers the mountain sides. House walls, mats, floors, and fences are made of it. It also makes an effective missile.

tandong, one of the principal payments made on family property. It corresponds to the initial payment made when an article is bought on installments among our people.

tanig, term applied to the principal marriage ceremony in the Benaue district. Corresponds to *bubun* in the Kiangan district.

tayap, wing.

te, because.

tikman, ceremony of tying up the bellies, appetites, passions, and desires of the guests at a feast.

tobong, spit on which edible water beetles are grilled.

tokop, the placing beside an article its equivalent.

tokom, fine assessed for putting another in the position of being an accomplice.

tombok, gossip.

tomok, fine for manslaughter, wounds.

tudong, woman's sweet-potato basket. It is used as a raincoat when at work in the fields.

tulang, brother (see Appendix 1).

tuldag, series of ceremonies at the time rice is put in the granaries.

tulud, a ceremony of witchcraft, in which, following the recitation of a myth for magic purposes, the characters of the myth recited are made to perform, or declare their will to perform, the desire of the priest.

tumuk, persons of the middle class. Persons are accounted of this class who have rice sufficient for the use of their family throughout the year, and those who, having surplus rice, have not been initiated into the ranks of the *kaḍangyang* by means of the *uyauwe* feast.

tungul, ceremony at the time of placing rice in granaries. One of the three greater ceremonials of rice culture.

ubunana, his seat.

ugâ, treachery.

ulitao, uncle (see Appendix 1).

ulitaon, spouse of uncle or aunt (see Appendix 1).

ulpitan, the placing on each side of an article its equivalent.

umuhun, burning off the grass preparatory to spading fields.

unud, follow, a term applied to a second payment of interest in advance. Thus, a man borrows a carabao, paying ₱30 as the interest in advance for one year, and if at the end of the year he cannot repay the carabao he makes a second payment, or *unud,* as interest in advance on the following year.

uyauwe, a series of pretentious and ostentatious ceremonies by which a person attains the rank of *kadangyang.* Sometimes it is combined with the last ceremony of marriage.

PLATES

Thanks to the help provided by the R. H. LOWIE MUSEUM OF ANTHROPOLOGY, University of California, Berkeley, in whose archives Barton's original photographs are catalogued, it is possible to reproduce here almost all of the illustrations in the original edition.

PLATE 1.

A NEGRITO SHACK

Often a Negrito's dwelling is the merest mockery of a house. This is an unusually good one, since it has a thatched roof. Often the roof is no more than a few curled banana leaves, and the dwelling without walls of any kind. Two or three bows stand to the right of the door. The Negrito puts into the making of his bow and arrows all the pains he neglects to put into the construction of his house.

PLATE 2. PURE-BLOOD NEGRITO AND AMERICAN

The American is 5 feet 9½ inches tall. Because of their mixed blood, the average height of the Negrito is above what one would expect in à tribe of dwarf blacks. These wiry little men are at home in the jungle, and inspire no little fear in their neighbors. The Ifugaos have quite poignant traditions of the time when Negritos lived in the surrounding forests. To this day in the general welfare ceremonials, they call a deity that is a Negrito spirit, and address him as follows: "We are also Negritos. Do not shoot us with your bow and arrow. Shoot our enemies instead because we are all Negritos together." *The American in the illustration is the author himself, Roy Franklin Barton. The identification was recently verified by a member of Barton's family.*

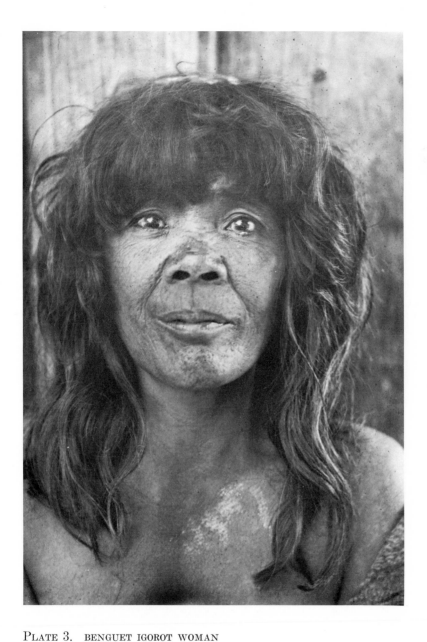

PLATE 3. BENGUET IGOROT WOMAN

The Benguet Igorots live to the south of the Ifugao. Notice that the hair is banged over the forehead.

PLATE 4.

A BENGUET GIRL OF THE BETTER CLASS

The Benguet and Lepanto women are the only women of the mountain tribes that habitually wear a garment above the waist.

PLATE 5.   LEPANTO WOMEN

Among the Lepanto the upper garment is frequently padded with rags and patched and repatched until it becomes "a coat of many colors." The women are stocky and hardy. They do a greater portion of the work than do the women of other tribes.

PLATE 6.   A BONTOC GIRL

The saucy, undomesticated expression is characteristic of the Bontoc Igorot. To describe in a word the dispositions of the three upper mountain tribes of northern Luzon, it could be said that the Kalinga is a rake, the Bontoc a dare-devil, the Ifugao a mystic.

PLATE 7. BONTOC HOUSE

The main room of the Bontoc house rests on piles and lies above the level of the eaves. It is used only as a granary and storeroom. Beneath it, protected from inclement weather by two or three planks on each side, the family cooks and eats. At one corner of this space beneath the house proper is a tight box in which husband, wife, and baby, if there be one, sleep. Older children sleep in the dormitories of the unmarried.

Sweet potato patches lie all about the house. Sharpened reeds are stuck in them to impale the serpent eagle should he swoop down upon the chickens.

PLATE 8.   A KALINGA MAN AND WOMAN.

The man wears flowers above his ears, feathers in his hair, and carries a gong which is held by a jawbone taken from an enemy's head. The woman wears ear ornaments and skirt spangles of mother-of-pearl; her wrists are wrapped with strands of beads nearly to her elbows. The Kalingas are the wealthiest of the mountain tribes and the fondest of ornaments.

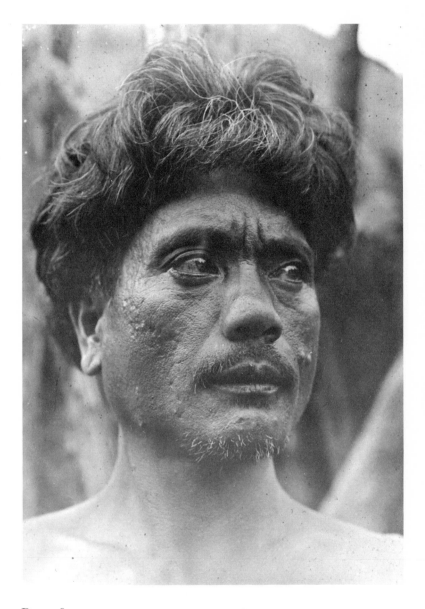

PLATE 9. IFUGAO OF PINDUANGAN VILLAGE

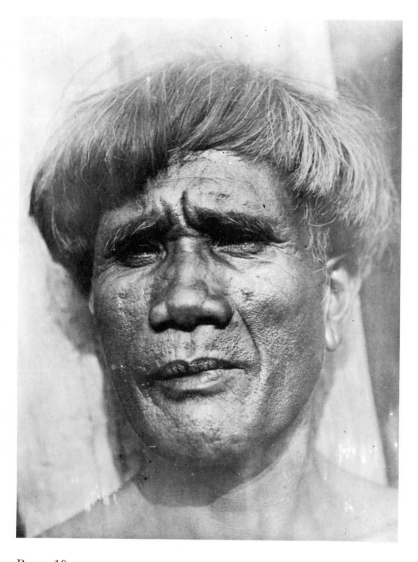

PLATE 10.   IFUGAO OF UMBUL VILLAGE

Patikwal, a strong character, famous in the whole region as a go-between and as a priest.

PLATE 11.   IFUGAO OF PINDUANGAN VILLAGE

According to Ifugao custom, Kuyapi must wear his hair long because he has not avenged the death of his father. The coming of the Americans prevented this vengeance.

PLATE 12.　THREE IFUGAO BELLES

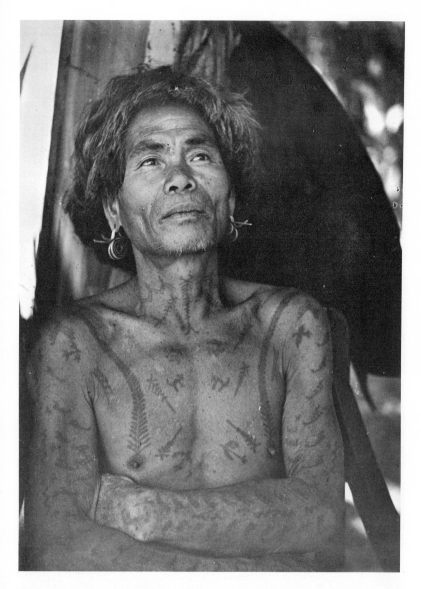

PLATE 13. A TATTOOED IFUGAO OF KABABUYAN DISTRICT

The following tattoo patterns may be distinguished: dog, eagle, centipede (running up from each breast), scorpion, lightning (zig-zag), and shield.

PLATE 14.   AN IFUGAO HOUSE

This is one of the best houses built by a Philippine population. Note the fenders on the pilings to prevent ingress of rats. The house is so constructed that its own weight holds the frame together.

PLATE 15.
HUNDUAN VALLEY,
IFUGAO

PLATE 16. PLANTING RICE, KIANGAN

Young rice plants are taken from the seed beds and transplanted in the field. Women do most of this work, since their hands are nimbler than men's. The men do most of the work of preparing the fields.

PLATE 17.
PREPARATION FOR IFUGAO
hagabi CEREMONY

The *hagabi*, or lounging bench, is the rich man's insignia of rank. The rice (in the large woven baskets) is thrown into the air for the poor, who scramble for it.

PLATE 18.   IFUGAO MOTHER AND CHILD

Ifugao babies are carried across the mother's back. The *oban* blanket
with which the child is held on the back is of great importance in
cases of illegitimate birth, since its gift by the father to the mother
constitutes a recognition of the child.

PLATE 19.   TWO IFUGAOS DRESSED FOR THE COCK-FIGHT DANCE

The man on the left has recently killed an enemy. About his neck he wears a string of crocodile teeth. Elements of his costume suggest a cock's comb, wings, and tail. The two men are about to perform a mimic dance in which one, representing a full-grown cock, overcomes the other, representing a half-grown cock. Priests in the background pray that the warriors of their village may have the success of the full-grown cock.

PLATE 20.

IFUGAO PRIESTS AT A
HEAD-TAKING CEREMONY

Priests are reciting myths and invocations against the enemy during the progress of the cock-fight dance.

PLATE 21.   FUNERAL PROCESSION OF A SLAIN IFUGAO

This is one of the most spectacular events the life of a barbarian people offers. The shield fronts are striped with zigzag white lines. The processions are often a mile long, and 1000 or even 2000 people may take part in them. The men wear gaudy head-dresses, women's beads, and strips of white fiber about the legs and arms. The participants dance along the way, turning from one side to the other. From a distance, one of these processions moving slowly along a rice field dike resembles nothing so much as a gigantic, squirming centipede.

PLATE 22.   BODY OF MURDERED IFUGAO GIRL

In one hand is placed a knife, in the other a spear. Corpses of the murdered are always propped against a house piling—never put in a death chair as are corpses of those dead from natural causes. The corpse, too, is neglected in order to make the soul angry and incline it to vengeance.

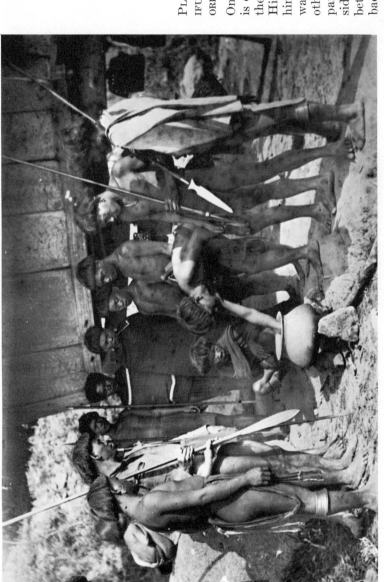

PLATE 23.

IFUGAO HOT-WATER
ORDEAL

One of the participants
is dipping his hand into
the pot of boiling water.
His party stands beside
him, spears pointed to-
ward the earth. The
other member and his
party are on the other
side of the pot. The go-
between squats directly
back of the pot.

PLATE 24.

AN IFUGAO FINE

Note the eight rice-wine jars, the knives and spears, two pigs, six rude cages containing chickens, eight copper pots, two coats (formerly part of the uniform of American soldiers), the baskets and dishes.

PLATE 25.
PARTICIPANTS IN
IFUGAO *uyauwe*
CEREMONY

The girl (fifth from left) and the boy next to her have been recently married and are being elevated to the rank of *kadangyang*, or wealthy. The boy carries a cock hanging from his belt; the girl a hen in her hand. The men and women are kindred of the boy and girl.

PLATE 26.   IFUGAO CORPSE IN THE DEATH CHAIR

When a person of *kadangyang* rank is placed in the death chair, he is dressed in the costume of that rank. These bodies are sometimes kept in the chair for as many as thirteen to fifteen days. The *mon-wahiwa* (undertaker) sits at the right. His duty is to care for the body and finally to carry it on his shoulders to the sepulchre on the mountainside. For these services he receives a very trifling compensation. Bodies of those dead from natural causes are treated with great care and respect, unlike the corpse; of the murdered. which are neglected.

אָמַר לוֹ אֱלֹהִים לְמֹשֶׁה:
מַתָּנָה טוֹבָה יֵשׁ לִי
בְּבֵית גְּנָזַי וְשַׁבָּת שְׁמָהּ
וַאֲנִי מְבַקֵּשׁ לִתְּנָהּ לְיִשְׂרָאֵל

(שבת י ע"ב)

*I have a precious gift
in My treasure-house,
said God to Moses:
"Sabbath" is its name;
go and tell Israel I wish
to present it to them.*

(SHABBATH 10B)

Fifth Edition, Revised and Expanded

THE SABBATH

A Guide to Its Understanding and Observance

Dayan Dr. I. Grunfeld

FELDHEIM PUBLISHERS
JERUSALEM · NEW YORK

Note: The translation of halakhic measurements into inches and centimeters is based on the opinion of the world-renowned halakhic authority, Rabbi Moshe Feinstein, *zt"l*, who determined an *amah* (one cubit) to be 21¼ inches – 54 cm.

ISBN 1-58330-607-2

First published 1954
Second edition 1956
Third edition 1959
Fourth, reset edition 1981
Fifth, revised and expanded edition 2003

FELDHEIM PUBLISHERS
POB 35002 / Jerusalem, Israel

202 Airport Executive Park
Nanuet, NY 10954

www.feldheim.com

Printed in Israel

Contents

Chapter Four
THE CELEBRATION OF SABBATH

Chapter Five
SABBATH IN THE MODERN WORLD

Introduction to the Fifth Edition

THIS BOOK WAS first written some fifty years ago. The present edition has been revised and expanded to cater to the styles and norms of the twenty-first century. Stories from our literature have been included to demonstrate how the principles outlined in the book affected the lives of Jews throughout the ages. A number of sections are entirely new. These are: The City Eruv, Sabbath Candles, and The Double Loaves. The halakhic sections have been revised to accommodate the rulings of more recent authorities. These additions are the work of my son, Rav Avraham Chaim, *shlita*, in consultation with halakhic authorities where necessary.

It is my fervent hope and prayer that this new presentation of Dayan Grunfeld's original efforts will be received with the same enthusiasm and appreciation as the former editions. We live in times when the threat of nuclear and biological warfare looms on the horizon. When the Sages of the Talmud peered into the distant future and foresaw this troubled period which heralds the "footsteps of the Messiah," they declared: "We shall have no one to rely on but our Father in Heaven." Now, more than ever, we need the powerful and reassuring message of Shabbos. In the long run, the world and all its resources and technologies are a heaven-sent gift for mankind to use for our moral and spiritual betterment.

Aryeh Carmell
Jerusalem
Iyar 5763/2003

In Memoriam

SINCE THE THIRD edition of this book appeared, Dayan Grunfeld, *zt"l*, has passed on to his eternal reward, and a few words on his life and work would certainly be appropriate here.

Dayan Isidor Grunfeld (1900–1975) — lawyer, Dayan of the Court of the Chief Rabbi, communal leader, educator and prolific writer — was above all an ardent follower of Rabbi Samson Raphael Hirsch. His whole life was dedicated to interpreting the ideas and works of the Master and making them accessible to our generation. He was an eloquent advocate for the application of the Hirschian approach to solving the problems of living in the 20th century.

From Rabbi Hirsch he inherited his breadth of vision. He was keenly aware of the currents of thought in the secular world and welcomed every opportunity to demonstrate the relevance of Torah to the wider problems of mankind. How he fought against the narrow *shtiebel* mentality which sees Torah as the possession and interest of only a small and isolated group of people! It says much for the man, however, that he remained on the best of terms with those very circles and gained their admiration, affection and respect.

This little book, on which the present writer had the privilege of collaborating, was the *bikkurim* — the first fruit — of his extensive literary activity. It has been called "the finest exposition of the Sabbath available in English" and has been translated into several languages, though strangely enough a Hebrew edition still awaits publication.[*]

The book is unique among expositions of the Sabbath in that it sets out to show the significance of the halakhic Sabbath and to demonstrate that abstention from *melakhah*, in all its ramifications, is the living heart and core of Sabbath observance. This is the aspect of the Jewish Sabbath so often decried by the ignorant as "senseless concentration on trivial details." Insightfully Rabbi Hirsch promulgated a majestic concept of *issur melakhah* as abstention for one day in seven from all creative activity, thus bearing eloquent testimony to the need to live in God's world as His creatures and to use all our human powers in His service. This concept, so well-presented in this book, must once and for all put an end to such unfortunate misunderstandings. And no one who has read this book will ever again be able honestly to use the outworn argument that the Sabbath law against kindling fire applied only to times when making a fire involved the hard labor of knocking heavy stones together (see p. 62).

The quarter-century that has passed since the book's first appearance, which has witnessed the increasing de-humanization and de-personalization of man and the worldwide erosion of moral standards, has served only to reinforce the message to which Dayan Grunfeld was so passionately committed — the eternal relevance of the laws of the Torah and particularly those of the Sabbath, to spiritual regeneration of the Jewish people and of all mankind.

A.C.
Jerusalem
Kislev 5741/1981

---

[*] A Hebrew translation entitled "*Matanah Genuzah*" was published by Feldheim in August 2002. [ed.]

Preface

THIS LITTLE VOLUME has mainly a practical purpose: to be a guide to the proper understanding and observance of the Sabbath, the foundation of our faith. Although the book is small in size, much time, work and thought have been spent on it.

At the outset I would like to express my deep gratitude to Rabbi Aryeh Carmell who has helped me throughout the preparation and publication of this book and has contributed various sections to it.

Any presentation of the Sabbath as the fundamental institution of Judaism must of necessity fall into two parts: an aggadic one, dealing with the underlying ideas of Sabbath, and a halakhic one, explaining the laws of its practical observance. I have tried to blend the one with the other.

For the aggadic part I have mostly drawn on the *aggadah* of Tractate *Shabbath* in the Babylonian Talmud; on the Midrashic literature; and among modern works, particularly on the writings of Rabbi Samson Raphael Hirsch, one of the outstanding Jewish thinkers of the last century. On the halakhic side, apart from the standard codes and works on Jewish Law, I have made use of Rabbi E. Biberfeld's *Sabbath-Vorschriften*, which was published in Germany some fifty years ago and proved very popular. My thanks are due to Mrs. Fanny Kahn, who put her translation of that little book at my disposal. The halakhic rulings follow Ashkenazi practice.

I am also grateful to Dayan A. Rapoport and Rabbi Dr. S. Mannes for their assistance in connection with the halakhic

11

part of this publication.

Thanks are due, as well, to Norman Solomons Esq., M.A., for many helpful suggestions.

I venture to hope that this book will deepen the under-standing of our holy Sabbath, serve as an introduction to the knowledge of its laws, and eventually lead the reader to the study of its halakhic and aggadic sources. I trust further that it will be helpful to Jewish educators. Finally, I pray that, with the help of God, this book will assist those who unfor-tunately have lost the Sabbath, to regain the peace and blessing which are to be found in its observance.

I.G.
London
5714/1954

THE TRAIN DRAGGED ON with its human freight. Pressed together like cattle in the crowded trucks, the unfortunate occupants were unable even to move. The atmosphere was stifling. As the Friday afternoon wore on, the Jewish men and women in the Nazi transport sank deeper and deeper into their misery.

Suddenly an old Jewish woman managed with a great effort to move and open her bundle. Laboriously she drew out — two candlesticks and two challoth. She had just prepared them for Sabbath when she was dragged from her home that morning. They were the only things she had thought worthwhile taking with her. Soon the Sabbath candles lit up the faces of the tortured Jews and the song of Lekhah Dodi transformed the scene. Sabbath with its atmosphere of peace had descended upon them all.

This story, reported to the author by an eyewitness who escaped, is by no means an isolated one in our long history. Countless similar episodes could be cited of Jews who clung to Sabbath in the face of death and in spite of death. What is the secret of Sabbath's hold over the Jewish heart? Mere sentiment will not account for it. Perhaps, consciously or unconsciously, it is a realization of the ancient word:

> *"Between Me and the children of Israel it is a sign forever..."*
>
> (Exodus 31:17)

For Sabbath expresses all the innermost longings of the Jewish soul, and each of its many facets reflects something of the Divine radiance.

Chapter One
The Spirit of Sabbath

I. THE MEANING OF THE SABBATH

Our Sages call the Sabbath *yesod ha-emunah*, the very foundation of our faith. This is no exaggeration. For the loftiest thoughts by which Judaism has ennobled the human mind, the highest ideals for which our people have been striving for thousands of years at the cost of innumerable lives, all are centered in the Sabbath.

Dignity of Work

"Six days shall you labor and do all your work." The basis of the Sabbath is thus work — labor dignified because it is God's commandment. Work is not a degradation but man's holy birthright. How many centuries, millennia even, did it take the world to grasp this fundamental truth! It is a long way indeed from the Greek and Roman conception of labor as degrading, with the resultant lack of rights of the laborer, to the present-day status of the working man. How much social unrest and misery, how many wars and revolutions, how much bloodshed could mankind have been spared, had the Biblical ideal of the dignity of labor been made from the very beginning the basis of the social order!

Jewish tradition tells us that Adam became reconciled to his fate only when he was told that he would have to work. Work is indeed the prerogative of free-born creative man. "Great is work," our Sages say, "for it honors him who does it."[1]

Spiritual Freedom

Yet work is not all. Work can make man free, but one can also be a slave to work. When God created heaven and earth, says the Talmud, they went on unreeling endlessly, "like two bobbins of thread," until their Creator called out to them, "Enough!"[2] God's creative activity was followed by the Sabbath, when He deliberately ceased from His creative work. This, more than anything, shows Him to us as the free Creator freely controlling and limiting the creation He brought into being according to His will — the Creator with a purpose.

It is thus not "work," but "ceasing from work" which God chose as the sign of His free creation of the world. By ceasing from work every Sabbath, in the manner prescribed by the Torah, the Jew bears witness to the creative power of God. He also reveals Man's true greatness. The stars and the planets, having once started on their eternal rounds, go on blindly, ceaselessly, driven by nature's law of cause and effect. Man, however, by an act of faith, can put a limit to his

---

1. *Nedarim* 49b. (All Talmudic references are to the Babylonian Talmud, unless otherwise stated.)
2. *Chagigah* 12a.

labor, so that it will not degenerate into purposeless drudgery. By keeping Sabbath the Jew becomes, as our Sages say, *domeh l'Yotzero* — "like his Creator." He is, like God, work's master, not its slave.

Man is truly great, however, only if he willingly co-operates in God's plan for the world, making use of his freedom to serve God and his fellow-men. Then he becomes, as the Sages put it, "a partner in the work of creation."[3]

Yet man's very freedom can lead to his downfall. His great powers over the world of nature, which enable him to control and master it, harness its energies, mold and adapt it to his will — these very powers make it fatally easy for man to think of himself in the guise of creator, responsible to no one higher than himself. In our time we have seen what happens to the world and to mankind when such ideas prevail.

But here Sabbath comes to the rescue. As we shall see later in greater detail, we have here perhaps the most fundamental aspect of Sabbath observance.

It is possible to recognize the basic truth of God's creation of the world. But what does this mean to the average man and woman? Very little indeed. But here, as always, the Torah is not satisfied with mere theory. The Torah is interested in deeds — the practical outcome. Put like this the doctrine comes to life: "Living in God's world as His creatures, we must use all our human powers in His service." Only thus can we justify our existence, and at the same time ensure our own welfare and that of the human race.

The unique provisions of the Sabbath law serve to

---

3. *Shabbath* 10a.

keep this very practical consideration in the forefront of our minds. We are stopped on this one day from exercising our characteristic human powers of producing and creating in the material world. By this very inactivity we lay these powers in homage at the feet of God Who gave them.

This basic Sabbath-idea will be developed more fully in later chapters. If we strain our ears, however, we may even now catch what the Sabbath is trying to say to us.

In fact, it says to us every week what God told the first human being:

> *I have placed you in this world of mine; everything I have created is for you. Set your mind to it that you do not corrupt and destroy My world.*
> (Midrash Rabbah, Ecclesiastes 7:9)

Here we have the pure essence of Sabbath. The same act that proclaims man's freedom also declares his subservience to God. To use all of one's powers in the service of God — there is no greater freedom than this.

2. Sabbath and Life

Another blessing flows from Sabbath — the blessing of *menuchah* — "rest." This *menuchah* is something much more than physical rest. It is an attitude of mind, a spiritual state, induced by the experience that is Sabbath. It is compounded of many things.

There is the joy at being released from bondage to the pressing demands of everyday life.

Quite apart from the bondage of work, there are

the insistent demands of our mechanical civilization — the bus, the car, the telephone; the demands, too, of our mechanical entertainment industry — radio, television, the cinema.... Until we reflect, most of us are unaware of the toll which these things take on our vital energy; we do not realize the extent of our enslavement. To take only one example: how many of us can sit alone in a room together with a ringing telephone without answering it? The summons is irresistible: we know that sooner or later we *must* answer it. On Sabbath this "must" does not exist. The relaxation, the relief of spirit, which a real Jewish Sabbath brings must be experienced to be believed.

The spirit of *menuchah* finds its positive expression in the Sabbath meals in which the happy companionship of family and friends, the enjoyment of good food, the table-songs in praise of God and the Sabbath, all combine to form an entirely unique experience.

In this Sabbath atmosphere it is easy to feel the nearness of God, and to face life without worry and without regrets, in the confidence that we are all in His care.

With body refreshed and nervous tension relaxed, the mind is stimulated in its turn to achieve closer contact with God by the study of His Torah, not as an intellectual pastime, but in the full knowledge that it is the only source of truth and true living for the Jew. If we make this spiritual activity the positive content of the Sabbath's leisure hours, then when Sabbath goes out it will leave us in all respects better equipped for the tasks of the coming week — better equipped, in fact, for the task of living.

The blessings of Sabbath are not confined to the life of the individual. After helping the Jew to find himself, Sabbath helps him to find his fellow-man. One of the basic motives given in the Torah for the Sabbath commandment is:

> ...*that your manservant and maidservant may rest as well as you.*
>
> (Deuteronomy 5:14)

The master like the servant — the servant like the master! Can anyone realize today what this equalization must have meant at a time when a bondservant was nothing but his master's animated tool, to be broken and destroyed at will? On the Sabbath servant and master meet as equals, as free human personalities. Sabbath restored to the slave his human dignity. Sabbath-rest and Sabbath-freedom applied also to the "stranger within the gates." Thus the foundation was laid for the brotherhood of man.

Indeed, as we shall see, even the cattle are not excluded from the heavenly blessing of Sabbath-rest. Not even the animal may be denied the dignity due a creature of God. "You.... and your ox, your donkey and all your animals" (ibid.).

Sabbath is thus a weekly-recurring Divine protest against slavery and oppression. Lifting up his Kiddush cup on Friday night, the Jew links the creation of the world with man's freedom, so declaring slavery and oppression deadly sins against the very foundation of the universe. Can one be surprised that tyrants of all times would not permit Israel to celebrate the Sabbath?

Spiritual Aspirations

We have seen that Sabbath is the root of all spiritual and social progress, that it is connected with the highest thoughts and aspirations of man: God, the dignity of the human soul, the freedom and equality of man, the supremacy of spirit over matter. Small wonder, then, that the prophets of Israel took the Sabbath as the symbol of everything that is morally good and noble.

> *Happy is the man who does this, and the son of man who holds fast by it: who keeps the Sabbath and refrains from profaning it — and keeps his hand from doing any evil.*

(Isaiah 56:2)

The same idea of identifying the Sabbath with man's highest aspirations on earth is expressed in Nehemiah (9:13):

> *You came down also upon Mount Sinai and spoke with them from heaven and gave them right judgments and true laws, good statutes and commandments — and You made known unto them Your holy Sabbath.*

Our Sages with their unique gift for epigram gave expression to the fact that the Sabbath contains the sum and substance of Jewish life and thought in the words: "If God had not brought us to Mount Sinai and had only given us the Sabbath it would have been enough."[4] It would indeed have been enough, for Sabbath epitomizes the whole of Judaism.

---

4. Haggadah of Pesach.

SABBATH IN EGYPT

Moshe will rejoice with the gift of his portion.
(Sabbath morning prayers)

"Moshe grew up and went out to his brethren and he saw their burdensome work" (Exodus 2:11). The Midrash relates that Moshe (who was saved from the Nile by Pharaoh's daughter and was raised in Pharaoh's palace) saw how his brethren were working seven days a week without any respite.

He came to Pharaoh with the following argument: "The Jewish labor-force is very important and beneficial for the realm. If you continue to work them without a chance to rest, they are going to grow weak and die."

"What do you suggest I do?" asked Pharaoh.

"Give them one day a week to rest up from their labor," Moshe replied, "and they will regain their energy for another week of productive work."

The idea appealed to Pharaoh, and he instructed Moshe to choose whichever day he felt most suitable. Moshe happened to choose the seventh day as their day off.

From that time on, the oppressed Jews would gather together every seventh day and their elders would read to them ancient scrolls that had been handed down as a legacy from the house of our forefather Jacob. They would tell them about the beginnings of the Jewish people and the lives and aspirations of their great ancestors, Abraham, Isaac and Jacob, and the promise that God had made to Abraham that He would one day redeem His children from bondage.

When, many decades later, the Jewish people left Egypt and were commanded to observe the Sabbath,

Moshe was delighted to find that the day he had chosen as a day of rest coincided with the Divine Sabbath; the day God has designated as the focal point of the week when the Jewish people connect with the Master of the World in a covenant of faith.[5]

---

5. Based on *Midrash Rabbah*, Exodus 1:28; 5:18 and Tur, *Orach Chayyim*, Chapter 281.

Chapter Two
The Concept of Melakhah

1. WHAT IS MELAKHAH?

How is the Sabbath to be observed to ensure that its sublime purpose may be realized in the Jewish soul?

The Torah's answer is unmistakable. As we have seen, it is by refraining from work; the very word *shabbath* (in Hebrew) means just this.

> *The seventh day shall be a Shabbath to the Lord your God; you shall do no manner of work...*
> (Exodus 19:9; Deuteronomy 5:14)

Again and again the Torah insists on this as the first condition, the center and essence of Sabbath observance.

We have now to consider exactly what the Torah means by "work" in this connection — and here we may be led to some rather unexpected conclusions.

Melakhah and Work

It is clear that "work" or, to use the Torah's own term, *melakhah*, is by no means identical with physical strain or exertion. This is shown by the simple legal fact that you are not a Sabbath-breaker if you carry a very heavy load inside your house, but if you carry

25

even a small article from your house into the street
you would be profaning the Sabbath. Nor is it true to
say that what the Torah forbids is merely the carrying
on of our everyday occupations. The Sabbath laws include this, but they include far more besides, and it is
clear that they must be based on some different principle.

What is really meant by "work" in the Biblical in-
junction, "You shall do no manner of work" can be ascertained only by careful study of the oral tradition.
And it is best not to use the confusing translation
"work" or "labor" but to keep to the technical term
melakhah. A clear appreciation of the nature of
melakhah is vitally important for the true understanding of Sabbath as the Torah itself means it to be observed, and as it is in fact observed to this day by
those Jews mindful of their great heritage.

Sabbath in the Torah

The main source in the Torah for the definition of
melakhah is the command that all the various activities necessary for the construction of the Tabernacle
in the desert — defined as *melakhah* — should cease
on Sabbath (Exodus 31:13). All these are thus ex-
pressly included in the term *melakhah*.

If we were to make a list of all the activities involved in the construction of the Tabernacle, we
would discover a surprising fact. They are seen to
form a cross-section of all the main types of human
productive activity. This can hardly be accidental.
However, it is not to our purpose now to inquire into
possible reasons for this so far as the building of the

Tabernacle is concerned. What does concern us is that the Torah has given us here a clear indication of the nature and scope of *melakhah*. In addition, certain types of *melakhah* are mentioned independently in the Torah, such as "carrying" (Exodus 16:29; Numbers 15:32), and "lighting fire" (Exodus 35:3), and in each case important light is shed on the Sabbath law as a whole.

Central Concept

The written law thus gives the outline of the Sabbath legislation. The oral tradition has only to fill in the details, by defining terms, and by applying the given principles to all the practical questions which arise in everyday life.

For all practical purposes, therefore, recourse must be had to the oral tradition — the *halakhah* (Jewish law).

Every student of the *halakhah* can see for himself the vast, logically constructed system of the Sabbath laws. The more deeply he studies, the more it will be borne in on him that it is indeed a system — not a haphazard mass of laws, but a consistent, coordinated body of legislation, derived from and conforming to one central, underlying idea.

What then is this unifying principle which underlies the concept of *melakhah*, and so forms the basis of the whole institution of Sabbath?

It is of the utmost importance to find such a general principle, for nothing has done so much harm to the proper observance of the Sabbath as the gross misconception that *melakhah* can be equated merely with physical effort or labor.

Many Jewish thinkers have tried to formulate a central concept of this sort, and so find the key to the whole vast system of the Sabbath laws. The exposition given by Rabbi Samson Raphael Hirsch, one of the foremost Jewish thinkers of the nineteenth century, is a most helpful one for the modern mind.

2. THE IDEA BEHIND MELAKHAH

In arriving at his interpretation of *melakhah*, Rabbi Samson Raphael Hirsch starts with the basic idea that the Sabbath testifies to God as the supreme Creator of heaven and earth and all they contain. Man, however, is engaged in a constant struggle to gain mastery over God's creation, to bring nature under his control. By the use of his God-given intelligence, skill and energy, he has in large measure succeeded in this. He is thus constantly in danger of forgetting his own creature-hood — his utter and complete dependence on the Lord of all things. He tends to forget that the very powers he uses in his conquest of nature are derived from his Creator, in Whose service his life and work should be conducted.

Israel's Task

In a world increasingly forgetful of God, Israel was entrusted with the task of preserving this all-important truth for the future salvation of all mankind. God willed therefore that the Jew, while subduing and controlling his environment like every other human being, must recognize, *and show that he recognizes*, that his powers are derived from One higher than himself. This recognition he is to express by dedicating one day in every week to God, and by refraining on this day from every activity which signifies human power over nature.

Renouncing Mastery

On this day we renounce every exercise of intelligent, purposeful control over natural objects and forces, we cease from every act of human power, in order to proclaim God as the Source of all power. By refraining from human creating, the Jew pays silent homage to the Creator.

The essential characteristic of human creativeness is the intelligent purpose which directs it. This, then, is the import of the fundamental halakhic principle which forms the basis of the whole of the Sabbath law: *Melekheth machasheveth aserah Torah*; i.e., "The Torah forbids as *melakhah* the realization of an intelligent purpose by practical skill."[6]

This, too, is the meaning of the principle (otherwise obscure), which states that any act of pure destruction, however strenuous, is not a *melakhah* — *Kol ha-mekalkelim peturim*.[7] Thus if one were to knock down a house simply with the idea of destroying it, one would not be doing a *melakhah* (although this would hardly be a recommended way of spending Sabbath, and the act would in any case be prohibited under the rabbinical legislation; see below, Chapter

---

6. *Sanhedrin* 62b.
7. *Shabbath* 106a.

3). If, however, one were to do precisely the same act with the constructive purpose of clearing the site for rebuilding, one's act would be a *melakhah*.

We see clearly that it is the purpose that counts, and the *melakhah*-act can only be an expression of human creative intelligence if that purpose is constructive.

Melakhah thus includes within its scope any activity of a constructive nature which makes some significant change in our material environment — significant, that is, in relation to its usefulness for human purposes. Any act, however small, which demonstrates man's mastery of nature in this way is a *melakhah*, be it striking a light or washing clothes, tying a knot or building a house.

We have thus arrived at the definition we have been searching for. A *melakhah* is:

an act that shows man's mastery over the world by the constructive exercise of his intelligence and skill.

Eloquent Restraint

In light of this exposition one can easily see how senseless is the oft-repeated argument that it is no exertion to switch on an electric light, or to write a word. As if the using of electricity were any less a conquest of nature because it happens to be effortless! Or as if writing a word were any less a manifestation of man's creative power because it seems so simple!

Actions can be more eloquent than words. By his complete renunciation of this type of activity on this day, the Jew, as the representative of mankind before God, solemnly affirms that it is only by the will of God that man has "dominion over all the earth," and that God alone is the Source of all creativeness.

Let it be clearly understood that giving up *melakhah* is a positive spiritual act. Man's work in the week, and the illusion which it fosters, is as a veil which hides from him the true nature of his purpose in the world. Giving up *melakhah* means lifting the veil. So long as there is the slightest trace of *melakhah* in our life on Sabbath, the veil hangs in place. In the spiritual sphere, the smallest act can have as great an effect as the largest.

He who presumes to do even one single *melakhah* on this day thereby denies God as Creator and Master of the world. This is why desecration of the Sabbath by *melakhah* is equivalent in the eyes of the Torah to apostasy and idol-worship. On the other hand, when we see a Jewish boy or girl refrain from plucking a single flower on Sabbath, we see something that is a greater testimony to God than all the high-sounding words of poets and philosophers.

We can understand, therefore, why cessation from *melakhah* is the essential requirement of Sabbath observance.

FIERY CONVICTION

One of the most difficult tests of a Jew's commitment to his Sabbath is when he finds his property on fire. Refraining from extinguishing the blaze (in a situation where the fire cannot possibly spread and endanger human life) represents a most powerful statement of the underlying mes-

sage of Sabbath — that we and all we possess are subject to the will of the Almighty.

The Talmud[8] relates a story of a wealthy Jew who served as the treasurer of the Roman governor of Galilee. One Sabbath a fire broke out in his private mansion. The non-Jewish inhabitants of the neighboring villages rushed to the scene to put out the conflagration.

But the Jew did not allow them to come close. "All that I possess I owe to the Creator of the World," he proclaimed. "Let Him take that which is His." As he was talking, the sky providentially became overcast and torrential rains came down and extinguished the flames.

After Sabbath was over, he made sure to reimburse all those who had attempted to help him.

[When the Sages heard this story, they said that, in actual fact, he could have allowed the non-Jews to put out the fire, since they had come of their own accord and not at his behest.]

3. CLASSIFICATION BY PURPOSE

We have defined *melakhah* as any act which shows man's mastery of the world by the purposeful and constructive exercise of his intelligence and skill. This is the type of activity he must cease from on Sabbath, in order to acknowledge and do homage to his Creator.

The activities included in this definition are those which bring about significant changes in our environment for productive purposes. They comprise the whole range of human productive activities.

---

8. *Shabbath* 121a; Jerusalem Talmud, *Shabbath* 16:7.

These are classified, for the purposes of the Sabbath law, into thirty-nine categories, derived, as mentioned above, from the building of the desert Tabernacle. In this classification it is not the physical nature of the activity, but its object or purpose that is the deciding factor. This is fully in accord with the *melakhah*-concept developed above. It is above all the productive purpose which gives to the act its distinctive *melakhah*-character.

For example, one of these categories (No. 2; see Table on page 34) unites under one heading such varied activities as: sowing, planting, grafting, pruning, and watering growing plants. All these have a common purpose, the promotion of plant growth — and they are therefore comprised in one *melakhah*-category. To take another example, the eleventh category (see Table) includes not only boiling, baking, frying, etc., but also industrial activities such as smelting iron, tempering steel, etc. The general principle in this case is: changing the physical or chemical state of a substance by means of heat.

Av and Toladah

A representative *melakhah* is selected by the oral tradition in each case, to give its name to the category. This is the one actually used in the construction of the Tabernacle and is known as the *Av Melakhah*. In the first example cited above the *Av* is "Sowing" and this is the name of the category. In the other example "Baking" is the *Av*. Other members of the category, whose status as *melakhoth* is derived from the common purpose they share with the *Av*, are known as

Toladoth (derivatives). For all practical purposes there is no difference between an *Av* and a *Toladah*. The Torah gives both of them equal status as *melakhoth*, and to do either of them intentionally is an equally grave desecration of the Sabbath.

Table of the Thirty-Nine Categories of *Melakhah*

1. Plowing
2. Sowing
3. Reaping
4. Sheaf-making
5. Threshing
6. Winnowing
7. Selecting
8. Sifting
9. Grinding
10. Kneading
11. Baking
12. Sheep-shearing
13. Bleaching
14. Combing raw materials
15. Dyeing
16. Spinning
17, 18, 19. Weaving operations
20. Separating into threads
21. Tying a knot
22. Untying a knot
23. Sewing
24. Tearing
25. Trapping or hunting
26. Slaughtering
27. Skinning
28. Tanning
29. Scraping pelts
30. Marking out
31. Cutting to shape
32. Writing
33. Erasing
34. Building
35. Demolishing
36. Kindling a fire
37. Extinguishing
38. The final hammer-blow (putting the finishing touch to a newly manufactured article)
39. Carrying from the private to the public domain (and vice versa)

Bearing in mind what we have written about the meaning of *melakhah* and the method of classification adopted, based on the activities employed in the construction of the Tabernacle, we have enumerated the thirty-nine classes of *melakhah* on page 34.

In effect, the oral tradition gives us here a masterly summary of the *productive purposes* of mankind.

In Chapter Three an attempt will be made to define the common purpose underlying the various activities comprised in each category, and to give a selection of some of the *melakhoth* and rabbinical safeguards likely to be met with in practice.

Before undertaking this survey, however, we must now consider the special character of the last of these thirty-nine categories — the *melakhah* known as "Carrying."

4. SPECIAL SIGNIFICANCE OF "CARRYING"[9]

If we consider the categories listed on page 34, we see that almost all of them are clearly *productive* activities.

But what of "carrying"? It is by no means clear at first sight how this *melakhah* fits in with the general concept we have developed above. Indeed, "carrying" seems of all *melakhoth* least obviously a "work," even in the special sense in which we have learned to apply this term in the Sabbath laws. No essential change, no productive process seems to be involved. Perhaps for this reason, and because it needs so little prepara-

---

9. See p. 66, "The City Eruv," for the practical application of this section, particularly in modern-day Israel.

tion and skill, there is unfortunately hardly another law of the Torah that is so widely ignored as this. Yet, as we have seen, the *halakhah* places "carrying" unmistakably among the *Avoth Melakhoth*. It is the first *melakhah* to be treated in the tractate *Shabbath*, and seven of the latter's twenty-four chapters are devoted to it.

Prophetic Warning

Moreover, when the prophet Jeremiah was told to warn Israel that the future of the Jewish state depended on the way Sabbath was observed in it, "carrying" was given special prominence in this connection.

The passage reads as follows:

Thus said the Lord unto me: Go and stand in the people's gate, whereby the kings of Judah come in and go out, and in all the gates of Jerusalem, and say unto them: Hear the word of the Lord, kings of Judah, and all Judah, and all the population of Jerusalem, who enter through these gates!

Thus says the Lord: Take heed for yourselves, and carry nothing on the Sabbath day, nor bring anything in by the gates of Jerusalem, neither carry out anything from your houses on the Sabbath day, neither do any other melakhah, but sanctify the Sabbath day as I commanded your fathers.... And it shall come to pass, if you obey Me implicitly, says the Lord, to bring nothing in through the gates of this city on the Sabbath day, to do no melakhah thereon,

*then shall there enter in by the gates of this city
kings and princes sitting upon the throne of David...and this city shall be inhabited forever....
But if you will not obey Me in keeping the Sabbath day holy, and not carrying anything when
entering in at the gates of Jerusalem on the Sabbath day; then I will kindle a fire in its gates, and
it shall devour the palaces of Jerusalem, and it
shall not be quenched.* (Jeremiah 17:19–27)

We have quoted this passage at length, firstly to show
the importance which the prophetic message ascribes
to the halakhic observance of the Sabbath, but even
more to remark on the way the *melakhah* of "carrying" is singled out from all the others and treated as if
in a class by itself. We are admonished "not to carry...
nor to do any other *melakhah*." This is something that
needs explaining.

What feature is common to all the thirty-eight categories of *melakhah* apart from "carrying"? Without
exception, as we have seen, they have to do with the
realm of nature. Their significance lies in the changes
they effect in natural objects, whether the change is
an actual, physical one, as in "reaping," "baking,"
"dyeing," lighting a fire," etc., or whether it consists in
taking the object out of the realm of nature and into
the sphere of human power and control, as in
"sheaf-making" and "trapping."

Social Organization

In the case of "carrying," however, neither of these
features is apparent. What is forbidden is to transfer

an object from the private to the public domain (and
vice versa), and from point to point in the public domain. The exact definition of these terms will be given
in Chapter 3; we may note for the present that the
most usual form of this *melakhah* is carrying between
the house and the street, or from house to house by
way of the street. We are dealing here with something
which is clearly quite different from the realm of nature. The house, the street, the city — these belong to
quite another sphere: the sphere of *human society*.

If the other *melakhoth* show us man mastering
and controlling his natural environment, this one
shows him active in the social realm, carrying on the
intercourse of the community, circulating its material
goods between house and house, through street and
thoroughfare; not for trade only, but also for the personal and social ends of everyday life. "Carrying" is the
characteristic *melakhah* by which man pursues and
attains his purposes in society. By ceasing from each
of the other *melakhoth*, we proclaim God as the
source of our power over nature. By ceasing from
"carrying" we acknowledge Him our Master in the
sphere of human society. This vast, complex world of
social organization — the world of house, street and
city — needs above all else the realization of God's
presence and God's purpose, the sanctification and
dedication which ceasing from *melakhah* expresses.
The community whose members refrain from
"carrying" on Sabbath places the seal of God upon its
social life.

Can we now perhaps understand the emphasis on
"carrying" in Jeremiah's message to the state of Judah? This is in line with the message of all the proph-

ets — that Israel can exist as a nation only if it knows itself to be the people of God. And what can better express this dedication of the community than ceasing from "carrying" on the Sabbath?

The picture is now complete. The concept of *melakhah* has been defined, and some of the ideas that may lie behind it have been sketched in. The most important, the vital task lies ahead. We have to see how the Torah wishes the sublime concept of Sabbath to be realized in practice, in detail, in our everyday lives.

AN INTERNATIONAL ASSOCIATION

Mr. S. was a traditional Jew who lived in England in the fifties. His connection to his Judaism was limited to eating kosher food and paying a visit to the synagogue a few times a year. The concept of keeping the Sabbath was foreign to him. On the contrary, the shoe shop he owned in one of the suburbs of London was most busy on Saturday, which is a half-day off in England.

Under the influence of an acquaintance, Mr. S. began to strengthen his connection to Judaism. He began to put on tefillin and pray on a daily basis and to participate in some Torah classes. Nevertheless, the idea of observing Sabbath appeared to him to be an insurmountable challenge.

He was convinced that closing his shop on Saturday would destroy his financial security. His regular customers would patronize other shops, not only on Saturday, but during the rest of the week too.

Yet numerous discussions about the importance of Sabbath observance and the central role it plays in the en-

tire framework of Jewish thought and life aroused within him a desire to somehow break through this barrier. But the fear of jeopardizing his financial standing prevented him from taking this crucial step.

One day his friend, who was both a learned person and a successful businessman, told him the following: "Okay, right now you have a well-established source of income. But just imagine if, God forbid, the wheel of fortune turns and you come on hard times. You will be left all alone to fend for yourself.

"However, if you join the ranks of the Sabbath observers, you will automatically become a member of the Association of Sabbath Observers. This association has no offices; it is not even a registered organization. But I can promise you that if you ever need any type of help, you will find all over the world friends who are members of this association who will be happy to give you a helping hand and set you back on your feet."

This promise gave Mr. S. the courage to accept upon himself full Sabbath observance. To his utter surprise, not only did he not lose even a single client, but his business prospered. As a Sabbath-observing Jew, he received a special permit to open his shop on Sunday, when all the other shops were closed, and his income grew substantially!

Chapter Three
Sabbath Observance in Practice

1. SAFEGUARDING THE SABBATH

We have seen the fundamental importance of the prohibition of *melakhah* on Sabbath. We have seen how
even one *melakhah*-act on Sabbath strikes at the roots
of the whole Torah and constitutes an arrogant denial
of God and His mastery of the world.

We can now perhaps begin to understand the extreme gravity of this offence in the eyes of the Torah.
We may now have an inkling of what lies behind such
sentences as:

> *Those who desecrate it shall die; anyone who
> does a melakhah on that day — that soul shall
> be cut off from the midst of his people.*
>
> (Exodus 31:14)

Indeed, who could commit such an act, while knowing its full implications, unless he were already dead
to all the spiritual aspirations of the Jewish people? It
is the simple truth, which we have unfortunately witnessed so many times in latter years, that when the
Sabbath goes out of the life of an individual, a family,
or a community, their Jewishness is turned into a hol-
low mockery, soon to be discarded altogether by

those who come after.

In matters of such seriousness, even unthinking transgressions must be guarded against. It is a very poor excuse, when fundamental questions of this nature are at stake, to say, "I wasn't thinking." Sabbath presents special dangers in this respect, since it concerns actions which we are in the habit of doing all the other six days of the week. Jews at all times, conscious of everything that is at stake, have been determined not to be dragged down from their high purposes by habit and forgetfulness. They have therefore sought ways and means to protect themselves against unintentional Sabbath-breaking.

The Sages have given practical effect to this endeavor by means of protective legislation, by the method known as "erecting a fence about the Law" (*seyag la-Torah*). A prohibition of this kind is called a *gezerah* (rabbinical decree), or, with special reference to the Sabbath laws, a *shevuth*.

In taking these measures, our Sages have acted with the full approval and authority of the Torah, which itself commands us to take effective precautions against the unwitting violation of its laws. Thus we find:

> *And concerning all that I have told you, you shall take measures to guard yourselves...*
>
> (Exodus 23:13)

and again:

> *And you shall safeguard that which I have given into your charge.* (Leviticus 18:30)

Referring to enactments made by the Sages in pursuance of this Divine command, the Torah says:

> ...*and you shall carefully carry out all that they teach you....* (Deuteronomy 17:10)

> *You shall not turn aside from the word that they declare unto you, to the right hand, nor to the left.* (Deuteronomy 17:11)

These *gezeroth* are thus as binding upon every Jew as the Torah itself. Moreover, since in every case the reason for the decree lies in the frailty and forgetfulness of human nature, they must remain binding for as long as human nature remains unchanged.

Our Sages have restrained us in this way from doing on Sabbath many acts which, although not themselves *melakhoth*, could very easily lead to our doing *melakhoth*. This may be for one of two reasons:

(1) They outwardly resemble *melakhoth*, and so can easily be confused with them; or

(2) Although they do not resemble any *melakhah*, they are linked with *melakhoth* by habit in everyday life or easily lead to a *melakhah* in practice.[10]

Tearing up a piece of paper is an example of the first kind. It is not a *melakhah* — the constructive *melakhah*-character is lacking — but it bears enough outward resemblance to one (viz. cutting material to a required shape) for it to be prohibited as a precautionary measure. Our Sages, with their deep insight into the ways of the human mind, saw clearly that if we were allowed to do the one, we would the more eas-

---

10. Maimonides, Laws of Sabbath 21:1.

ily be led into doing the other — the real *melakhah* — when the occasion arose.

Agreeing to buy an article is an example of the second kind. This is a situation habitually linked with a *melakhah* (viz. writing down a note of the agreement); it is therefore forbidden to enter into such an agreement, even verbally, on the Sabbath.

Another example of the second type would be climbing a tree. It may easily lead to unintentionally breaking off a twig or tearing a leaf, either of which is, of course, an actual *melakhah*.

Touchstone

It has been proved countless times that if all these safeguards are conscientiously observed in practice as an integral part of the Sabbath law, the probability of actual desecration of the Sabbath is greatly lessened.

One's attitude to this safeguarding legislation is the touchstone of one's attitude to the entire institution of Sabbath — indeed to the Divine Torah as a whole. The Jew who decides to take a *gezerah* lightly has already decided in his heart to treat lightly the Torah itself. He has forfeited the right to call himself an observant Jew.

It should be noted however that the Sages, in their great practical wisdom, restricted this type of legislation to the minimum necessary to avoid transgression of the actual Torah-laws. It is a halakhic rule that "a protective measure is never enacted to safeguard another protective measure" (*Bava Metzia* 5b).

This reflects the realistic standpoint of the Torah itself, which, while insisting on the high standard demanded of the servant of God, nevertheless gives full weight to the practical necessities of everyday life.

THE FIVE-MINUTE NIGHT

The Steipler Gaon, Rabbi Yaakov Yisrael Kanievsky, zt"l, was one of the leaders of Torah Jewry during the latter half of the twentieth century. In his youth he was drafted into the Russian army. The coarse talk and vulgar behavior of the Russian soldiers were an anathema to the refined, delicate nature of this young yeshiva student. So as to avoid their company, he applied for a regular position on the night watch, preferring to endure the long, freezing nights at sub-zero temperatures. The soldier who stood out on the watch received a thick fur coat and hat to protect him from the biting Russian winter frost.

One Friday evening, when Rabbi Kanievsky arrived at the watch point to relieve the soldier who had had the afternoon watch, the latter pointed to a nearby tree on which he had hung the coat and hat. Apparently, it had been warm enough that afternoon that he had not needed to wear the heavy coat.

The sun had set and the Sabbath had begun. Placing things onto or removing them from a tree is forbidden by a rabbinical decree. However, before Rabbi Kanievsky could ask the soldier to remove the items from the tree, he had left the area.

The Steipler Gaon was left with a dilemma: On the one hand, he of course didn't want to transgress even a rabbinical decree. On the other hand, he knew that very soon the frosty Russian night would descend and the temperature would drop below zero. Standing outside the entire night in the freezing cold without a coat or a hat was a potentially life-threatening situation that would require transgressing

*the Sabbath even if this involved transgressing a Torah pro-
hibition.*

*In his later years, the Steipler would tell the story of how
he spent that freezing night. His first thought was that at
the present his health was not yet in such danger that
would warrant desecrating the Sabbath. As the cold increased he said to himself, "I am sure I can last another
five minutes without the coat and hat without endangering
my life." And after those five minutes had passed, he reck-
oned that he could push himself for another five minutes,
and so on.... In this manner, he managed to stand through
the entire night without transgressing even a rabbinical
decree!*

2. PRACTICAL SURVEY OF THE MELAKHAH CATEGORIES

It must be emphasized that the notes which follow are
intended only to give a general idea of the scope of
this legislation, and of its systematic nature. They are
by no means intended to be exhaustive. For the detailed knowledge essential to proper Sabbath observance there is only one course — *tzei u-lemad*: Go
and learn! The laws must be studied under the guidance of a competent *talmid chakham* (Torah scholar).
If possible they should be learned at the source —
Tractate *Shabbath* in the Talmud, and in the *Shulchan
Arukh*, the standard compilation of the *halakhah* (Part
I: *Orach Chayyim*, sections 242–416).

[In recent years a number of books have been
written in English that discuss in detail the practical
applications of keeping Sabbath in the context of
modern technological developments in the twentieth
century and beyond. Suggested English reading is

Shemirath Shabbath Kehilchathah, by Rav Yehoshua Y. Neuwirth (Jerusalem: Feldheim Publishers, 2002), *Shaarei Halachah*, by Rabbi Ze'ev Greenwald (Jerusalem: Feldheim Publishers, 2000), *The 39 Melochos*, by Rabbi Dovid Ribiat (Jerusalem: Feldheim Publishers, 1999), and *The 39 Avoth Melacha of Shabbath*, which includes lavish illustrations, by Rabbi Baruch Chait (Jerusalem: Feldheim Publishers, 1992).]

In the following brief survey, a description of the type of activity included in each class will be followed by some of the *melakhoth* frequently met with in practice, and some of the relevant *gezeroth*.

Category 1: *Plowing.*

The class bearing this name comprises every activity by which the soil is made receptive for seed or plant; also the removal from the soil of anything that might hinder plant growth.

MELAKHOTH include: digging arable land; fertilizing the soil; removing stones from the soil; leveling the ground.

GEZEROTH include: dragging a bench or other heavy item across the garden if it will definitely make a groove in the soil. This bears an outward resemblance to plowing.

This is the basic *melakhah* by which man prepares the earth to yield its produce. By desisting from it on Sabbath in all its forms, we acknowledge that "The earth is the Lord's, and the fullness thereof" (Psalms 24:1).

Category 2: *Sowing*.

This class comprises every activity by which the growth of plants is caused or promoted.

> MELAKHOTH include: placing seeds or fruit-pits in receptive soil (even in a flowerpot); pruning trees or bushes; watering the lawn, or plants or flowers; weeding.

> GEZEROTH include: renewing the water in a vase with cut flowers.

Category 3: *Reaping*.

This class comprises every activity by which any growing plant is severed from its place of growth.

> MELAKHOTH include: cutting or plucking flowers, grass, leaves, twigs, berries or fruits, from trees, bushes, etc., growing in the ground or in a flowerpot. This applies equally to mushrooms or other fungi, wherever they may be growing.

> GEZEROTH include: climbing a tree; leaning against a tree that moves under one's weight, or using it in any way; horse-back riding (because one might easily be led to break off a branch in passing, to use as a switch. These are *gezeroth* of the "habit" type — see page 43.).

Category 4: *Sheaf-making*.

This comprises every activity by which natural products are gathered together into a unit serving some useful purpose.

MELAKHOTH include: gathering fruit together into a pile in their place of growth in order to store or sell them.

GEZEROTH include: gathering up eggs in a chicken coop.

Category 5: *Threshing.*

This comprises every activity by which a natural product (solid or liquid) is separated from its husk, or other natural container, or from the organic whole of which it is a part.

MELAKHOTH include: shelling nuts, peas, etc., for some purpose other than immediate consumption; pressing out the juice of fruits grown primarily for their juice: for example, grapes, olives; milking.

GEZEROTH include: pressing out the juice of other fruits as a drink.

Categories 6–8: *Winnowing, Selecting, Sifting.*

These comprise activities by which a mixture is improved by removing its less desirable parts.

MELAKHOTH include: sifting flour; straining liquids; skimming the cream off milk (except for immediate consumption of the cream). In a heap containing both good and wormy fruit, to make the heap more suitable for consumption by removing the bad or even removing the desirable parts for later use, or by using a utensil, e.g. a colander, even for immediate use.

GEZEROTH include: separating the good from the bad even for immediate use, using a utensil not specifically designed for separating. One may remove the *desired* part, for *immediate* use, by *hand*, i.e. without using a utensil. Washing and peeling fruit and vegetables using a knife is similarly allowed for immediate consumption only.

NOTE: This *melakhah* is not confined to foodstuffs only, but can apply to the sorting of a mixture of jumbled collection of any articles; for example, removing the broken ones from a pile of chairs or sorting out a pile of silverware in order to return them to their respective places in the drawer.

These are essentially "sorting" *melakhoth* and represent a characteristic of human activity. By ceasing from them on the Sabbath in all their forms, we acknowledge the God-given nature of our human intellect. Great care should be taken when learning the details of this *halakhah*; it has not been possible to give more than a short outline in this brief summary.

Category 9: *Grinding.*

Every activity by which a natural product or other substance is divided (by means of an appropriate instrument) into small particles, in order to make better use of it.

MELAKHOTH include: milling or grinding corn, coffee or pepper, dicing fruits and vegetables (chopping them into pieces larger than usual is permitted for immediate use, filing metals; pounding or crushing substances in a mortar.

GEZEROTH include: grating vegetables, cheese, etc. by means of a grater; rubbing off clots of dried mud or clay from boots or clothes.

It is further forbidden (by a *gezerah* of Type [2] — the "habit" type): to take medicine, and to carry out any treatment, for the relief of discomfort or pain or slight ailments (since to do these things is habitually connected with the pounding of medicinal ingredients). This *gezerah* does not apply in cases of acute pain or actual illness. For further discussion of this question see section 4 of this chapter, page 72.

Category 10: *Kneading.*

Activities by which small particles of a substance are combined by means of a liquid to form a dough or paste.

Category 11: *Baking.*

Any activity which changes the state of a substance by means of heat, thereby improving it for consumption or use.

MELAKHOTH include: cooking in all its forms; heating water to over 104° Fahrenheit (40°C); adding ingredients to a boiling pot; stirring boiling food; pouring hot water onto tea-leaves; melting down any solid (fat, wax, metals, etc.).

GEZEROTH include: wrapping a pot in a blanket or towel to retain its heat (*hatmanah*); adding cold, non-pasteurized milk to hot tea, unless the latter is at two removes from the fire (that is, the hot liquid must first be poured into a "second vessel," for example, a tea-pot, and from this into the teacup, to which milk may then be added).

The prohibition of cooking does not mean that we may eat only cold food on the Sabbath. On the contrary, no Sabbath is considered complete without some hot food.

How is this result achieved? By setting up the "Sabbath-Stove":

This means that one arranges the stove before Sabbath in such a way that the actual burners are covered, so that it is unlikely that one would come to regulate the heat on Sabbath. (This is usually done by means of a sheet of metal placed on top of the cooker with the edges bent down to cover the controls.) Hot cooked food and an urn of hot water can then be placed on the stove before the commencement of Sabbath, with the heat adjusted to keep them hot during Sabbath until needed. (On Sabbath itself it is of course forbidden to adjust the flame.) One can also use an electric Sabbath hot-plate for this purpose.

Category 12: *Sheep-shearing.*

This comprises every activity which severs from the human or animal organism those parts which serve it as outer covering, such as hair or nails.

MELAKHOTH include: cutting off or otherwise removing (by the appropriate means) hair, nails, wool, or feathers from a living organism.

GEZEROTH include: pulling off nails, etc. by hand; combing the hair, (because this invariably severs hair). (It is, however, permitted to brush the hair with a soft brush, designated specifically for Sabbath use.)

Category 13: *Bleaching.*

This class includes all activities by which garments or cloth are freed from dirt, dust or stains, or by which a gloss is imparted to them.

MELAKHOTH include: soaking clothes; rubbing; wringing; ironing; removing stains or mud by water or otherwise.

GEZEROTH include: brushing clothes; handling wet washing (lest one come to wring it out); hanging washing out to dry (since it might appear as if it was laundered on Sabbath).

Category 14: *Combing raw materials.*

Activities whose effect is to turn compact or entangled raw materials into separate strands or fibers.

MELAKHOTH include: combing raw wool; beating flax stalks to make fibers.

GEZEROTH include: winding thread onto a bobbin or wool onto a card; disentangling woolen or other threads.

Category 15: *Dyeing*.

Any activity which changes the existing color (natural or artificial) of an object or substance.

MELAKHOTH include: applying paint or white-wash to wall surfaces, etc.; applying dyestuffs to clothes; dissolving colors in water; mixing or blending colors; making color reaction tests in medicine.

GEZEROTH include: adding coloring matter to food (unless done to improve the taste). The application of makeup, rouge, etc. is forbidden on Sabbath; cosmetics can, however, be obtained which last over the Sabbath.

Category 16: *Spinning*.

Extraction of thread from raw material by drawing out, twisting or turning.

MELAKHOTH include: manufacture of plush and felt, and rope making.

Categories 17–19: *Weaving operations*.

These three categories comprise the whole range of the weaving technique, from the insertion of thread into the loom to the removal of the finished article, as well as everything similar in effect.

MELAKHOTH include: knitting; crocheting; darning; embroidering; plaiting; basketwork.

GEZEROTH include: plaiting hair on a wig.[11]

Category 20: *Separating into threads.*

The separation of woven or other material into its constituent threads.

MELAKHOTH include: unraveling any part of a knitted garment, tearing off a piece of cotton wool.

GEZEROTH include: Separating a twisted thread into strands.

Category 21: *Tying a knot.*

Any activity which effects a lasting connection between two objects. See Category 22.

Category 22: *Untying a knot.*

Undoing such a combination for some useful purpose.

MELAKHOTH under the above two categories include: tying and untying a double knot between two ends of string, thread, laces, etc.; tying together two ends of a string or rope, or even tying a single knot at the end of a string, for example knotting the end of a sewing thread.

GEZEROTH include: tying any type of knot even if it will not last. It is, however, permissible to tie and untie a bow that one plans to untie within twenty-four hours, since this is considered

11. Plaiting human hair that is still attached to the head is also forbidden for another reason (cf. *Shabbath* 95a).

merely as a temporary connection. For the same reason it is permissible to break or cut the string around food containers if it cannot be slipped off, when the container's contents are required for immediate consumption. (For details of how to deal with various types of containers on Shabbos, see *Shemirath Shabbath Kehilchathah*, Chapter 9.) One should refrain from tying or untying a wire "twistee"; it should be cut or slipped off.

Category 23: *Sewing*.

Any activity by which two materials (similar or dissimilar), or two surfaces, are permanently joined together by means of a third substance. See category 24.

Category 24: *Tearing*.

Undoing a combination of the sort referred to in Category 23 to facilitate re-joining.

> MELAKHOTH under the above two categories include: sewing or undoing two stitches; sticking papers together with paste; stapling papers.

> GEZEROTH include: tearing toilet paper (cut paper should be prepared before Sabbath). Fastening two pieces of fabric together by a safety pin is permitted, since this is only a temporary fastening.

Category 25: *Trapping*.

This class comprises every activity which so restricts

the freedom of movement of an animal, bird, etc., that it comes under the control of a human being.

MELAKHOTH include: fishing, catching or trapping animals or insects by hand or in nets, traps, etc. (This does not, however, apply to domestic animals, unless control over them has been lost.)

GEZEROTH include: closing a window to prevent the escape of a bird or butterfly which happened to fly in.

Category 26: *Slaughtering*.

Any activity which terminates the life of any living thing, or causes loss of blood.

MELAKHOTH include: killing by any means (this applies equally to animal, bird, fish or insect); drawing blood for a positive purpose (for example, for a blood test, except in case of serious illness. See "Illness on the Sabbath," p. 72).

Category 27: *Skinning* or *flaying*.

Separating the skin of a dead animal from its flesh as a process of manufacture.

Category 28: *Tanning*.

Activities by which raw materials are made more durable or otherwise more valuable for human use, by chemical or physical processing.

MELAKHOTH include: all of the stages of the tanning process.

GEZEROTH include: polishing boots or shoes
with shoe polish; salting and pickling fish, meat,
etc.

Category 29: *Scraping.*

This includes every activity which removes roughness
from the surface of a material by means of grinding,
rubbing, polishing or otherwise.

MELAKHOTH include: cleaning silver or copper
utensils with scouring powder or by machine;
smoothening the surface of any substance; rubbing soap to make lather; application of oint-
ment, face cream, etc.; brushing boots or shoes;
playing with Playdough or clay, plaster, etc. (because it also involves smoothing).

Category 30: *Marking out.*

This comprises the activities of marking or scoring
lines on a surface, in preparation for cutting, or for
writing, or for any other useful purpose.

Category 31: *Cutting to shape.*

This comprises every activity by which the size or
shape of an object is altered to one more suitable for
human use, as a process of manufacture.

MELAKHOTH include: cutting or tearing any material to a definite shape or pattern; cutting out a
newspaper paragraph. (Cutting up foodstuffs for
immediate consumption is, however, permitted

[see above, Category 9, *Grinding*]. Similarly, tearing the string or paper wrapping of a food package in order to use its contents is permitted. See above, Categories 21 and 22.)

Category 32: *Writing*.

Comprises every activity by which significant signs are made in a durable manner on durable material.

MELAKHOTH include: writing, drawing, painting, etc., by pencil, ink or other writing materials; embroidering patterns, letters or figures; making impressions on wax; typewriting; printing.

GEZEROTH include: making signs of a non-durable nature, e.g. drawing with the finger on a moist window-pane or tracing patterns in the sand; doing anything that is usually accompanied by writing, note-taking, etc., e.g. buying or selling or agreeing to buy or sell; measuring and weighing; reading business correspondence; judicial acts; marriage, divorce; playing games for money (or promises of money!); betting.

Category 33: *Erasing*.

Activities whose effect is the production of a clean surface for writing.

MELAKHOTH include: any obliteration of writing whereby space is gained for new writing.

GEZEROTH include: erasing letters or symbols of a non-durable nature; tearing through the words or pictures on a food wrapper (unless the contents are urgently required).

Category 34: *Building*.

This category comprises a wide range of activities connected with the concepts of structure and form; namely, all those which have as their purpose and effect:

▶ Constructing, repairing, improving or making habitable or usable any structure or part of a structure;

▶ Permanently joining together two or more things so as to make of them a usable whole, and

▶ Permanently changing the configuration of any mass or substance for a useful purpose.

MELAKHOTH include:

▶ The whole range of building operations; leveling or smoothing roughness or unevenness in wall or floor; knocking a nail into a wall; hanging a door; inserting a window frame or window pane; erecting a tent.

▶ Fixing together the haft and blade of an axe, or broom-handle and broom-end.

▶ Digging a hole in the ground for storage; pressing substances into a mold, e.g. cheese-making; clay modeling.

GEZEROTH include: opening or closing a cover or awning (unless it was opened at least 9 cm. (3.5 in.) before Sabbath entered); attaching a hood to a baby stroller. One should not use an umbrella on Sabbath.

At first sight it may be difficult for us to see how, for example, opening an umbrella is similar to the *melakhah* as described. A little reflection, however, will reveal to us something of the depths of our Sages' formulation of *gezeroth*. In fact, in this example, besides the similarity in the activity (erection), there is also a similarity in the resulting structures (the umbrella open; the tent erect), and, further, an essential similarity of purpose (protection from the elements). We see how the Sages penetrated beyond ordinary appearances to the essentials beneath.

Category 35: *Demolishing.*

Preparation of space for building operations by demolishing an existing building, or by undoing any of the operations comprised in the preceding category.

Category 36: *Kindling a fire.*

Any activity which initiates or prolongs combustion (or similar light- and heat-producing processes).

> MELAKHOTH include: fire production by any means, including lighting one flame from another; poking the fire or otherwise increasing the flow of oxygen thereto; regulating a flame by turning it up or down; smoking a cigarette; producing an electric spark; starting or driving a car; using the telephone; switching on an electric light or any electrical apparatus.

> GEZEROTH include: reading alone by lamplight, as one is liable to adjust the lamp. (Reading by candlelight is permitted.) Opening a door or window opposite an oil lamp or candles, and traveling in a bus or car, even if driven by a

non-Jew, are also forbidden (see section 3 of this chapter: "Work by a Non-Jew," page 71). With reference to long-distance sea or train journeys, see Chapter 4, section 10: "Travel on the Sabbath" (page 92).

It is hoped that by now enough will have been said to leave no room for the foolish argument, so often heard in conversation about this *melakhah*, to the effect that "this was all very well in the olden days, when kindling a fire meant hard work — knocking heavy stones together and so on; but it cannot be meant to apply at the present day." This is so obviously based on ignorance of the Sabbath idea that it hardly needs refuting. (Incidentally, the use of this argument reveals the user to be as ignorant of the history of civilization as of the basic principles of the Sabbath. The method of kindling fire in use in Egypt at the time of the Exodus was based on the principle of the tinder-box and involved hardly more effort than striking a match.[12]) In reality, of course, this — and particularly in its modern forms — is one of the most fundamental and characteristic of all *melakhoth*, since it is the key to man's control of nature. It is fitting that many of the modern trappings of civilization, such as electric light, telephone, radio, etc., involving the closing of an electric circuit, should fall under this heading. By keeping us from this type of activity on Sabbath, the Torah wishes to dig out from us the very roots of *melakhah*.

---

12. Sir E.A. Wallis Budge, *The Dwellers on the Nile* (1926), p. 63.

Category 37: *Extinguishing a fire.*

Any activity which terminates, shortens or slows down any of the above-named processes in order to use the extinguished material.

> MELAKHOTH include: putting out a candle to improve the wick.

> GEZEROTH include: extinguishing in any way for any purpose, e.g. turning out gas, switching off electric light. (This *gezerah* does not, of course, apply where the spread of fire might cause danger to life.)

Category 38: *The final hammer-blow.*

This is a general category, comprising all activities which put the finishing touches to any manufactured article, according to the nature of the article and the usages of the trade concerned; also those which repair or improve any article.

> MELAKHOTH include: imparting a glossy finish to an article; removing hanging threads from a new suit; sharpening knives or scissors; repairing a clock or any machine or instrument.

> GEZEROTH include: winding up or setting the hands of a watch or clock. Specialized activities requiring the use of complex or delicate instruments are in general forbidden, owing to the danger of inadvertently adjusting or repairing the instrument. For this reason it is forbidden to produce any musical sound on an instrument, or indeed to make any sound with an instru-

ment designed for the purpose. Rowing and cycling are also forbidden under this heading (see also Chapter 4, section 9: "'Sabbath' and 'Weekday' Activities," page 86).

Category 39: *Carrying.*[13]

This category comprises:

▶ removing an object, for any purpose, from an enclosed "private domain" (*reshuth ha-yachid*) to a "public domain" (*reshuth ha-rabbim*) or vice versa; and

▶ moving any object a distance of four cubits (approximately 7 ft.) in a "public domain."

Whether a "domain" is termed "public" or "private" in this connection is not at all a question of ownership.

Private domain means, for this purpose, any enclosed space not less than four handbreadths (approximately 14 in.) square, bounded by walls not less than ten handbreadths (approximately 3 ft.) high. The usual form of this "domain" is a house, garden, etc. The term also includes a depression or elevation of not less than the above dimensions in a public space; for example, a pit or a block of stone. A movable object of this size, for example, a box or a car, also constitutes a "private domain," if situated in a public space. The Oral Law contains a number of halakhic definitions of what constitutes an enclosure. For example, the "outline of a door" (*tzurath ha-pethach*), i.e. two poles joined at the top by a third pole or even by a

13. See "The City Eruv," p. 66.

string or wire is in certain circumstances considered a complete wall.

Public domain means a street, road or square, frequented by the public, unroofed, open at both ends, and having a width of not less than sixteen cubits (approximately 28 ft.) and frequented by 600,000 people daily (as was the encampment of the Jews during their sojourn in the desert).

> MELAKHOTH under this heading include: carrying by hand, over the arm, over the shoulder, in the pockets, in a bag or case; throwing, pushing, pulling (in a container, on wheels, or otherwise), and removing objects from one "domain" to the other, or four cubits (approximately 7 ft.) from point to point within the "public domain." There is no *melakhah* in carrying any object within the boundaries of a "private domain." If, however, the "private domain" exceeds a certain size, and in certain cases when it is in the occupation of two or more families, this is forbidden by the Sages as a *gezerah* (see *Eruv Chatzeroth*, below, and *Carmelith* [page 69]).

> *Eruv Chatzeroth* (literally, "mixing" or "pooling of rights" in relation to occupied premises). If two or more Jewish families live in adjoining houses having direct communication with one another, or in separate dwellings in the same house, they are not allowed to carry from one dwelling to the other, nor in the parts used by all the tenants in common, unless an *eruv* has been made. This means that the various Jewish

families combine, and pool their rights of possession, so that their dwellings are the joint property of them all, in which case the *gezerah* no longer applies. The symbol of this joint possession is the *eruv* — as a rule a loaf of bread or a box of matzoth deposited as their joint property in the custody of one of them. If there are also non-Jewish families in the building, one must first hire from them the right of way for the Sabbath. The same laws apply to an enclosed square, a cul-de-sac, or garden used by several householders in common.

The City Eruv

Nowadays, all towns in Israel and many Jewish neighborhoods in the Diaspora use an expanded application of this concept of *eruv chatzeroth* to permit carrying items from the house to the street and through the streets.

This idea most likely originated during the times when most towns were enclosed by a protective wall. This meant that technically the entire town was considered one large private domain, all the more so when the gates were closed at night.

We mentioned above the concept of a halakhic "wall," e.g. the *tzurath ha-pethach*, which can serve to enclose an area instead of an actual wall. As a result, even after Jews moved into non-walled cities they could surround their neighborhood, or even the entire city, with a series of such symbolic "walls," thereby transforming the entire area into one huge "courtyard." All they needed to do then was to pool their rights of possession as described above by designating a loaf of bread or a box of matzoth to be owned by all the Jewish members of the town, thereby uniting them all as one large "family." The custom is to leave this *eruv* in a prominent place in the central synagogue as a reminder to all that it is by the means of this combined property that they are allowed to carry in the streets.

This is the concept of the "city *eruv*" that exists in all towns and in many settlements in Israel. Obviously, the *eruv* must be under constant supervision to ensure that the poles, etc., are in place in accordance with the requirements of the *halakhah* — in particular, after stormy weather. One can say that this constant concern that the *eruv* is in order serves the same purpose of imprinting the seal of God's sovereignty on our social lives, which is the essence of the *melakhah* of carrying, as explained above on page 35.

If someone lives in a place where there is no *eruv* or the *eruv* is found to be damaged, he must abide by all the restrictions on carrying that are included in this *melakhah*.

As we have seen above (page 38), this is the characteristic activity of man in society, and by ceasing from it on the Sabbath we acknowledge God's sovereignty over the world of social relations. The circulation of material goods, whether for commercial, personal or social ends, is the life-blood of the community; and it is this which must be dedicated in its entirety to God on the Sabbath.

The *melakhah*-character of the activity appears only when the article is transported by the method normally employed to move such things from place to place during the week; i.e. by hand, in the pocket, in a case or in some similar manner. If the article is worn as part of one's personal attire, however, it is no longer an "object" which is being transported in the above sense. It belongs rather to the "person" of the wearer. Thus, carrying an overcoat over one's arm is a *melakhah*, but wearing one is not. Anything which is capable of being worn is — if worn — not within the compass of this *melakhah*. Thus a handkerchief may be worn as a scarf, or two tied together may be worn as a belt. It is also quite permissible to wear two overcoats one on top of the other, if required for any reason.[14] In none of these cases is there anything in the nature of a *melakhah*. On the other hand, to qualify, the clothing must be worn in the proper way. (Such so-called "subterfuges" have often been the object of mockery on the part of those who have no conception of the depth of these laws.)

> GEZEROTH include: wearing in the street such articles or ornaments which one might easily take off and so might inadvertently carry; for example, eyeglasses not permanently required.
>
> A child may not be carried in the street on Sabbath; it is therefore advisable not to take little children too far from home. Children may also not be taken out in a stroller or carriage. In case of need, however, this may be done by a non-Jew.

In addition, several regulations have been made by our Sages in connection with this *melakhah*, some

---

14. *Shulchan Arukh, Orach Chayyim*, section 301:36.

of which may be conveniently summarized under the following headings:

Carmelith (literally, "unfrequented place"[15]). This is the name given by our Sages to certain types of places which, while not having the special characteristics described above, are nevertheless liable to be confused with the "domains" of the Torah.

These include:

▸ A street less than 28 feet wide, or lacking any of the other characteristics of a "public domain" — for example, a cul-de-sac. It follows that most streets, except for major thoroughfares in the largest cities, that are not used by 600,000 people daily, fall under this category, i.e. a "public domain" only by rabbinical decree.

▸ An enclosed space more than 50 yards square, which is not the area attached to a house; for example, a park.

▸ Open country

▸ Seas, rivers and shores

It is forbidden as a *gezerah* to carry from a *carmelith* to either a public or private domain and from either of these to a *carmelith*, and to carry a distance of 7 feet within a *carmelith*.

Mekom Petur (literally, "free place"). This is the name given to places which have the characteristics neither of the "domains" of the Torah nor

---

15. Rashi, *Shabbath* 3b.

of the *carmelith*, and concerning which no *gezerah* was made; for example, an enclosed space less than 14 inches square in a public domain, enclosed by walls at least three handbreadths (11 in.) high, or an area of these dimensions above or lower than the street.

We have already noted the deplorable ignorance and neglect among large sections of the Jewish public of these laws against carrying on Sabbath. Yet, as we have seen, they are of fundamental importance in the Sabbath scheme. Our Sages have decreed that the mitzvoth of *shofar* and *lulav* shall not be observed if the occasion for performing them falls on Sabbath. The only reason for this decree is: lest an over-enthusiastic Jew might forget it was Sabbath and inadvertently carry the *shofar* or the *lulav* in the street. Our great teachers considered the mere possibility of a desecration of the Sabbath by carrying to be of such consequence that they decreed the omission of these two important mitzvoth of the Torah rather than take that risk. Anyone who, for reasons of personal convenience, is inclined to treat the *melakhah* of "carrying" lightly is thus making a very grave mistake.

It is hoped that this survey of the *melakhah* categories has given the reader some little insight into the practical aspect of true Sabbath observance. With a little thought, it will be seen how each productive purpose, each individual *melakhah* which we have discussed, is a practical application of the fundamental Sabbath-concept developed at length in Chapter 2. It will be seen, too, how each *gezerah* is an expression of true Jewish *yir'ath Shamayim* — of reverence for God and His commandments — and of the determination of the Jewish people not to let momentary weakness or forgetfulness rob them of their unique act of homage and service — cessation from *melakhah* on Sabbath.

3. WORK BY A NON-JEW

See: God has given you *the Sabbath...*
(Exodus 16:29)

It is thus the Jew who was blessed with — and who bears the responsibility of — the Sabbath. Nevertheless, in order to safeguard our observance of the Sabbath, our Sages have decreed that we may not ask a non-Jew to do for us on Sabbath anything that we are not permitted to do ourselves. We are not allowed to benefit from a *melakhah* done for us by a non-Jew, even unasked.

Since the Sages enacted this measure as an additional protection for the Sabbath, they were able to make certain exceptions; for example:

▶ in case of illness (see below, section 4) or other emergency;
▶ lighting a fire in cold weather;
▶ to relieve an animal in pain;
▶ where the act is done for both non-Jews and Jews, and the former are in the majority.

It is further forbidden to engage a non-Jew before Sabbath to carry out work on Sabbath, except under the following conditions:

(1) The non-Jew must work as an independent contractor, for a fixed sum for the job;

(2) The work may not be done on the premises of

the Jew;

(3) The non-Jew must not be bound to carry out the work on Sabbath.

4. ILLNESS ON THE SABBATH

Minor Ailments: A normally healthy person is not allowed to take medicine or receive medical attention, even from a non-Jew, in cases of slight indisposition or localized pain, such as heartburn, headache, toothache, constipation, etc. (This *gezerah* has already been referred to above under Category 9, pages 50-51.)

Illness (not involving danger to life): Where, however, the person has to go to bed, or the pain is so severe that the whole body is affected, or the temperature is above normal, the above *gezerah* does not apply. In such cases everything that is necessary for the patient may be done by a non-Jew, medicines may be taken and treatment received. If no non-Jew is available, a Jew may do things otherwise forbidden as *gezeroth*, but these should be done a little differently from usual, in order to keep in mind the exceptional circumstances.

It is permitted to take the patient's temperature with a mercury thermometer.

Serious Illness: Where there is any suspicion that the person's life may be in danger, it is not only allowed, but a duty for every Jew himself to do whatever may be necessary to save the patient's life. "Desecrate one Sabbath, so that he may live to fulfill many Sabbaths" (*Yoma* 86a). The potential glorification of God's name which is inherent in every Jewish life outweighs the momentary desecration which saving that life may entail.

Further information on this subject is given in a booklet published by the Gateshead Jewish Religious Publications Committee, entitled *Care of Children on the Sabbath* (Chapter 6), as well as in the books mentioned on page 47.

5. RESTING THE ANIMALS

In the Ten Commandments and elsewhere the Torah commands us to let our animals rest on Sabbath.

This means that we may not allow any animal of ours to do any *melakhah*, nor may we place any burden on it, apart from bridle and reins and anything needed for its protection.

To induce an animal to do a *melakhah* by leading it, driving it or calling it to a desired place (except for its own benefit) is forbidden, even when the animal is not our own (*mechamer*).

If, however, the animal wishes to do a *melakhah* for its own satisfaction, for example, to crop grass, we are of course not to prevent it; the Torah says, "so that your ox and your donkey may rest..." and depriving it of its satisfaction can hardly be called "rest" (*Mekhilta*, Exodus 23:12).

It is interesting to note here the essential difference between the prohibition of *melakhah* as applied to man and as applied to animals. For man, *issur melakhah* (prohibition of work) has the positive significance we have seen above; the prohibition flows from a higher concept than that of physical rest. In the case of the animal this is not so. The superficial argument against true Sabbath observance ("...after all, the Torah only wants me to enjoy myself, and if my enjoyment is a cigarette...?") can now be seen for exactly what it is worth. It expresses a desire to exchange the Sabbath of man for the Sabbath of the animal.

THE SABBATH-OBSERVANT COW

There was once a Jew who possessed a cow that was very efficient at plowing fields. Being in need of money, he offered it for sale. A non-Jew came to check the cow and, finding it fit for his needs, he agreed to buy it.

During the first week, the cow worked very diligently and the new owner was extremely pleased with his new acquisition. However, when he tried to take the cow out to work on Saturday, she absolutely refused to budge. All his cajoling and hitting were of no avail. The cow just would not move.

Rather disappointed, he returned to the Jew and told him that if the cow was beset by such bouts of crazy behavior, the sale was invalid.

The Jew immediately grasped what was going on and asked to be taken to see the cow. He bent down and whispered into its ear, "Until now you were in my possession and you rested on the Sabbath as commanded by our Torah. Now that you have been transferred to a non-Jewish owner, you must work on Sabbath!" The cow immediately got up and went out to work as usual.

At first the non-Jew suspected that there was some magic at play. But the Jew explained to him that the cow's strange behavior was a result of the Torah lifestyle she had grown accustomed to.

The non-Jew was very impressed by what he had heard

and began to inquire into the nature of the Jewish Sabbath that even affected animals. Eventually, he became a proselyte and later a rabbi, and was known as "Rabbi Yochanan the son of a cow"! According to some opinions, he was one of the rabbis of the Mishnah and a colleague of the famous Rabbi Akiva.[16]

16. *Pesikta Rabbathi, Parashath Parah*, Chapter 2.

Chapter Four
The Celebration of Sabbath

1. THE SPIRIT OF MENUCHAH

All the week we have worked. All the week we have lived in the illusion that power over the world is in our own hands. This has been a veil hiding from our eyes the truth that God is the source of all power.

On Sabbath we have ceased from work. We have given up all *melakhah*, down to the last detail. As a result, the veil has been lifted. Now we can glimpse in all its glory that truth which lies behind our purpose in the world.

This is a moment which must fill us with wonder and joy. It must awaken our hearts towards that spiritual contentment which is the secret of Sabbath rest.

This is *menuchah* — the blessing of Sabbath experienced to the full, in the ways the Torah has shown us.

2. WELCOMING THE SABBATH

The deep insight of the Torah into the human soul, and the genius of the Jewish people, have combined to ensure that this joy shall overflow into and transform our material surroundings. Sabbath, itself a great spiritual experience, is to be welcomed with wine and song and festive meal.

Throughout the thousands of years of its history Sabbath has always been a day of joy and gladness in the Jewish home. Its coming is an eagerly awaited event for which the family begins preparing days in advance. In fact, Sabbath casts its radiant glow over the whole week. The days themselves are named in Hebrew in relation to the Sabbath: "the first day to Sabbath," "the second day to Sabbath," etc. This is how the week looks to Jewish eyes:

SABBATH

Friday

Thursday

Wednesday

Tuesday

Monday

Sunday

Everything looks forward to Sabbath. Business and social arrangements are made in such a way that they will not interfere with the Sabbath. Little luxuries bought during the week are stored up for the Sabbath. When Friday comes the tempo increases. Every member of the household plays his and her part in the preparations. Above all, of course, it is the Jewish housewife who now comes into her own. It is her proud duty to ensure that the royal guest is received in a worthy manner. She must see that all the Sabbath food is prepared and cooked before Sabbath comes in, the "Sabbath-stove" is on, the table decked with fresh linen and sparkling silver, with wine and challah and the Sabbath lights. The whole family changes into their Sabbath clothes and a festive air overhangs the house. The scene is set for Sabbath, the royal bride, to enter.

3. SABBATH CANDLES

One of the most familiar symbols of the Jewish Sabbath is the Sabbath candles. It should be noted that this is not merely a folk custom. Lighting the candles is another one of the institutions of the Sages to ensure that every Jewish home is well-lit on Sabbath eve.

One might be tempted to argue that in today's modern world where electric lighting transforms night into day, lighting the candles is no longer of any significance. However, when we examine the reasons the Sages gave for this institution, we will find that it has not lost its relevance.

The first reason given is "the peace of the home." Groping around in a dark house causes frustration and irritability that will mar the relaxed, peaceful atmosphere of Sabbath. Another reason given is *Oneg Shabbath* — "the Enjoyment of Sabbath." A meal eaten at a well-lit table is far more enjoyable than one eaten in the dark.[17] These reasons no longer apply.

But the third reason is "the Honor of Sabbath." It is customary to light candles in honor of a distinguished guest. True, our electric lighting systems ensure that we no longer have to grope in the dark; nevertheless, it is still accepted practice to add flavor and dignity to

---

17. "Abaye said: 'If you have a meal, eat it by day'" (*Yoma* 74b).

festive occasions by lighting candles. This then is the function and significance of the Sabbath candles in our modern world and, as such, they should be lit on or close to the table where the family will eat their Sabbath meal.

[It is worth noting that many a family can attest to the fact that remaining faithful to this instruction of the Sages has saved them from sitting in the dark in the event of a power failure!]

Although technically this mitzvah is equally incumbent on men and women, it has become customary for lighting the candles to be the privilege of the lady of the house. This can be seen to be a token of appreciation of the efforts she expends in creating the unique Sabbath atmosphere that pervades the home.

SAVED BY THE CANDLES

Jeffrey was a graduate student at Tel Aviv University. He would occasionally meet a young rabbi from the nearby religious town of Bnei Brak and discuss topics in Judaism, such as the purpose of life, the role of a Jew, the wisdom of the Torah, etc. Every now and then the rabbi would invite him to his home for a Sabbath meal. But Jeffrey refused; he was hesitant to "cross the border" into the distant world of Torah-observant Jews.

As time went on, Jeffrey's inhibitions waned and he finally accepted an invitation for a Sabbath dinner. When he and his host returned from the Friday night service at the synagogue, his host opened the door... and found the house shrouded in darkness. Apparently, an electrical fault had flipped the automatic cutoff switch, leaving the Sabbath candles casting their warm glow in the dining room as the only light in the house.

Jeffrey's host was rather concerned over the negative impression this first encounter with Sabbath would have on his guest. After a few words of apology about the mishap and explaining that it couldn't be fixed on Sabbath, he began reciting the Kiddush by the dim light of the Sabbath candles. The meal continued in its usual festive manner, accompanied by the Sabbath songs sung by all the children in unison and the excellent culinary efforts of the hostess. Various topics of the Torah portion to be read the next morning were discussed by the rabbi, with the children piping up with ideas that they had learned in school.

After the meal was over, the children were sent off to bed. But Jeffrey and his host continued their discussion until well past midnight.

Jeffrey eventually got up to leave and thanked his host profusely for the unique evening — the likes of which he had never experienced before. He added that one thing had impressed him most of all. "We live in the technological age. We are constantly connected to and dependent on the inventions of the twentieth century. I saw in your home that one can enjoy a life full of meaning and pleasantness without having to rely on all these modernizations. As we sat by the ancient Sabbath lights, I felt I was in a different world, a world of true, unfettered freedom. I doubt whether a thousand hours of talking about the Sabbath could have given me such an appreciation of the profound impact of Sabbath as this one meal did."

4. ENTRY OF THE SABBATH

Sabbath commences on Friday, eighteen minutes before sunset (some communities start earlier), and lasts until nightfall on Saturday (in Israel until about half an hour after sunset; in other countries up to an hour or more after sunset depending on latitude and time of year). The housewife has to kindle the Sabbath lights before the Sabbath comes in. As soon as she has said the blessing over the lights (*le'hadlik ner shel Shabbath*), Sabbath commences for her even if the official time has not yet arrived, and she may no longer do any *melakhah*.

For the other members of the family Sabbath commences at the official time, or at the moment Psalm 92 ("A Song for the Sabbath Day") is recited in the synagogue (whichever is the earlier).

5. Sanctification (Kiddush)

We are bidden to "remember the Sabbath day." This means that each Sabbath we are to utter words which will serve to impress on our minds the holiness of the day. This is the Kiddush or "sanctification."

Although Kiddush is often made in the synagogue, it is everyone's duty to make Kiddush at home, before the Sabbath meal, over a full glass of wine or grape juice. In the absence of wine or grape juice, Kiddush may be said over the two challoth (Sabbath loaves) or any bread. It is forbidden to eat on Sabbath before Kiddush is made. The Kiddush must be followed by a meal (or at least some baked goods) eaten in the same room.

In the morning, before the first meal, another Kiddush is made. If possible, this should also be made over wine or grape juice, but other alcoholic liquor may be used (but not challoth).

6. THE DOUBLE LOAVES

At the onset of each of the Sabbath meals we place two whole loaves of bread or challah on the table. One of them, at least, is used for the meal. These loaves are called *lechem mishneh* — "the double loaves." The two loaves come to remind us of the double portion of Manna the Jews received during the forty years they spent in the desert before entering the Land of Israel. Every day, except for Sabbath, one portion of Manna came down from Heaven for the sustenance of each household member. On Friday a double portion came down for Friday and Sabbath (cf. Exodus 16:22). The double loaves on the Sabbath table remind us that our sustenance is a gift from Heaven and keeping Sabbath ensures us a double portion of blessing.

7. SABBATH JOY

Three festive meals (*shalosh seudoth*) are to be enjoyed on the Sabbath: one in the evening and two during the day. These are accompanied by table-hymns (*zemiroth*) extolling the greatness of the day and the glory of God. It is a happy experience to see how the children revel in the lively tunes of these *zemiroth* and in the other eagerly awaited features of the traditional Sabbath meal.

All these things contribute to "the feeling of happiness and joy which the Jew experiences, after having worked diligently and uprightly all the week, when surrounded by wife and children, he lifts up the cup to God to greet the Sabbath. No lip has been able to utter nor pen to describe such happiness; it is the ineffable reward, the foretaste of the World to Come, that remains forever a secret between God and the feeling Jewish heart" (Samson Raphael Hirsch).

"YOSEF WHO HONORS SABBATH"

The Talmud tells about a certain Jew who was known by the title "Yosef who honors Sabbath." He would never skimp on his Sabbath expenses and would always buy the most special and tasty foods to enhance his Sabbath meals.

His neighbor was a wealthy non-Jew, the richest man in the town. One day he was accosted by a soothsayer who told him that the stars had foretold that all his wealth would be transferred to the ownership of his Jewish neighbor, "Yosef who honors Sabbath." The non-Jew was very upset by this prediction. He therefore decided to move to a far-off country in order to prevent it from becoming true.

He sold all his extensive property and invested the entire proceeds in a large-size diamond. He had the diamond sewn into the large turban he wore, and he thus set off for his new destination overseas. As he was sitting on the deck of the ship, seeing his home country recede into the distance, a strong gust of wind caught his turban and cast it into the sea. Amidst his horror at seeing all his wealth swallowed up by the waves, he comforted himself with the thought that at least he could be sure that the Jew would no longer be able to get it!

That Friday the local fishermen caught a very large fish. By the time they brought it to the market, it was already late on Friday afternoon. They said to themselves, "Who is going to want to buy such a big fish at this time of day? Let's offer it to 'Yosef who honors Sabbath.' He will definitely buy it from us as he always does."

Yosef was delighted to have obtained such a magnificent portion to adorn his Sabbath meal, and paid them a good price for the fish.

When Yosef and his wife cut open the fish, they found in its stomach a large diamond. Apparently, the fish had swallowed the jewel after it had fallen into the ocean. And so the entire wealth of the non-Jew became the possession of Yosef as predicted.

The Sages of Yosef's town told him that in the merit of the extensive expenditures he had laid out in order to honor the Sabbath, the Sabbath had repaid him manifold.[18]

8. Farewell (Havdalah)

We bid farewell to the Sabbath by making Havdalah (literally, "division" — between the holy and the profane). This is best said over a full cup of wine or grape juice, but other liquors, such as beer, may be used. We take, too, sweet-smelling spices, as if to compensate us for that fragrant breath of added spiritual life which only the Sabbath can give us, and which our Sages call *neshamah yetherah*, the "extra soul."

With a blessing for the gift of fire we mark our return to the world of production and the conquest of nature, with the lessons of the departing Sabbath in our hearts to fortify and direct us in the toil of the coming week.

Nothing may be eaten after Sabbath before

---

18. *Shabbath* 119a.

Havdalah is made. *Melakhoth* may however be done as soon as Sabbath is out, provided the Havdalah is mentioned as prescribed in the fourth blessing of the *Shemoneh Esrei* of *Ma'ariv* (the evening service). Alternatively, the words *Baruch ha-mavdil bein kodesh lechol* ("Blessed be He Who separates the holy from the profane") may be said.

If otherwise impossible (for example, if no wine, grape juice or liquor was obtainable previously), Havdalah may still be said on Sunday, Monday or Tuesday, for these three days still belong to the outgoing Sabbath. Wednesday would, however, be too late; because the next three days already belong to the Sabbath that is to come. Here, then, is another view of the week, as it looks to the Jew:

SABBATH

Friday   Sunday

Thursday   Monday

Wednesday   Tuesday

Thus Sabbath dominates the week, casting its radiance before and behind.

9. "Sabbath" and "Weekday" Activities

Sabbath has the power to release in us hidden springs of spiritual energy.

This spirit of Sabbath should express itself in all that we do on that day. Listen to how Isaiah the prophet instructs us to honor Sabbath:

If you restrain your steps on Sabbath,
[From] pursuing your interests on My holy day,

And you will call the Sabbath a day of pleasure,
Giving honor to that sanctified by God,
And you will honor it by not doing that which
*   you do usually —*
Pursuing your interests and talking about such
*   matters,*
Then you will find pleasure with God...
(Isaiah 58:13–14)

Our Sages derived from these verses that "The way that you walk on the Sabbath should not be the way you walk on a weekday; what you speak of on the Sabbath should not be what you speak of on a weekday" (*Shabbath* 113a). All our activities should be consonant with the dignity and restfulness of the Sabbath.

Thus we should not rush or hurry; nor pursue athletic sports. [Youngsters may play running games since this is their form of pleasure. However, they may not run in order to exercise.] We should not use our time on Sabbath to do heavy jobs, for instance re-arranging the furniture in the house (although, as we have seen, no question of *melakhah* is involved). Again, we should not make any kind of preparation on Sabbath for a weekday, e.g. packing a suitcase or looking up an airline timetable for a journey to be undertaken after Sabbath. Similarly, we may not read business correspondence or engage in conversation on business matters. These restrictions help us to disengage ourselves from the bustle of our weekday lives and enable us to fully enter the peaceful atmosphere of the Sabbath.

REFRAINED FROM FIXING AND GAINED A BLESSING

A pious Jew was once strolling in his garden one Sabbath afternoon. As he was walking, he noticed a breach in the wall and began to think to himself how he could fix it after Sabbath.

Then he remembered that it was Sabbath and he shouldn't be thinking about such things. In order to censure himself for such non-Sabbath-like thoughts, he decided that he would never mend the breach in the wall.

A miracle happened and a large, thick berry bush grew up exactly where the wall was breached and sealed off the wall. The pious man and his entire family lived for many years off the proceeds of the sale of those berries.[19]

Muktzeh

Our sense of Sabbath as holy and unique must be carefully nurtured. The unnecessary handling of objects for which there is no use on Sabbath is not conducive to this end, and in addition is likely to lead to *melakhoth*.

This is the basis of the rabbinical measure known as *muktzeh*. The effect of this is that we are not to handle on Sabbath any objects which, for one reason or another, were not intended by us for Sabbath use. This may be because their nature makes them unfit for use on Sabbath (e.g. money); or because they are not normally used at all (e.g. pebbles); or because they simply were not there when Sabbath commenced (e.g. a newly laid egg). The meaning of *muktzeh* is "set aside," or "excluded" — that is "excluded

---

19. *Shabbath* 150b.

from our minds": that which was not in our minds to use on Sabbath.

There are several different types of *muktzeh*, of which the following may be considered the chief ones:

▶ Objects which, when Sabbath commenced, were inaccessible to use. Examples: fruit fallen from a tree on Sabbath; eggs laid on Sabbath.

▶ Objects which can never be brought into use on Sabbath without transgressing the Sabbath laws. Examples: animals; a lamp; money.

▶ Objects whose normal use is for a *melakhah* purpose. Example: tools. These may not be handled for their own sake, for example, to show them to a friend, but they may be used for a purpose not involving a *melakhah*. (For example, a hammer may be used to crack nuts.) They may also be moved if they are in one's way.

▶ Useless objects. Examples: broken crockery, pebbles, peelings, etc. (These may however be cleared away with a broom; see below.)

▶ Any object which, at the commencement of the Sabbath, served as a basis or support for a *muktzeh* object, and was intended to continue this function throughout Sabbath even after the *muktzeh* item has been in any way removed from it. Example: a drawer containing money. (However, if the drawer contains other things besides money, this does not apply.)

It must be understood that what we are considering is a *gezerah* against *using* and *handling* certain objects. There is nothing against *muktzeh* objects being moved indirectly, where necessary — i.e. so long as they are not moved directly by hand. For example, broken crockery may be cleared away by using a broom and dust-pan. Similarly one is allowed to have a *muktzeh* object moved by a non-Jew.

If one takes up a *muktzeh* object by mistake, one need not drop it on the spot, but may put it down in its proper place.

Freedom

The full effect of Sabbath is only felt when both body *and mind* are given over to the Sabbath ideal. "Six days shall you labor, and do all your work." This indicates, say our Sages (*Mekhilta*, Exodus 20:9) that when Sabbath enters we should feel as if all our work were completed, leaving our minds and bodies completely free.

In effect, this means that there should be no "hangover" from the world of the "weekday" to the world of Sabbath. The author personally knows people who, the moment they close the office door behind them on Friday afternoon, leave all worries and problems behind, and enter the Sabbath world as if such things no longer existed.

Sabbath Activities

From this Sabbath world we have banished all traces of *melakhah*, all "weekday" activities — even "weekday" thoughts and cares. For six days they have claimed all our interest and attention. What have we to put in their place?

The answer is: *menuchah*, and the interests and activities which flow from this.

For this *menuchah* is not merely a negative concept. It does not mean that Sabbath should be spent in the armchair. On the contrary, our release from weekday acts and attachments should set free in us latent spiritual forces. New interests and activities should arise to take the place of those set aside. For example, here the family comes into its own. The Sabbath meals should be focal points of family interest, when each member of the family should be encouraged to take an active part in the celebration of the day. Above all, the Sabbath provides opportunity and energy for that greatest of all spiritual pursuits — learning the Torah.

Reading the Torah in public is one of our most ancient rabbinical enactments that dates back to the period shortly after we received the Torah at Sinai. Moses himself introduced the idea that a section of the Written Law should be read in public on Sabbath, Rosh Chodesh, and the festivals. At a much later period the Torah was subdivided into fifty-four sections and the Sages arranged that one section should be read each week. This is known as the *"parashath ha-shavua"* — the weekly portion. This portion is read in the synagogue from a Torah scroll after the first half of the Sabbath morning prayers and is a main topic of discussion during the entire day.

Here the greatest and the least can meet. Here is wisdom, to be partaken of by each according to his powers and capabilities. Here is the voice of God, lovingly and faithfully transmitted by the Sages and scholars down through the ages. A Sabbath on which this voice has not been heard is a Sabbath strangely mis-spent. The home where it is heard has found in Sabbath a heightened spiritual experience.

10. TRAVEL ON THE SABBATH

The spirit of Sabbath is essentially restful. It is understandable therefore that our Sages should have imposed certain well-defined limits to journeys undertaken on Sabbath. Normally, one may not proceed more than 2,000 cubits (about three-quarters of a mile) outside the town or place in which one is spending Sabbath. This limit is known as the *techum Shabbath*, the "Sabbath boundary." Vehicular travel is forbidden for other reasons (see pages 61 and 64).

Long sea-journeys and the like may be commenced before Sabbath; the ship then becomes one's temporary domicile for the Sabbath.

11. CHILDREN AND THE SABBATH

Jewish parents have a religious duty to train their children in the way of the Torah from their very earliest years. This training must of course be by degrees, according to the capacity and intelligence of the child.

> *Train up a child in the way that suits him best;*
> *even when he grows old he will not depart from*
> *it.*   (Proverbs 22:6)

Certain rules have been laid down by our Sages as to the form this training should take at the various stages of the child's development.[20]

Stage 1. According to the wisdom of the Sages, the first stage in this training starts at birth. Even when the child cannot yet understand simple commands (i.e. from birth until about 1 or 1½ years), his parents should not induce him to do any *issur* (forbidden act) unnecessarily, whether it is forbidden directly by the Torah or by the Sages. (Thus one should not, except on medical advice, give him forbidden foods; neither should one, for example, give him paper to tear up on Sabbath.) There is, however, no need to prevent him from doing any such act if he initiates it himself. Training in positive commands is of course not yet applicable.

Stage 2. As soon as the child can understand simple commands, he should be restrained from doing any *issurim* unnecessarily, even when he initiates them himself. Training in positive acts is not yet applicable so long as the child has no appreciation of the nature of the acts involved. This stage may last from 1 (or 1½) to 3 (or 4) years old.

Stage 3. When the child begins to appreciate the nature of the various acts concerned, he may be progressively introduced to certain positive mitzvoth, and encouraged to participate in them according to his ability and intelligence. *Shema Yisrael, berakhoth, tzitzith*, listening to Kiddush and Havdalah, eating in the *sukkah*, are among the first mitzvoth to which the child is usually introduced during the early part of this period. From the age of 5 or 6 onwards the child should receive practical training in all the mitzvoth ap-

---

20. See *Orach Chayyim*, section 343: *Mishnah Berurah* (3).

plicable to him or her, so that in reaching religious maturity at 13 (or 12 in the case of a girl) the transition to full responsibility is effected without undue difficulty.

These rules apply to the mitzvoth in general, but they have special application to the Sabbath, because of its unique function in the training and dedication of the Jewish soul.

In the Jewish home the child sees everything centered around the Sabbath. All the "best things" are kept for Sabbath: the best clothes and best dishes, favorite cakes and candies, table hymns, Kiddush and Havdalah, his parents' company and attention; all the things in which the soul of the child delights are concentrated in these twenty-four hours. In this way Sabbath becomes the central point in the child's life. The restrictions which true Sabbath observance imposes are no longer felt as restrictions at all, but are accepted by the child as part and parcel of the glory of Sabbath.

(For a full treatment of problems connected with the care of children on Sabbath, see the books referred to on page 47.)

Chapter Five
Sabbath in the Modern World

I. The Economics of Sabbath Observance

About two-hundred years ago the so-called emancipation of the Jews began. Until then Sabbath observance had been almost universal among Jews. When they stepped out of the Ghetto to take part in the economic life outside, they gained wealth — some of them — and, for a short while, political freedom. But they lost the Sabbath, and with it the soul of our people. For the ethical values that have become ingrained in the Jewish character are largely due to the hallowing influence of the Sabbath.

A similar situation arose over a hundred years ago, with the mass emigration from the great centers of Jewish population in Eastern Europe to England and America. Now those centers themselves are unfortunately no more. In spite of the amazing resurgence of Orthodoxy in America and other parts of the Diaspora during the past fifty years, it remains a fact that the great majority of Jews at the present day have become almost completely estranged from the Sabbath. In so many cases, observance is limited to the meaningless lighting of candles in a darkened room.

The majority of Jews felt the loss involved in giving

up the Jewish Sabbath. But their plea was, "We cannot help ourselves; present-day economic conditions force us to work on Sabbath."

Standing Firm

But do they? There are thousands upon thousands of Jews at the present time who keep the Sabbath in spite of all economic difficulties. How do they manage it?

The truth is that present-day conditions are by no means exceptional in this respect. It has never been easy to keep the Sabbath.

Was it easy for the farmer in ancient times, dependent on his own labor and that of his household, when a day lost in the urgency of plowing and harvest-time might mean the difference between sufficiency and starvation?

And was it easier for the medieval Jew, living in intolerable conditions and in complete insecurity, to call for a halt for twenty-four hours to his efforts to earn the meager pittance that was his livelihood?

Yet these Jews stood firm. The difference between their times and ours lies not in the external difficulties but in the will to fight where Sabbath is concerned — the determination to hold on to the Jewish Sabbath as to a life-line. Contact with a non-Jewish scale of values has robbed the Jews of their sense of Sabbath's supreme importance.

Will to Conquer

After all, what decent man, whatever difficulties he

had in earning a living, would accept a job as a paid spy to betray his country to the enemy? Only contempt would meet a man who pleaded that, economic conditions being what they were, he was forced to do this in order to earn a living. If only our Jewish people realized that the same applies to the Sabbath, which is the secret of our nation's existence, they would never agree to sacrifice the Sabbath for the sake of bread and butter, or as is more often the case, for the sake of increased comfort in life. A Jew would say, "Sabbath is the supreme value in life. It must not be touched. I must conquer or die"; and he would conquer.

For if the Jew is convinced that by breaking the Sabbath he is destroying what is most precious in himself, and breaking the link that binds him to God and the Jewish nation, and if he stands firm in this conviction, however great his difficulties may be, then in the end God will help him. The old promise of the Torah still holds good: "See that the Lord has given you the Sabbath; therefore He gives you on the sixth day the bread of two days" (Exodus 16:29). The present writer has seen so many examples of the fulfillment of this promise among Sabbath-observant Jews that he can only pity those who call this argument naive. No Jew has ever died of hunger on account of the Sabbath. But many Jews and even whole Jewish communities have disappeared from the stage of their people's history through breaking the Sabbath.

In the last resort Sabbath is the great measuring rod of *bitachon*, the touchstone of our belief that a higher force rules and guides our lives.

He who knows that his livelihood depends not on

men, nor on "nature," nor on "economic forces," but on God Himself, knows also that no real gain can come from work done in defiance of God on the Sabbath. How often can one see the imagined gains from such soul-destroying work canceled by unexpected losses in other fields! And on the other hand, the person who stands firm and refuses to betray the Sabbath for the prospects of apparent monetary gain, will often find that the loss was after all only illusory.

THE DISTURBED SABBATH

Jakob de Vries was a gem merchant in eighteenth-century Amsterdam. He had good relations with all his customers and particularly with his main customer, the local Duke. Jakob was a Torah-observant Jew and it was well-known that he could never be induced to do business, or even to talk about business, on the Sabbath.

One Sabbath morning Jakob was sitting with his family over Kiddush when a ducal herald accompanied by two army sergeants appeared at the door. "A message from his Grace the Duke for Mijnheer Jakob de Vries." Jakob read the message and his face grew pale. It requested him politely, but firmly, to appear before the Duke within an hour with a selection of his choicest gems, since the Duke had urgent business to transact. A very large profit for the merchant would be forthcoming.

"My humblest respects to the Duke," said Jakob to the herald. "Tell him that there is nothing I would like more than to oblige him, but he knows that I never do business on the Jewish Sabbath. As soon as Sabbath is out I shall be glad to do his bidding."

But the Duke would not take no for an answer. Within

the hour another delegation arrived, more numerous than the first. "The Duke's business brooks no delay," they said. Jakob again politely refused.

Throughout the day more and more messages came from the ducal palace, more and more threatening in tone. "Jakob de Vries should know that if he disobeys this command the Duke will break off all business relations with him and revoke his license to sell jewels in the whole province."

Beads of perspiration stood out on his forehead but Jakob de Vries stood firm. "Tell the Duke," he said, "that I am loyal to him but I owe a higher loyalty to my God."

After the termination of the Sabbath — and Jakob curtailed none of the ceremonies and songs with which observant Jews say farewell to the Holy Sabbath — he hastened to the palace, not knowing what to expect there.

To his amazement, as soon as he entered the great hall the Duke rose from his throne and clasped him in a warm embrace.

"Thank you, my friend," said the Duke. "You were great! And what's more you have added 10,000 guilders to my coffers. You see, I had a guest here today, the Duke of Brabant, and I told him about your loyalty to your Jewish laws. He laughed and said that no Jew could resist making a big profit, and he bet me 10,000 guilders that a combination of monetary incentives and threats would surely break your resolve. I had faith in you and bet 10,000 guilders that you would stand firm. Thank you for living up to my expectations!"

Reeducation

The first step to be taken, if we wish to regain for the Jewish masses their lost Sabbath, is the reeducation of public opinion to appreciate the Jewish Sabbath in its entirety, with all that it stands for.

Nevertheless there are solid economic factors which must be taken into account, for the Torah is on earth and not in heaven. It is based on the realities of everyday life. We must therefore do whatever we can to make Sabbath observance easier, and not rely on miracles. Planning, foresight and careful preparation are needed if an occupation is to be found in which Sabbath can be observed without undue difficulty.

Career Guidance

This should be borne in mind in the first instance by parents when helping their children choose a career. When the difficulties have already arisen, it may be too late to do anything about it.

A "Sabbath Observance Employment Bureau" can do fine work in this connection. Its activities can be extended to include vocational guidance, in conjunction with other Jewish bodies, with a view to giving parents and the public the fullest details of careers and occupations in relation to Sabbath observance.

If only as much thought and determination were devoted to this problem as to other aspects of earning a living, many obstacles would disappear.

The Complete Sabbath

Yet one thing must not be forgotten. It is true that there can be no Sabbath without stopping work, in the economic sense. But it is also true that this alone does not make a Jewish Sabbath, as we have endeavored to show in the earlier chapters of this little book.

The *neshamah yetherah*, the "additional soul," which, as our Sages say, brings us that highest form of spiritual happiness created by the Sabbath, is bestowed only on a person *ha-meshamer Shabbath kehilkhathah* — who keeps it in strict accordance with the Torah. Cessation from work must be supplemented by cessation from *melakhah* if our Sabbath is to be what God intended.

In spite of all difficulties and of all indifference, the fight for the Jewish Sabbath must and will continue. The infinite blessing of this Sabbath must again become the possession of the Jewish masses. Until we achieve this aim any words about Jewish spiritual revival will be no more than empty talk.

2. SABBATH AND THE JEWISH STATE

Israel is the only country in the world in which the Sabbath is the national day of rest. In modern Israel, therefore, the focus of the Sabbath question is quite different. For the individual, at any rate, the economic problem is no longer acute. If one wishes to have Sabbath-free employment there are ample opportunities at hand. Sabbath is the official rest day, and enterprises working on Sabbath are the exception rather than the rule.

This solves the problem only partially however. Just as an individual can have a rest day without having a real Sabbath, so can a state.

One can conceive Sabbath as a social necessity, or even as a time-honored national custom or tradition, and still miss the whole point of the Jewish Sabbath.

It must be kept as a God-ordained day, a day of cessation from *melakhah*, as defined by the Torah, undiminished by the demands of ignorance and undistorted by ideas gained from outside sources. Only then will it appear in its true form as the proclamation of God's presence in the midst of human endeavor and human society. Only then shall we clearly see its basic relevance to the problems of the age.

Out of the Rut

It is well over three thousand years since the Sabbath was given to the Jewish nation, but no age has ever had more need of it than our own. Never has there been a generation with minds so obsessed as ours by *melakhah* — the control of nature by the power of the human intelligence. Our achievements in this sphere have driven us to a delusion of self-sufficiency; they have driven us away from God and the roots of our own being. Instead of giving us a stable world to live in, they have increased instability beyond all imagination and produced a mass of rootless, hopeless, fear-ridden humanity.

The Jewish Sabbath frees us from our bondage to *melakhah*, and points the way to sanity and to the recovery of the real roots of our existence. The Sabbath of the *halakhah* is a spark of hope in the dark vista of the modern world.

We, the Jewish nation, gave Sabbath to the world, preserved and cherished it throughout the millennia, for just such an age as this. Surely we ourselves should have ears for its saving message! After all, it is to us, in the first instance, that its message is addressed.

The Jewish state has a particular responsibility — and a unique opportunity — in this matter. It could, if it wishes, quell for once the raucous, insistent clamor of the modern world, and so let the voice of Sabbath be heard.

What does this voice say? It proclaims to the Jewish nation, and through it to the world, the necessity of serving a purpose higher than itself. It shows them the way out of the spiritual rut in which humanity is caught. It shows them that the labors of state and society, if they are to have value and meaning, must be devoted to only one end — the service of God.

Era of Redemption

Seen in this light, the observance of the true Jewish Sabbath of the *halakhah* becomes a basic necessity if the Jewish state is to fulfill its high destiny.

Many problems of *halakhah* do of course arise in connection with Sabbath observance in a modern state. There are questions of the maintenance of power stations, essential services, international communications and internal and external security, to name only a few. This is not the place for a detailed examination of these questions. Once the fundamental importance of the Sabbath law to the Jewish nation and state is realized and accepted, however, all problems of this kind will be found to have a solution within the framework of true Sabbath observance.

Here again it is fitting to point out that if only the ingenuity, vigor and determination evinced in other spheres were devoted to this highest of all ends, many practical problems would cease to exist.

Modern science has posed many of these problems, and modern science can do much to solve them. For example, automatic milking machines, controlled by a time-switch, are now in use in some *kibbutzim*. Accumulators can be, and in some places in Israel in fact are, used to store during the week sufficient electricity to supply Sabbath needs. In some cases electronic devices — such as a simplified form of "electronic brain" — could be adapted to provide a solution. Set for example in a power station, these could be arranged before Sabbath to react to many different eventualities, so that no Jewish hand does a *melakhah* except when the Torah demands it, i.e. in case of danger to life. Thus science can contribute to that great glorification of God's name — the full observance of the Jewish Sabbath by the people and institutions of the Jewish state. Once it was accepted by the bulk of the Jewish nation, this unique act of homage and service would indeed be a herald of the Messianic era, when the nations will set aside their destructive ends, and unite in the service of the living God.

This is the meaning of a profound saying of our Sages:

> *If the whole of Jewry were to observe but two Sabbaths according to the halakhah, they would at once be redeemed.*

> (Shabbath 118b)

Index

Index to Passages Cited